More pra
another bull
in suck city

"*Another Bullshit Night in Suck City* succeeds in a way most writers can only dream of: It is intense, lyrical, moving and ultimately enlightening. This is a book about no less than the value of blood and the permanence of familial relations. A strangely poignant meditation on the debt sons owe their fathers, even bad fathers, even fathers that weren't around. And if none of that interests you, read it for the sentences, each one a poem, and the flow of the narrative that hurtles toward a conclusion both stunning and unexpected."

—Stephen Elliot, *San Francisco Chronicle*

"Told with energy, critical reflection and sensitivity, *Another Bullshit Night in Suck City* is less a memoir than a study of one of America's darker conundrums: homelessness. . . . One chapter is a play, another a thesaurus-like gloss on inebriation. Some advance the story; others are more visceral, suggesting Lear, Beckett, Faulkner, Genet and forcing us to decide which is more painful: a parent's lost dreams or a child's lost innocence."

—Thomas Curwen, *Los Angeles Times Book Review*

"Flynn's tough, lovely memoir *Another Bullshit Night in Suck City* is a swift, accomplished weaving of two trajectories: his father's and his own. . . . His story is eerie testimony to the potent influence of an absent parent. But Nick, a poet, is too subtle a writer to say so outright, and instead lets us draw our own conclusions with a delicate, poetic logic. In place of a straight narrative he builds a spine of interlocking memories and fragments that, for all its gentle overlapping, still pushes the story forward page by page."

—Kate Bolick, *Boston Globe*

"A remarkable feat: a clear-eyed, inventive, and astonishingly honest guided tour of hell. . . . As fascinating as the story of the reconnection between father and son is, equally remarkable is the way Flynn soberly and poignantly captures the true lives of outcast and marginal men without ever being preachy or scolding. 'Hey,' he says, 'none of us are saints.' " —Elissa Schappel, *Vanity Fair*

"Flynn's a poet by trade, and like good poetry, *Suck City* is small without being slight. There's a lot of sadness in it, but it's really about the human capacity—our somewhat reluctant instinct—for compassion, and I don't think I'm crazy for saying it's a hopeful book."

—Devin Friedman, *GQ*

"From Ponzi schemes to homeless shelters, Flynn traces the life of his indigent father with unsentimental clarity."

—*Esquire*

"Unlike the pity parties that too many memoirs have become, *Night* has no maudlin gestures, no 'inspirational' tones, no hysterics; it stares down emptiness with clear, dry eyes." —Troy Patterson, *Entertainment Weekly*

"Tapping equally the grace of poetry and the power of story-telling . . . [Flynn] creates one of the finest Boston-set works of non-fiction this year. . . . This fascinating, wrenching book in your hands is proof that at least one survivor made it to land." —J. L. Johnson, *Boston Herald*

"There is reason to celebrate when a good memoir comes our way, one whose author has taken the raw material of experience and turned it into art. Nick Flynn has written that kind of memoir. . . . Among a surfeit of books by celebrities with profoundly uninteresting lives, or examples of the more self-pitying brand of 'literary' memoir, Nick Flynn's book is a tremendous tonic."

—Gordon Haber, *New York Sun*

"Flynn's vibrant prose strikes an elegant balance between terse, chiseled chapters and evocative prose poems in a manner reminiscent of Eduardo Galleano. Never maudlin or sentimental, even in the most wrenching of circumstances, Flynn offers an unflinching vision of homelessness in which no detail is spared. Throughout the book, he never loses sight of the basic human dignity of his broken subjects—his father included." —Steve Smith, *TimeOut New York*

"*Another Bull—— Night in Suck City* . . . is an unsparing, unsentimental, often darkly comic piece of work. . . . What he has done in this clear-eyed book is bear witness to the inscrutable human personality."

—*Houston Chronicle*

"With his new memoir, Nick Flynn has crafted an astonishing, affecting work about a father and a son, and the dark worlds they each inhabit. It's a bracing, briskly paced excavation of Nick's conflicted reaction to Jonathan's jarring re-entry, drunk and without a home, into his life. Exquisitely and often experimentally written, it's an unsparing look at his father's struggles, and his own."

—*Boston Phoenix*

"*Another Bullshit Night in Suck City* is a remarkable memoir: uneasy, evocative, sometimes funny." —*Spectator*

"Flynn has a flair for striking images." —*Sunday Times*

"This remarkable memoir is far more than a portrait of a grimly fascinating man. It is about our response to those who demand so much from us that they could take us down with them." —Lavinia Greenlaw, *Financial Times*

"Taking for a title his father's description of living rough, he's written a brilliant, blistering book, driven by emotional honesty and raw compassion." —*Daily Mail*

"*Another Bullshit Night in Suck City* is a formidably graceful book." —*New Statesman*

"*Another Bullshit Night* is among the best contemporary memoirs I've read, though it reads like a novel. . . . It's an unsentimental, eloquent study in disillusionment, and a cleverly structured story about a father and son living parallel lives with a supporting cast of colourful crazies, told in bursts of blazing prose. . . . Nick has succeeded in transforming a wasted life into impressive literature."

—*Independent on Sunday*

"Nick Flynn's devastating memoir does what only significant works of art can do—it shows us a world we know, but fail to see or understand. No one who reads *Another Bullshit Night in Suck City* will ever walk through a city in the same way again. If I say that Flynn's book ranks with Frank Conroy's *Stop-Time*, I mean it as the highest possible praise."

—Michael Cunningham, author of *The Hours*

"What a piece of work. I don't usually like memoirs, but if they were all like Nick Flynn's *Another Bullshit Night in Suck City*—eloquent, funny, unsentimental, and bravely inventive—I'd read them by the truckload."

—Dennis Lehane, author of *Mystic River*

"Nick Flynn has given us one of the most terrifying families in American letters, though he approaches each character in this ferocious, inventive memoir with an almost radical sense of compassion, as if all that any of us could do were to stumble ahead with the burdens we're given.

The result is a book so singular, harrowing, and loving as to be indelible." —Mark Doty, author of *Firebird*

"My favorite book of the past few years, and the best memoir since *Stop-Time*, *This Boy's Life*, and *The Liar's Club*."
—Chris Offutt, author of *The Strange River Twice* and *Kentucky Straight*

"*Another Bullshit Night in Suck City* is a wonder, both sweet and agonizing, a fusion of the lyric and the well-wrought story. Nick Flynn finds, through the assemblage, piece by piece, of his own breakneck life and father, what all of us must see: our fathers (living, dead, mercurial, solid, never glimpsed) are amazing and wretched; they are genius; they are filthy and naked; they are gut drunk beautiful. This book, in both story and language, shatters convention with every word, and Flynn makes that destruction flawless." —Brad Land, author of *Goat*

"*Another Bullshit Night* is one of the best books I've read in years—a heartbreaking, searing story—the perfect memoir. Nick Flynn hurls himself toward the blunt trauma of history, toward his fear of what he himself might become. It is a story of self-discovery in the best sense, and also a story of the dissembling of history, the fight to keep oneself whole, and the inherent obligations of biology. In the end it is about family, about fathers and sons and how painful it is to know the depth of that relation at its fullest." —A. M. Homes, author of *Music for Torching*

"Flynn gets the details of the family down cold—egomaniacs with inferiority complexes, forever burning the bridges in front of themselves, cursed with a thirst for which enough is never enough. Gorgeously wrought."

—Thomas Lynch, author of *Booking Passage* and *The Undertaking*

another bullshit night
in suck city

also by Nick Flynn

Memoir

This Is the Night Our House Will Catch Fire

The Reenactments

The Ticking Is the Bomb

Poetry

Low

I Will Destroy You

My Feelings

The Captain Asks for a Show of Hands

Blind Huber

Some Ether

Criticism

A Note Slipped Under the Door: Teaching from Poems We Love (with Shirley McPhillips)

Plays

Alice Invents a Little Game and Alice Always Wins

Hybrid

Stay: threads, conversations, collaborations

another bullshit night in suck city

a memoir

nick flynn

foreword by Andre Dubus III

W. W. NORTON & COMPANY

Independent Publishers Since 1923

disclaimer Although this is a work of nonfiction, the names of those mentioned have often been altered, especially the names of those who found themselves homeless for any length of time, or still find themselves "there." The names of those who may have transgressed the law have also been altered, except for the name of my father, who has done his time and is proud of it.

Printed in the United States of America

For information about special discounts for bulk purchases, please contact W. W. Norton Special Sales at specialsales@wwnorton.com or 800-233-4830

Manufacturing by Lakeside Book Company
Book design by Lovedog Studio
Production manager: Daniel Van Ostenbridge

ISBN 978-1-324-10537-4 (pbk)

W. W. Norton & Company, Inc., 500 Fifth Avenue, New York, NY 10110
www.wwnorton.com

W. W. Norton & Company Ltd., 15 Carlisle Street, London W1D 3BS

10 9 8 7 6 5 4 3 2 1

foreword to the 20th anniversary edition

Deep into this heartbreakingly beautiful memoir, Nick Flynn writes, ". . . and I see that I don't really know what I'm doing, that I'm adrift, as the Buddhists say, on a river of forgetfulness. A hungry ghost." This insight comes when Nick is twenty-eight, six years after his mother's suicide, when he is indeed adrift: working off and on at Boston's largest homeless shelter, the Pine Street Inn; living off and on aboard his mostly restored boat; being off and on with his girlfriend, Emily; drinking and getting high; and now having to see and care for the bombastic, alcoholic, homeless father he never knew. Yes, young Nick Flynn is adrift on the river of forgetfulness, and in the Buddhist tradition those who fail, after death, to drink from it will never be free of the memories from their past life and will be tortured in the "in-between" until willing to move on. But it is this in-between, Nick Flynn so movingly shows us here, that holds our very lives. And we readers are so fortunate that instead of drinking from that river, Nick Flynn, the man and now the writer of this groundbreaking memoir, works while adrift to gather the floating shards of his own memory into some recognizable shape he might be able to call Nick Flynn.

Any descent with words back into a writer's life and its various wounds is a brave act, one rife with "psychic bombs," as Flynn later describes his father's letters to him. But because Nick Flynn began writing *Another Bullshit Night in Suck City* only ten years after his father became a client of the shelter where Nick worked, the emotional stakes of the actual prose here feel so much higher than they might have otherwise. There is none of that helpful distance in time so many memoirists take before their own descents, and so the writing here feels as urgent yet disembodied as someone in shock, as if a family has literally been blown to bits, and we are now witnessing one of its only survivors on his hands and knees picking up one jagged piece after another and holding it up to the light.

Rumi reminds us to "Sell our cleverness and purchase bewilderment," and yet so many contemporary memoirs, as well-written as they may be, seem fueled not by any bewilderment on the writer's part, but more by a deep need to express a story the writer knows all too well and now it's our turn to know it too. This approach can yield fine work, but it seems to me to undercut the very nature of memory itself.

The opposite of the word *to remember* is not *to forget* but *to dismember*. In this sense then, every act of memory is a reaching for a fragment, each one often elusive and in no particular chronology. Maybe the gathering will bring about some sort of recognizable whole, or maybe it won't, but for a young man who has just begun to grieve the loss of his mother by her own hand, a young man whose forever-absent father is now "circling close," the structure Nick Flynn employs here is near perfect: eighty-three short chapters, each with its own thematic and often ironic title, divided into six parts.

One of the principal dangers of the memoir form is that its writer, as the novelist Richard Yates said about autobiographical fiction, must walk a fine line between self-pity and self-aggrandizement. This is a perilous line for most of us, especially when writing about those who've perhaps hurt us in some way, either by direct action or through neglect. And if there is a more neglectful father than Jonathan Flynn, I cannot think of one, yet his son begins this story by slipping into his father's skin and imagining what it's like to be him, trying to get some sleep in an ATM booth in 1989.

> Please, she whispers, how may I help you? The screen lights up with her voice. A room you enter, numbers you finger, heated, sterile almost. The phone beside her never rings, like a toy, like a prop. My father lifts the receiver in the night, speaks into it, asks, Where's the money? asks, Why can't I sleep? asks, Who left me outside?

This is a remarkable beginning: first, we quickly learn that Nick Flynn, the accomplished poet and playwright, will be crafting these evocative sentences as much as Nick Flynn, the lost and grieving son, will be; but more important, we see that Nick's first step back into the shattering darkness of his youth begins with a creative act of immense compassion and generosity: *What's it like to be you, my father?* And very soon comes the harder question: *How much of you is inside me? Am I like you, too?*

This is the central shadow that rises up throughout the entire course of this spellbinding memoir: How much of our parents are in us, anyway? Are their fates *our* fates? And what about our parents' parents? And theirs and theirs and theirs? How much has been passed down to me? The question itself expands the interior scope here to one of even deeper emotional resonance, starting with, only four pages into the book, the one paragraph chapter *The Inventor of the Life Raft*:

> His father, my father claims, invented both the life raft and the power window, though sometimes it is the life raft and the push-button locks on car doors. . . . In this story my father's family is rich, with gardeners and chauffeurs during the Depression.

In this story. This is a telling phrase, for not only does it signal the habitually egomaniacal ramblings of a man Flynn knows not to trust, it also reflects Nick Flynn's creative and perhaps personal relationship to traditional narrative itself: What's *true*, anyway? Aren't our stories and, therefore, our very truths always changing?

Apologist, the third chapter, begins with:

> If you asked me about my father then—the years he lived in a doorway, in a shelter, in an ATM—I'd say, *Dead*, I'd say, *Missing*, I'd say, *I don't know where he is.* I'd say whatever I felt like saying, and it would all be true. I don't know him, I'd say, my mother left him shortly after I was born, or just before. But this story did not hold still for long. It wavered.

It wavered because Nick Flynn had heard rumors that his father was living in a rooming house up on Beacon Hill, that he drove a cab, maybe in the same Boston neighborhoods where his grown son he'd never known worked and lived. That Nick would "involuntarily check the driver of each that passed, uncertain what it would mean, what I would do, if it was my father behind the wheel." But the story also wavered, we soon discover, because Nick Flynn the memoirist doesn't quite trust stories to stay still because they don't: Just one page later, he tells us: "Ask me about him now and I'll say, *Housed*. . . . Ask now and I'll say he's a goddamned tree stump . . ." The "now" Nick Flynn refers to here is the moment of writing the memoir itself; we are only in its third chapter of eighty-three, yet it's a prelude to the symphony that will follow, a scanning of the fragments that will be picked up and examined along the way, beginning with one of the heaviest of them all, the distillation of these years into a tv game show called "*The Apologist.* Today's show: 'Fathers Left Outside to Rot.'"

Why "left outside to rot"? Because if Flynn offers his homeless father a place to stay, if he takes him in, then he ". . . would become him, the line between us would blur, my own slow-motion car wreck would speed up."

And what *is* that "car wreck"? It is young Nick flying down the hot highway on his motorcycle barefoot in search of his lost shoes; it's Nick cruising the back streets of his hometown with his friend while getting high on marijuana laced with methamphetamines; it's Nick stealing a Christmas tree with his mother's Vietnam Vet boyfriend who suffers from severe PTSD; it's Nick drinking too much and waking up in the bed of a woman who is not his girlfriend; it's finding an early draft of a suicide note by his mother, burning it, and keeping a more vigilant eye on her; it's working on the fish pier for local mobsters after "forgetting" to apply to college; it's his mother finding Nick's notebook, one with a story-in-progress in it "about a woman who works two jobs and tries to fit in a couple hours between each to be with her kids"; and it's Nick's mother's suicide halfway between Thanksgiving and Christmas.

Yet when Nick Flynn tells us of his own "slow-motion car wreck," we are only at the end of the third chapter, with eighty more to follow, and we have still not lived through any of what he ultimately takes us through above, as well as all that will follow. But because he has already come clean about his own story wavering, we begin to trust him fully to bring us into truth. And then, by trying to put himself into his father's experience, an act of artistic benevolence we already see may be psychically hazardous to the author, Nick Flynn has galvanized our trust, and we will follow him anywhere.

And so he takes us back four years before his own birth to his parents' courtship: his future father home for the summer from Palm Beach where he works on charter fishing boats; Nick's future mother, Jody, a pretty seventeen-year-old working in a coffee shop in Scituate Harbor. Thirty miles south of Boston, this old fishing village will become Nick's future hometown, and it—as well as the streets of Boston and Provincetown and the waterways in between—become essential in the telling of Nick's story. For while this riveting memoir is wonderfully and movingly interior, so many of its chapters the son's imaginings of his parents' lives, including their own interior monologues, there is also the steady, nonjudgmental eye of the social documentarian. In creative nonfiction circles, this is called the "I" as well as the "eye," and here Flynn, while remaining fully his young, wounded self on the page, also captures the ravages of addiction and homelessness, the deep divisions of social class, and the harrowing nature of single motherhood in late twentieth century America.

But perhaps Nick Flynn's greatest artistic triumph in *Another Bullshit Night in Suck City* is his ability to render three-dimensional, flesh and blood characters on the page, most notably that of a man he has only just begun to know, his own putative father, Jonathan Flynn. We are in a time when many creative writers appear to be more influenced by feature films than they are literature, when characters are created largely by what they say and do and how they appear while doing it. This can, of course, be an effective way to tell human stories, but it leaves behind the writer's most powerful tool, which is the license to descend into the psyches of our characters, to become them from the inside out and not the other way around.

From the opening pages here to the very end, Nick Flynn floats, like "a hungry ghost" into his imaginings of his father's vision of the world. The chapter "Family Friend" begins this way:

> No one would notice Jonathan wandering upstairs as Ray and Clare's annual New Year's party rages below. Maybe he's looking for a free bathroom, maybe a little air, a place to clear his head. . . . He stands before the sink and checks his eyes in the mirror. How long can he hold his own gaze? Does he look as loaded as he feels? . . . *A party, for chrissakes, let's get to it.* He can hear the girls singing below, angels calling him. He wakes up with his cheek pressed to the tile floor. *Must've dozed off.*

As we read this wonderfully novelistic rendering of the drunk man who happens to be the author's father, we know that young Nick Flynn is beginning to deal with his own drinking and his own self-destructive tendencies, and so this passage and many others—imagining his young father selling Renaults in the doomed business his new father-in-law sets up for him; imagining his father's first arrest for stealing a sheriff's car while blacked out and now referring to his jail time as "My Dostoyevsky," yet one more opportunity for Jonathan Flynn to write his masterpiece; imagining him skipping his own mother's funeral; imagining him paranoid and locked inside an apartment he's about to be evicted from; imagining him searching for a place to sleep in the streets—all feel as if the son is not only flying close to the flame, he's willing to burn in it if it will bring him any closer to the varying and conflicting truths of what it means to be the child of a man whose first ever letter to his son came when Nick was sixteen, and it came from prison:

> *Tell me of yourself—I regret our mutual loss—perhaps—soon—in our future—we can regain our lost knowledge of each other.*

Jonathan Flynn sends his son dozens and dozens of letters, and his son keeps them all, quoting from many of them throughout this increasingly devastating memoir to great effect. For we begin to see just how toxically solipsistic and sadly delusional his alcoholic father is, this man who says that his masterpiece is "going very, very well," this man who sends his son many photocopies of a personal rejection from Viking Press and a letter from Patty Hearst, this man who claims to be the greatest writer America ever produced, but also this man who shows glimmers of actually thinking and maybe even caring a bit about his son:

> Dear Nick, 6/22/87
>
> Many deep thanks for your recent help. All grist for the mill. . . . I've really enjoyed as a writer—my time at

> the Pine Street Inn. It's been a pure pleasure to merely stand with my back against a wall—watching my son at work. It has been a very, very long 25 years.
>
> Whether you like it or not—you are me. I know.

He then writes:

> I thought if your very beautiful mother were alive and if she could somehow see this scene—her youngest son at work and Father a resident—in Pine Street—a shelter for the homeless—the beaten—the sad—the losers in life's great game—Jody would have laughed loudly at the entire macabre scene.

But once again, whatever nascent pride for his son begins to show here, its central subject always comes back to him, Jonathan Flynn, the real hero of this "macabre scene." In fact, the letter ends with Jonathan Flynn absolving himself once again of being any sort of genuine father to his son whatsoever. "Eno the Beano . . . tells me you are into drugs—if so—good luck."

Yet Nick Flynn does not intrude here to amplify any of this or to make some sort of didactic point about his neglectful father and his tenuous, at best, relationship with him. Instead, Flynn simply holds up to us yet one more shard, trusting us to bring our own life experience to the page, to perhaps see and feel what he may have as well.

A common, yet understandable misstep for many memoirists is to try to become the biographer of one's family. This impulse seems to be rooted in an admirable sense not only of fairness, but the knowledge that the life experience of each of us is entirely our own, that one's mother or father will be a different mother or father for our siblings, that my view of this life is not your view. And so this sort of memoirist may interview others in the family for *their* perspective, which begins to read more like an act of investigative journalism, a desire to get the full story.

But what Nick Flynn wrestles so bravely and movingly with here feels to me to be much more accurate and honest questions: What if there *is* no full story? What if the desire to go back in time to put the pieces back into some sort of shape *is* the story? For at the heart of *Another Bullshit Night in Suck City*, one of the great American memoirs, is a flame that burns steadily in the stark air of loss and grief and yearning, a flame that yields a wisp of hope in the slowly growing warmth of forgiveness.

—Andre Dubus III

another bullshit night
in suck city

HAMM: Scoundrel! Why did you engender me?

NAGG: I didn't know.

HAMM: What? What didn't you know?

NAGG: That it'd be you.

— Beckett, *Endgame*

one

automatic teller

(1989) *Please*, she whispers, *how may I help you?* The screen lights up with her voice. A room you enter, numbers you finger, heated, sterile almost. The phone beside her never rings, like a toy, like a prop. My father lifts the receiver in the night, speaks into it, asks, *Where's the money?* asks, *Why can't I sleep?* asks, *Who left me outside?* The phone rings on a desk when he lifts it, the desk somewhere in Texas, someone is always supposed to be at that desk but no one ever is, not at night. A machine speaks while my father tries to speak, it doesn't listen, it only speaks, my father's face reflected dimly on the screen.

Any card with a magnetic strip will let you in, all the street guys know this, or learn quick. It's never night inside this room, the lights hum a deafening white. My father stands at the desk, filling out deposit slips—*Five hundred to savings, twenty-five thousand to checking, all cash*—then puts the slips in an envelope and tosses it into the trash. Drive past and it's like a window display, a diorama—*Late Twentieth Century Man Pretending to Be Banking*—brought to you by the Museum of the Homeless. The people who enter, those with money to withdraw, most of them don't even glance at my father, don't give him a second look. Dressed well, clean, his graying hair long and swept back from his forehead—just like them, doing a little banking after midnight, on his way to an after-hours club, a late dinner, a lady waiting in the car, *that* car, by the curb, the engine running, the heat blowing on her legs while she listens to the radio—*A little honey in my pot*, or, *Baby it's cold outside.* Skid is curled beneath the desk—semiconscious or out cold, hard to tell, his boombox cranked up full, he holds it tight to his chest like a screaming child. My father hums. The lights hum. The couple at the automatic teller kiss, the machine clicks out a small pile of bills, my father bends to his deposit slip, *Six hundred and seventy thousand, cash*, he puts it in an envelope, licks the envelope shut. The couple stand by the door, still kissing, like they have no place better to be, like this is the most romantic spot in the city.

Others find their way to the ATM after midnight, after the last Dunkin' Donuts closes. They rattle the magnetic door to get my father's attention, but unless he knows them he'll feign sleep or pretend he's absorbed with his banking. After midnight it's hard to find an open lobby, a dry place to enter, and for some it's hard to scrounge even so much as a magnetic card. My father knows Beady-Eyed Bill, another harmless weirdo, unlatches the door. The Beady-Eyed One talks out of the side of his mouth, glancing over my father's shoulder to scope what's coming. He fears he's being watched, and inside this room who can say he's not? Someone behind that wall is making a goddamn movie of his life.

Alice, hunched by the trash, swears people come in at night and carve their initials into her flesh. She holds an upturned palm to Bill accusingly, asks, *Who's "J.L."?* The scratches on her hand do look like the letters "J" and "L," this is true. Bill glances at my father conspiratorially. Alice glares at Bill. *And which Bill are you tonight? The one in the gray slacks, or the one that snuck in last night and branded my hand?* My father, finished depositing his cash, curls up on the ceramic floor, turns his face to the baseboard, tucked below the window so the fake police won't see him. Phony sheriff stars painted on their little jeeps, if he can stay below their line of sight it might buy ten minutes of sleep.

In Boston the bars close at one. The next wave of revelers, more gregarious than the earlier crowd, bleary and headed home, push their way inside. Sometimes they give you a hassle, sometimes they flip you a few bucks. A little lit, sometimes they try to start up a conversation, sit on the floor next to you, offer you a drink, want to know your name. *You seem like a regular guy, how'd you end up here?*

Where? my father asks.

the inventor of the life raft

His father, my father claims, invented both the life raft and the power window, though sometimes it is the life raft and the push-button locks on car doors. Or some sort of *four-gig carburetor that saves gas.* In this story my father's family is rich, with gardeners and chauffeurs during the Depression. His grandfather owned a roofing company that had the contracts for Faneuil Hall and the Boston Museum of Fine Arts—big public works projects that kept them flush while the country struggled. Look inside the grasshopper weathervane on the roof of Faneuil Hall and you will see my great-grandfather's name, Thaddeus, which is also my brother's name. My father tells me this, but how to get inside this grasshopper he doesn't say.

apologist

If you asked me about my father then—the years he lived in a doorway, in a shelter, in an ATM—I'd say, *Dead*, I'd say, *Missing*, I'd say, *I don't know where he is*. I'd say whatever I felt like saying, and it would all be true. I don't know him, I'd say, my mother left him shortly after I was born, or just before. But this story did not hold still for long. It wavered.

Even before he became homeless I'd heard whispers, sensed he was circling close, that we were circling each other, like planets unmoored. I knew he drove a cab, maybe my mother told me that, though she said almost nothing about him, except that it was better he wasn't around. I even knew what kind, a Town Taxi, a black and white. In my early twenties, after I dropped out of college and moved to Boston, I would involuntarily check the driver of each that passed, uncertain what it would mean, what I would do, if it was my father behind the wheel.

I knew he lived in a rooming house on Beacon Hill, I'd heard about it a couple years before they evicted him, before he moved into his cab, leasing it twenty-four hours at a stretch, before he blacked out on a vodka jag, hit *someone or something*, before they took his license away. The day he was evicted was the first face-to-face I had with him as an adult, the second time in my life I can remember meeting him—he'd called on the phone, told me to get over to his room with my truck. It was the first time I'd heard his voice on the phone. Two months later he appeared at the shelter where I worked and demanded a bed.

The Pine Street Inn was and still is the largest homeless shelter in Boston. State-of-the-art. When my father arrived I'd already been working there for three years, first as a counselor, then as a caseworker. He wasn't homeless when I first started—marginal, sure, but not homeless. I remember the day he arrived the nights could still be cold. He raised his arms to enter, because every "guest" has to be frisked—no bottles, no weapons. This is the first rule.

Ask me about him now and I'll say, *Housed*. Twelve years. Subsidized. A Section 8. A disability. I'll thank you for paying his rent, unless you're also a Section 8. Unless by the time you read this he's been evicted again. Ask now and I'll say he's a goddamned tree stump, it'll take dynamite to get rid of that motherfucker.

Before he lost his room I could have met him, if I'd chosen to, at any time. He was never difficult to find. No one is, really. Even the months he was barred from the shelter I knew the three or four spots outside where he slept, each one burned into my internal map of the city. Nowadays I can look at a calendar and roughly pinpoint his location. I've seen the inside of his apartment, I know his routine. The first of the month he gets his check, and from this he (hopefully) pays his rent, then buys a gallon or three of vodka. If it is near the first he will be in his room drinking. Easy to find near the first. If it is later in the month he will have to venture out, to soup kitchens for meals, and then he will be harder to track down, at least at midday. He has no phone. If I want to see him I have to go to his apartment building and ring his bell, the bell with my last name taped to it. It will take about a minute for him to buzz me in, his finger stuttering on the button. Or else his apartment will be empty and I will not be buzzed inside. I will then either wander down Commonwealth Avenue looking for him or sit in the local Dunkin' Donuts and wait for him to appear.

If I could distill those years into a television game show I'd call it *The Apologist.* Today's show: "Fathers Left Outside to Rot." And there I'd sit in an ill-fitting suit, one of three or four contestants, looking contrite or defiant or inscrutable under the life-draining lights. At some point, after I tell an abridged version of my story, the host will parade my father out, and we will have a reunion of sorts, on national tv as the camera pans the reactions of the studio audience. Before we go to a commercial break a caption will appear under my face—*He wished his father dead.*

The abridged story:

I worked with the homeless from 1984 until 1990. In 1987 my father became homeless, and remained homeless for nearly five years.

If it snowed I'd turn up the heat in my loft in the Combat Zone, a whole floor of a building above an abandoned strip joint, look out the window at Boston's so-called "adult entertainment district."

The sign of the Naked Eye, a woman's neon legs opening and closing on an enormous flashing eye. The Glass Slipper. Playland.

Cars skidding slightly, footprints filling in. Tiny lights bouncing off whitened streets. I knew precisely the risks involved.

Many, most of the homeless die, sooner or later, turn up dead, in the most unimaginable, in the most ordinary ways. Robert Kuneman propped upright against a wall in the South End, seemingly waiting for a bus, frozen solid. Fergus Woods sleeping in a cardboard box in his sister's garage, trying to keep warm with a can of sterno, sets it, and himself, on fire.

In the summer I'd hear about someone found face-down near the railyard and wonder if the body was my father's. A reflex. White male, fifties, sixties, could be anyone.

Sometimes I'd see my father, walking past my building on his way to another nowhere. I could have given him a key, offered a piece of my floor. A futon. A bed. But I never did. If I let him inside I would become him, the line between us would blur, my own slow-motion car wreck would speed up. The slogan on the side of a moving company truck read TOGETHER WE ARE GOING PLACES—modified by a vandal or a disgruntled employee to read TOGETHER WE ARE GOING DOWN. If I went to the drowning man the drowning man would pull me under. I couldn't be his life raft.

barracuda

(1956) Jonathan, years before he will become my father, is back north for another summer. For the past few winters, since he dropped out of college, he's been working on charter fishing boats out of Palm Beach. When back in Massachusetts he ranges from his parents' house in Scituate to friends' couches in Boston. A vapor. Everywhere. Nowhere. Scituate (sit-tchoo-it, from the Native American *satuit*, meaning "cold brook"), a fishing village about thirty miles south of Boston, is the summer home to a few of the city's politicians, who've dubbed it "The Irish Riviera." During the week Jonathan lives at home, working for a local construction mogul. On weekends he skips north to Boston, crashes on Beacon Hill with Ray, his best friend. Ray is from working-class French Canadian Catholic stock—he pays his bills on time and is generous with his friends, which is becoming more and more important for someone like Jonathan. Steady Ray. *You didn't need much* *money in your pocket, not a whole lot was expected of you. You could live well as a struggling artist, you could rise up or you could drift along.* Cocky, his dark hair slicked back, Jonathan's rising, making a name for himself—*The Next Great American Poet*—saying it and then moving toward being it, possessing what passes for ambition in those beatnik days. He often wanders Harvard Square dressed in tennis whites, a racket tucked under his arm, though he doesn't play tennis. *Trawling for Radcliffe girls*, he calls it. He'd always been slight, and he'd overcompensate with his swagger. Ray's making jewelry, bending forks into rings, moonstones in spider settings. In later years Ray will open his own factory and make a fair bit of money manufacturing plastics used in missiles—"Daddy Warbucks," his family will call him.

One afternoon on Charles Street Jonathan nudges Ray, nods into the crowded sidewalk—*You watch*, he says, *there's going to be a girl walking down that street, and she'll be from a wealthy family. She'll have artistic aspirations but not much talent. She's coming to Beacon Hill to be part of the scene, looking for someone with talent that she can latch on to, looking to be the power behind a diamond in the rough, even if she still believes that she is the one with talent.* Jonathan squints into his sun-drenched future. *She doesn't know it yet, but she's looking for me.*

Jody, seventeen, home for the summer, works in a coffee shop in Scituate Harbor. A photograph from that time shows a girl with a dark brown ponytail, deep green eyes, a difficult smile. Jonathan orders coffee, chats her up. As he recalls it, *I think we went on a date the first night I met her. Your mother was beautiful, for chrissakes. I had a car, some shit-*

box I'd borrowed or finessed. We went on a date in it that first night. His charm, less tattered than it would later become, before several liquid tons of alcohol crush it out of him, appeals to Jody on some level. Rebellious and adrift, bounced from one boarding school to another (now between Dana Hall and House in the Pines), she comes from money. Her father was running his father's wool business, and during the war—uniforms, blankets, felt—wool had made money. Jonathan tells Jody he's back in town for the summer, doing construction, though in fact he's a laborer, digging ditches. In Palm Beach he's known as "Barracuda Buck, Native Guide." *Native to what?* Jody asks. He tells her about the novel he has yet to write, his faith in it. Barracuda. Half hot air, but Scituate's a small town—she tells him what time she gets off. After her shift he's waiting. They drive to Peggotty Beach, park facing the water as the sun sets behind their heads. He knows her family, knows their summer house on First Cliff, the biggest house in town. He'd seen her at the beach before, but she'd been just a child then. He uncorks a pint of whiskey, offers her some. They talk about their families, he tells her how he had to get away from his father (*that bald-headed fuck, playing his violin*), away from this small town, in order to become his own man. *If I'd've stayed here I'd be dead.* She struggles with her father also, feels he doesn't know her, has never tried. For the past year he's been sleeping with his secretary, Jody found a letter ("Not long now, dearest, before we're in Reno and all this is behind us"). They're both reading Salinger—*Catcher in the Rye* in her bag. She reads aloud her favorite passage so far:

> "When I was *really* drunk, I started that stupid business with the bullet in my guts again. I was the only guy at the bar with a bullet in their guts. I kept putting my hand under my jacket, on my stomach and all, to keep the blood from dripping all over the place. I didn't want anybody to know I was even wounded. I was con*ceal*ing the fact that I was a wounded sonuvabitch. . . ."

Jonathan puts his hand under his jacket and doubles over in pain. *No*, she says, *he's con*ceal*ing it.* His face goes stoic. They laugh. Jonathan sees his novel like that, breaking the world open, and Jody's willing to believe him, at least this night, and for many nights to follow. For the rest of the summer they'll meet on the beach that connects the two cliffs, lean against the seawall, out of the wind, out of sight, compare the size of their feet, press their palms together. He'll tell her more about his book, about Florida, about life on the docks. *To be a poet digging ditches is very different from being a mere ditch digger.* His family had thrived through the Depression, and he will also, but on his own terms. For a writer the place to be is Beacon Hill, he has friends there, he is known—he promises to take her.

beacon hill

Jonathan makes a couple trips back north from Palm Beach over the winter, to carouse Beacon Hill, to see Jody. A trolley connects House in the Pines with Boston—Jody meets him for parties, then for weekends. She's forbidden to stay out all night but she does anyway, sneaks back into her dorm the next afternoon, takes her punishment. By then her father has moved out, flown to Reno for six months to finalize his divorce, and her mother has stopped answering the phone. Years later she will tell me that when teachers yelled at her she simply blurred her eyes until they ceased to matter. She even shows me how, looking straight at me, narrowing her eyes slightly, heavy-lidded. She tells me this when I am having trouble at school. I try it but it never seems to work.

That winter Ray meets Clare, a student at Radcliffe. Jonathan will always claim to have introduced the two of them, as he likes to imagine his influence far-reaching, but this is not how they remember it. Clare describes Jody as "the most beautiful woman she had ever seen." *But not too bright*, she will quickly add, *after all, she was just a child. We'd have these big parties, and she'd always help out, get very concerned that everyone had enough to eat. In the kitchen at one of the parties I remember she asked, "Is China a country or a continent?" Can you imagine?*

In May Jonathan leaves Palm Beach for Boston and moves into Ray's apartment. Jody has let him know that she's three months pregnant. Already she's been spirited out of House in the Pines to the Florence Crittenton House, a home for unwed mothers. At this point no one knows what will happen. Anything could happen. Adoption is a possibility. Abortion, though illegal, is a possibility. There are places to go, back-alley doctors, a girl could take a bus to Providence. It's up to Jody, of course, but there is a lot of pressure for her to make a decision, soon. Her father by now is back in Scituate with his new wife, back in the big house on First Cliff, having set his first wife, my mother's mother, up in a new, smaller house across town. He arranges a meeting with Jonathan at Locke-Ober, a restaurant in Boston, demands to know what he intends. *Don't worry,* Jonathan assures him, *I'm not going down to Florida anymore. I'll marry the poor girl.* A proposition made, a deal struck, whereby Jody's father will set Jonathan up in business, a car dealership, the details to be ironed out later.

My mother, though, already has second thoughts about Barracuda. In a letter she never sends to my father, or perhaps the draft of a letter she does send, she writes,

> Christ, how much can a girl stand when the one she love<u>d</u> is always drunk—always up late with another and being tired and bitchy around her, out all the time. . . .

That August Ray drives Jonathan to the home for unwed mothers, and is the one witness to my parents' shotgun wedding. My brother is born a few months later. Ray drives my mother to the hospital, Jonathan shows up just after the birth—car trouble. That winter they all live together in Ray's apartment on the Hill. Clare remembers changing my brother's diapers.

Years later, when asked about his two marriages, first to my mother and then to his second wife, both young women from money, my father will say—*I never even asked them, they both asked me so I jumped on it.* We are alone in his apartment when he tells me this, years after the divorces, the jail time, the homelessness. *I've known a lot of poor women, and they were very nice, but not marriage material.* He glances at a photograph of my brother as an infant in my mother's arms, propped beside a photo of his second wife helping their daughter to walk. *I was thinking of the children we would have together—it was important what their background was, that they came from culture.* He looks me in the eye. *It was all for the children*, my father insists.

trader jon

Renault is the only spot open for them in the foreign car market, and they don't sell especially well. *Who the hell wants a Renault?* My father is set up as president, though my grandfather maintains ownership himself. They dub this doomed enterprise European Engineering, its world headquarters in Belmont, Massachusetts, one in a row of other dealerships. My father gets to wear a suit to work each morning and drives a new car and his pretty young wife is at home with their newborn and a few people work under him and it all seems to be unfolding nicely. Except my father has no talent for selling cars. And his father-in-law, his backer, his silent partner, is a businessman, and expects a return on his investment. The new son-in-law is expected to show his worth. But soon there is a cash-flow problem. My father has hired several of his old drinking buddies to work alongside, including Ray, and none of them knows the first thing about selling cars. Nothing much moves for the first few months, until my father hires an acquaintance named Duffy. Duffy, my grandfather will claim to this day, could sell sand to a beach. The cars start moving, and things look bright, until the folks that bought the cars began returning, to redeem the new radios, or the custom paint jobs, or the whitewall tires Duffy had promised them.

(1960) After two years of diminishing returns, after they had sold perhaps the only Renaults they would ever sell, my grandfather cans Jonathan as president of European Engineering, cuts his losses, folds up shop. My mother, though wary of her ne'er-do-well husband, is relieved to be no longer beholden to her father. My father decides to take in used foreign cars and sell them on commission, full-time, after having done it on the side, piecemeal, for a while. He leases another garage next door and christens himself "Trader Jon." His clients are rich, away in Europe for the summer, and these cars—BMWs and Mercedes, Fiats and MGs—sell themselves. But come fall there's another cash-flow problem. My father takes his time notifying his clients that their cars have sold, waiting instead for them to contact him. And when they do, often the money isn't there, already spent, and my father can't say on what. He assumed they were so rich that they wouldn't miss the money, not right away, but he was wrong. In another version he claims not to have kept track of the books, that he was born to be a president, not a treasurer, and it was the treasurer who set him up. But in the next breath he will claim, gleefully, that the entire "caper" made front-page news. A search through microfilm records of newspapers from that time reveals not a word.

In January I am born. Again Ray drives my mother to the hospital, just as he did when my brother was born. That June my mother, twenty years old, packs us up and leaves my father. She will never receive any child support from him, nor will she ever take any money from her father. Or perhaps none will be offered, at least not in a way that she will feel comfortable accepting. Perhaps she wanted to make it on her own. Perhaps she saw that money hadn't really ever made anything right. Perhaps her father did not want to confuse money with love, not again, and so he withheld the money, confusing them even more. *I lost a lot in that car business*, is all my grandfather will say now.

ulysses

Many fathers are gone. Some leave, some are left. Some return, unknown and hungry. Only the dog remembers. Even if around, most disappear all day, to jobs their children only slightly understand. Gone to office, gone to shop, men in suits hiding behind closed doors, yelling into phones, men in coveralls, reading pornography in pickup trucks. The carpenter. The electrician. They drive to strangers' houses, a woman in a robe answers the door, they sit at the table with her, she offers coffee and cake, they talk about the day ahead. By nightfall you won't recognize the bathroom, he promises. Monday we start in on the roof. Many end up sitting around the house all day, sneaking sips in the woodshed. Many drive to other towns, make love to a woman they've been making love to for years. Some continue to yell at their sons from the grave, some are less than a tattered photograph. Some sons need to exhume the body, some need to see a name written in a ledger. Some drive past a house the father once lived in as a child, park across from it, some swear that if they could gaze into his face just once their hearts would settle. One friend inherited some money and hired a private investigator to track down his lost father, paid a thousand dollars to find out his father was dead. All my life my father had been manifest as an absence, a nonpresence, a name without a body. The three of us sat around the table, my mother, brother and I, all carrying his name. *Flynn*?

Some part of me knew he would show up, that if I stood in one place long enough he would find me, like you're taught to do when you're lost. But they never taught us what to do if both of you are lost, and you both end up in the same place, waiting.

winter

(1989) My father wraps himself in newspaper some nights, stuffs his coat with newspaper, the headlines finally about him, though he isn't named. Just more heartstring pieces about "the homeless." *Get it straight, I've never flung a knife or shot a bullet at anyone. I've only been locked up for two of my fifty-nine years. I'm no jailbird.* The nights drop below freezing and still he sleeps outside. "My toes," he writes me, "are being cut off." On wet nights he wraps himself in plastic, a Hefty trashbag sealed with duct tape, he weaves himself a cocoon, lies on the ground, puts his feet into the bag and pushes until they reach the bottom. Leaning forward, he tightens the plastic around his ankles and tapes them, and then he tapes the bag around his waist. This way, in the night, the bag won't slide down his body.

two hundred years ago

If you had been raised in a village two hundred years ago, somewhere in Eastern Europe, say, or even on the coast of Massachusetts, and your father was a drunk, or a little off, or both, then everyone in the village, those you grew up with and those who knew you only from a distance, they would all know that the town drunk or the village idiot was your father. It couldn't be hidden or denied. Everything he did, as long as you stayed in the village, whether shouting obscenities at passing children or sleeping in the cemetery, all would be remembered when they looked at you, they would say to themselves or to whomever they were with, *It's his father, you know, the crazy one, the drunk,* and they couldn't help but wonder what part of his madness had passed on to you, which part you had escaped. They would look into your eyes to see if they were his eyes, they would notice if you were to stumble slightly as you stepped into a shop, they would remember that your father too had started with promise, like you. They would know he was a burden, they could read the struggle in your face, they would watch as you passed and nod, knowing that around the next corner your father had fallen and pissed himself. And they would watch you watch him, note the days you simply kept walking, as if you didn't see, note the days you knelt beside him, tried to get him to rise, to prop him up. If they were friends and they came by your house they couldn't help but notice whether you had an extra room, or whether your own situation seemed precarious, marginal. And they might not say anything but they would take it in and wonder, either way it meant something. If this was two hundred years ago you left the village maybe once a month, to bring whatever it was you grew or fabricated—onions or oil, wine or cloth—to a distant market to sell, only to return in a day or two to the village, and you might get the sense, perhaps rightly, that there was nowhere else on earth for you to be, that to leave the village would be akin to banishment, to enter into a lifetime of wandering, to become open to speculation that you'd abandoned your father to his fate, turned your back, left him to die. Taken and not given back. For if you are not responsible for your own father, who is? Who is going to pick him up off the ground if not you?

the cage

(1984) I'm twenty-four when I start at Pine Street, full of nonspecific, scattershot longing. "Dissatisfied" is an emotion. When my shift gets off at eleven I go out with my co-workers and drink to the eventual collapse of the capitalist system, to the hollowness of the go-go eighties. Working with the homeless we can hear the buildings crumble. Yet each night we close Foley's and step out, faintly disappointed, into the still-standing city.

As a newcomer I often work the Cage, where the bed tickets are given out, and the valuables, if any, are stored. Controlled, in terms of contact with the guests—four hours a night, one-on-one, easy. It is also the busiest time in the shelter, when the lobbies are at their most chaotic, the building just reopened after being shut all day. Three hundred to six hundred men will swell through the doors in the next few hours. This is when dinner is served, when the clinic is open, when the men are shepherded upstairs and into beds, those who managed to score a bed. Slowly I am getting to know them by name, trying to be responsible, to count their money out where they can see my hands.

4011. Yes sir, sleep will feel fine tonight.

And your name . . . ?

What's the name beside the number? That's my name.

Ah yes, the ever-satisfied Jamal Dexter. Smokes dope in the park all day, they say, sells loose joints to the youngbloods. Followed in line by the nearly unintelligible Randy Phillips, who cannot utter his own name, who cannot look me in the eye, who unfolds yesterday's bed ticket and slides it through the slot, both hands on it, precious.

Carlos, a co-worker, shows me the ropes. Make sure they sign for everything, make sure the number on the envelope matches their bed number, call a counselor if something isn't right. During a lull one night he tells the story of how he shot a guy under the tracks of the old Dudley Station, how he'd been looking for this guy to avenge a wrong done to his little brother, how the guy pulled a gun when Carlos found him, shot once but Carlos knew to turn sideways, take the bullet in his biceps. He even turns sideways as he tells the story, *Like this, flex, your arm can take it, better than making your whole body a target.* After he took the bullet he knocked the gun from the guy's hand, leveled him with a punch, picked up the gun and unloaded the rest into the guy's head. In telling the story he holds two fingers like a gun to show how he kept pulling the trigger, *click click, click click*, long after the gun was empty. He went into hiding for a year, disappeared upstate, came back, began working the shelter.

Inside the shelter the tension is inescapable—the walls exude cigarette smoke and anxiety. The air is thick, stale, dreamy, though barely masking the overpowering smell of stale sweat. When open the lobbies fill with a constant nameless din, the murmur of hundreds of men, the narcotic drone of a television, punctuated by the occasional freak-out—an altercation here, someone shouting down a private demon there. All heads turn toward the sound, register it, turn away. When blows are being exchanged, if a staff member is there to intervene, he or she will intervene. A balance between escalating and defusing, stepping in and backing the fuck off. The ground floor is divided into the Brown Lobby and the Yellow Lobby, each lobby its own city, cities within the city, each with its own rules, its own physics. Brown is mostly oldtimers—drunks, mellow, regular; Yellow is the youngbloods—psych, addicts, wilder. From my perch behind the steel-mesh screen, when there is a lull in giving out bed tickets, in putting pennies into envelopes, the rhythm of these cities can slowly enter my bloodstream.

I work the Cage for a few months through that first fall, until the cycle of life within the shelter begins to make some sense to me. Patterns emerge. On Fridays, payday, there's more money to check in, more drunken men pushing it at me through the slot. The drunks show up later and are, depending on the man, either more boisterous or more sullen. Jimmy's got the shakes again, after a month of doing so well. He's perfected the trick of stashing a fifth in his sleeve, of raising his arms with a flourish above his head for the frisk. Eddie is carried in by the cops again—not only did he lose his leg beneath a bus a few winters before, but now he's lost his fake leg. More than likely he took it off himself and brandished it at a passerby, some "punk-assed bitch." Some get government checks, either for a physical disability or a mental one. They call the mental ones "nut checks." These checks come on the first of the month, a time when the predators, usually the young addicts, show up at the shelter, lurking, waiting for a mark. Staff that have worked the shelter longer know the thieves, know their targets. But the old guys are easily lured away by a bottle, down the alley, only to limp back, sheepish, a pocket torn, a bloodied ear, broke again.

Joy works the front desk. She'd been a cokehead and a prostitute and is now an oversized redheaded mother to the guys. Years later she will end up in a room with a shotgun across her lap, back to dealing and smoking crack 24/7. When I first land at Pine Street she is benign and ravaged, a failed queen who seldom leaves her throne at the front door. *We catch them on the way down,* Joy says. *Next stop, the morgue.* Each year we count a hundred, a hundred and fifty, dead from the year before. These are just the ones we can name, the ones we know. In a few years we will begin holding a memorial service for them, reading off the names of those we can remember, mostly as a way to stave off our own sense of desperation, of hopelessness. We will build two hundred crosses in my loft, paint them white, paint the name of someone who had died on each one, hammer them into the Common one night, an instant graveyard.

funeral, unattended

(1963) Sunglasses in the visor, wallet in the glove compartment, satchel in the back. A sports coat on a hanger so it doesn't wrinkle. Look the cop in the eye, nod, don't look at the cop at all, adjust the mirror, the ashtray empty, the window down. Drive with both hands so as not to draw heat—respectable citizen, upright. The red light turns green but no one's behind, no one honks.

My father drives back to Scituate one day and everything's been replaced. Houses have changed color and there are more of them—the bookstore's now a knickknack shop, the bookie's a barber, the package store's a bank. He digs his heel in below the gas pedal as he steers, his heel wears a hole in the carpet, beneath the carpet is steel. Sweat drips from his ankle in summer, collects in the hole, eats away at the steel. Without thinking he will end up outside the house he grew up in, he will look at the front door but he will not enter. His legs will not carry him, his hand will not work the latch, as in the dream when you come to the threshold you know you must pass but cannot. Open your mouth to scream but nothing comes out.

My mother by now has a warrant out on him for nonpayment of child support. "Nonsupport" we call it around my house. I'm three, and cannot remember my father, who is thirty-three. After my mother left him he drifted, south again, eventually ending up back in Palm Beach. There he's found the title for his book—*The Little World of Pier 5*. It's all mapped out in his head, he just has to write it down.

Idling outside his family home my father sits in his car, a wood-grained Ford station wagon, a "Woodie," a car the Beach Boys sing about. The springs buried in the seat dig into his back. This is the house he lived in, off and on, until he married my mother. He looks up to his mother's bedroom window, the shade pulled half down, how he left it when he left, his mother bedridden then. If he opens the car door the inside light will click on and he will be illuminated, he will turn from shadow to object, become solid, something you could attach handcuffs to. Two brothers he went to school with have become town cops, the Breen boys, *those ignorant fucks*. They know my father's face, know about the warrant, one even stops by my grandmother's for coffee, promises to keep a sharp eye out. If my father's foot comes off the clutch, touches down on the tar, the sirens will sound, the Breen boys will appear with their warrant, their clubs, say, "Aha," say, "Gotcha," carry him away, the car left at the stoplight, the door sprung open, the interior light lighting the now-empty seat, the seat shaped like his body, the radio playing Top 40.

Move your foot from the brake to the gas, keep your foot on the clutch—the house stays where it is, stays where you left it. Close your eyes and you see it—open them and it's there. A sunspot on your eyelid, that's home. Cover one eye and it flattens, it shifts to one side. Cover the other, it shifts to the left. Blink slowly back and forth—the house swings like a pendulum on a grandfather clock, your mother laid out in the parlor.

Did he know he would never return, never walk up the front steps, never enter the kitchen again? A woman he almost recognizes carries a platter up to the door, sandwiches maybe, but what is her name? Inside there will be plenty of liquor, a sea of booze, but not enough. If he steps into the house again not even the walls will stand where he remembers. Each room will be smaller, rooms he'd forgotten will appear between them. The paint will be wrong and he will not find the hole where he kicked his foot through the plaster the night of the storm when he knew his boat was badly anchored. If he pushes open the door his mother will be dead inside and if he doesn't, well, what will that mean? If he pushes open the door he can say goodbye to her body but what is the body? If he crosses the threshold the police will be waiting in one of two small rooms, *ignorant fucks*, waiting for his return, they have waited all these years. Blood from a stone. Once he could outrun them but he no longer knows the way through his own house.

hiss & fall

Spring-timed, the showers run maybe thirty seconds before the valve twists shut and you are forced to hit the stainless steel button again. When the water shuts off sometimes the man beneath the spray beside you doesn't notice. Hands in his hair, lather running in streams down his face, eyes straight ahead—the sound of water surrounds him, you keep hitting your button, but this one man is lost—lost in the white tiles, lost in the fluorescence, lost in the hiss and the fall.

After the Cage, Housing is the next level of work open to newcomers. Or at least this is where newcomers are encouraged to work. Only a few hours a night, like the Cage, but it's more intense. No longer are you protected behind steel mesh. This is where the men bring the bed tickets that were handed out earlier at the Cage, this is where they strip down naked and hand in their clothes, to be stored overnight in the Hot Room. The Hot Room has a door like an old freezer, with that kind of pull handle, but inside it's a sauna, wood-lined, set for maybe 180 degrees fahrenheit. To kill any bugs, to vaguely sanitize the clothes. Inside the Hot Room the smell is of superheated sweat, quick-fermented, an almost shiny smell, as shiny as an overworn coat. The joke is that it's a good place to go to make out. Meet me in the Hot Room in ten minutes, we joke with our co-workers. If I'm not there start without me, they joke back. An as-yet-unnamed inner ring of Hell. A counter separates the guests from the two workers who take their clothes, live-in staff, formerly homeless guys who now live at the shelter, have their own rooms. A transitional step, theoretically, back into the world. Normally there are two counselors working Housing, one for the Brown side, one for the Yellow, but often one fails to show, which can make things difficult. The live-in staff worker takes the bed ticket, hands back a plastic bin with a wooden hanger and a wrist tag inside. The guest hangs his jacket, pants and shirt on the hanger, then puts his shoes, socks, underwear and whatever else into the bin. Both the hanger and bin are then given back to the live-in staff worker, who walks the hanger into the Hot Room, puts the bin on a shelf. Similar to a coat check at a museum, the number on the hanger corresponds to the number on the wrist tag, except this is also the number of a bed. Each man is allowed to store one bag overnight—by nine there is a mountain of bags to negotiate around. My job is to oversee this operation, to see it moves along smoothly, defuse any incidents. Mirrors are screwed to the walls along the benches the guests sit on while they undress, only these mirrors are made of stainless steel, not glass—glass could break, become a weapon. Someone might punch the face looking the wrong way back at him. The screws that attach the metal to the wall cause slight indentations, the indentations cause distortions, creating a funhouse effect. Your head in this mirror, if held at a certain level, becomes massive. Your chin vanishes. Move slightly and you can have superman arms, or a belly that takes over your body. You can open your mouth and it keeps on opening, becomes your whole head. Some of the drunk guys, some of the psych guys, you see them, halfway naked on a bench, staring at their reflections, openmouthed—*When did I become a gargoyle?*

How do they navigate an hour, I wonder, let alone a city, a lifetime? One of my first nights upstairs a man needs a new set of clothes—maybe he'd pissed himself, maybe he had bugs, maybe it was just time. As I head for the room where the donated clothing is sorted and stored, I stop, whisper to Gabriel, a salt-of-the-earth Midwesterner who approaches the job with a mixture of gravitas and levity that I aspire to, *How do I know what size he wears?* Gabriel just looks at me and smiles—*You ask him.*

Just off the changing room are the showers, a tiled room with a dozen showerheads, where the men pass through and hopefully linger, if only for a few moments. I move between the men undressing and the showers, stand between the two rooms, subtly looking over their bodies, checking for rashes or discolorations or anything weird, which I will report to the clinic. I will check the condition of their clothes and offer replacements. If a man is too drunk I will send him back downstairs to sleep it off in the lobby rather than risk a scene in the dorms. But I won't do any of this at first, at first I won't know what I am doing, beyond watching them wash, beyond steering them upstairs without any hassles. At first I will count how many times the button must be pressed for a man to take a shower. Some drunks seem to find the water an annoyance, some psych guys speak directly into the spigot, arguing with the pressure, pleading. Most hit the button five or six times, enough for a quick lather and rinse. Sometimes a drunk will go over to the other side, turn psychotic. Sometimes the psych guys will start drinking, some call it "self-medicating" but it looks like clinging to an anvil in the middle of the sea. Like everywhere, some are ashamed of their bodies, turn their faces to the tiles, hold their hands over their privates as they walk. Some glance at others' bodies, some glance longer. Some stand defiant, with their hand on the button, pressing it like a gambler murmuring, *Hit me*. Burt comes in every night, stands under the shower for an hour, slams the button over and over with the side of his fist. I don't know his story. To chat is difficult up in Housing, difficult to start up a conversation with a naked man. Burt looks like he works construction, at least he wears a hardhat, and his clothes are often covered with plaster dust. A big man, barrel-chested, he comes upstairs in the last hour, stands under the hot water until it's time to close up, his legs spread wide. He looks like a construction worker, but perhaps it's just a costume. Perhaps he was a construction worker, once, and at some point he lost his job, got laid off. Maybe he never was, technically, constructing anything, maybe he did demolition, maybe they handed him a sledgehammer and a pry bar, pointed to a wall. Maybe he drank, maybe the job dried up, maybe he swung the sledgehammer at the boss one day, maybe one day they pointed to the door. In subsequent months I'll see Burt walking downtown. Once or twice I'll see him dozing on a bench in the Common, still wearing that yellow plastic hardhat.

my dostoyevsky

(1964) Head bowed, faux contrite, my father stands in the dock, listens to what he's done, awaits his sentence. It could be a year, it could be five. The judge asks if he has anything to say in his own defense and my father says nothing. The arresting officer tells the story of finding him behind the wheel of the Palm Beach sheriff's family car. In the backseat were the passengers he'd picked up, as if he were driving a taxi and they were his fares. It's against the law to impersonate a taxi in Florida, but this lesser charge is dropped for the greater charge of stealing an automobile. My father was drunk at the time and in a blackout, though he never uses that word. The words he uses are "toxic amnesia." Still bleary, he remembers none of it.

He's been held in the "stockade" since his arrest, five weeks ago, awaiting trial. But now there is no trial, just the formality of sentencing, as he enters a guilty plea. He stands in the dock, does not fight what the judge hands down—six months' hard labor in the county jail. In lieu of doing time he could pay a fine, not much, really, a few hundred dollars, he could wire his father and ask for the money, but maybe both of them know it's better this way. My father, it seems, cannot stop drinking. Not on the outside, not on his own. For almost twenty years, since high school, he has identified himself as a writer, but he has yet to write much, beyond notes scribbled out on cocktail napkins, titles for his novels-to-be. He's been locked up before—a week here, an overnight there—so he knows what the inside of a cell is like. No leniency begged—he will be sober for a few months and he will write out the novel that sits in his head. Something inside him knows it won't get done otherwise, that the booze is eating away at his talents, his energies. In six months (no, *five*, he gets credit for time served), he will emerge with a draft. This setback will be turned into a victory. It will quiet the chatter in his head.

He thinks:

> *This will be my prison novel. My Dostoyevsky. My Solzhenitsyn. Solzhenitsyn will be green with envy when he reads this shit.*

Except this isn't a prison—it's a county jail. Palm Beach, no less, hardly Siberia. Here the prisoners play Monopoly in the hallways. He isn't doing time for any grand or noble purpose—it's an everyday drunk charge, a car stolen in a blackout. But prison sounds more grandiose than jail, and grandiose is preferable to commonplace. Years later he will be arrested again, for robbing banks, though really it'll be for passing forged checks. This time he *will* end up in prison, and he will be given more time, three to five, but by then his powers, whatever they once were or might have been, will be gone. He may imagine another novel will come from it but nothing will. By the time he gets out this second time he will be nearly fifty, having drunk heavily for thirty years, and he will live in Boston from flophouse to flophouse, driving a real taxi now, not a sheriff's car, twenty years after going to jail for impersonating a taxi.

exterminator!

Just off the showers is the drying room, where a live-in staff worker sits in a closet, handing out towels and soap, flip-flops and johnnies. One flight up to the dorms another live-in staff worker leads each man to the right bed, after silently aiming his flashlight at the wrist tag. Sometimes it goes smoothly, often not. At nine o'clock we hurry the last guy upstairs, close the Hot Room, set the thermostat, go down to the lobby, write up the night in the log:

9:10 Housing firsts—
Tonight I was called to the fourth floor to rescue Isaac Clegg, who not only fell out of bed, but had the bed fall on him. Upon extrication Isaac was found to have a cut above his eye, and was brought

to the clinic for a look. The bed was returned to its proper position.

Amazing how easily the skin of a drunk splits open, their blood really does flow more freely, thinned out by the booze. I helped Isaac to his feet, walked him downstairs, leaving tiny crimson drops all the way. The nurses had gone for the day so I dressed the wound myself.

And Russell Pagano had a Kwell.

In the beginning this is my true purpose, the thing I can do that seems to help, that seems to do *something*. "Kwell" is the brand name for a skin lotion/shampoo used to kill bugs—head lice, pubic lice, scabies—which feast on human blood. Kwell's active ingredient is DDT, the banned pesticide, and the warning states it's not to be administered to the same body more than once in thirty days, though we sometimes do, if the bugs are especially pernicious, if they have taken up residence, built cities. I've been trained to kill bugs from an early age. To keep me busy my grandmother would send me into her yard with a bottle of bleach to pour down the anthills—a thrill to see thousands of ants stream out of their underground world and writhe. Later, the last house my family lived in was infested with carpenter ants, bigger than the ants I'd bleach, meaner, named (or misnamed) for their tendency to eat through wooden sills and joists. Hours were spent with a hammer on the sewer cap in the backyard under the spotlight, crushing those that scurried into the light.

At Pine Street I continue in my role of exterminator. I have a way with the psych guys, a certain patience to sit and engage them in twisted ramblings, about aliens invading their bodies, about self-dentistry and handmade shoes, then gently steer the conversation back to their need for a Kwell. George likes to set trashbarrels on fire in the Common and warm his hands over the flames, muttering about his lost kingdoms. George, to hear him tell it, is a deposed, and sometimes a beheaded, queen. Queen George. Lice thrive so well on his body that they can be seen crawling over him from twenty paces. I sit beside him as he picks one the size of a corn kernel off his neck. He holds it to his eye and speaks, a benediction. To get George upstairs is a coup, to convince him to peel off the layers of clothing collected over god knows how many months and stand before me naked, six-four and muttering, to allow me to apply the poison to his back, between his legs, to the red spots that cover his chest—this is my destiny. First I bring him to the clothing room to pick out a complete new outfit—a pair of gray wool pants, not covering his ankles, as is his style; high lace boots; a thermal t-shirt; three wool sweaters; a long snorkel jacket with fur trim around the hood. To Kwell George can take an hour or two—first he needs to strip, then shower, then the lotion needs to seep into his skin, then he has to shower again. I sit beneath the fluorescents, listening to how they tried to burn him at the stake but he wouldn't catch fire, his big hands still working his flesh, searching for his dying minions. Nothing in the shelter makes more sense to me, makes me understand my purpose more, than to kill bugs on a homeless man's flesh, to dress him well in donated, cast-off clothes, to see him the next day, laughing beside a burning barrel.

button man

(1964) While in the Palm Beach County Jail my father's job will be to sit in a booth and work the switch that lets people in and out of the front gate. Button Man. In from the outside, out from the inside. If he lets a man escape he will have to serve that man's time, that's what they tell him. *The Button Man* will be the title of his novel. I'm too young to know what prison is, nearly too young to know what a father is, or that mine is gone.

He thinks (approximately):

> *My father saw bodies falling and he imagined a machine. The* Titanic *went down while he was drawing his plans. They ran for the lifeboats but there weren't enough, not enough room on deck for that many lifeboats. My father's*

invention could be stacked like cordwood, he showed me how with a little model he made—simply cut the line and they all float free. A seat in the dark ocean for every man, woman and child.

He thinks:

Self-made man, success at twenty-eight, my father saw the ship sinking, saw bodies falling, and he made a net to catch them. I'm proud of that. He could have invented anything—the machine gun, dynamite—killed millions. Ten years later he made me, an afterthought. Already his prototype was in production, the patent sold to seven countries, already he was known. And I was no one. Not yet.

He thinks:

We never got along, I never understood why. I was the only one who did any work around that goddamn house—I filled the oil tanks, mowed the lawn—my two half-brothers never lifted a twig. I stood beside my father while he had a new and improved raft dropped over and over from a crane into Scituate Harbor, perfecting it. He was madly in love with my sister—me, never.

He thinks:

Prisons are not unlike ships—men of all types huddle in the hold, some stroll freely above, all aware it's going down.

I too see bodies falling—habeus corpus, deliver the body of ______, and the sheriff comes, leading ______ in shackles. Maybe this is the root of the anxiety—something terrible is about to happen. Or nothing good is about to happen.

Sherrie writes:

Dear Buckie, 3 April 1964

All your pals were sorry to hear about your misfortune, but everyone expects great things to come out of it. I know how good it must feel to have the writing urge and be able to develop it. Please, Buckie, do some writing, this is your chance. I told the gang about your ideas for your novel, and they can't wait to see it.

Pogo writes:

Barracuda, 13 May 1964

You're sorely missed back here on the Hill.

I've been dating a guy the last couple weeks who thinks a lot like you do—that he is bright and can't see himself taking a mickey-mouse job. That the world owes him a living. He considers himself a writer, like you, but I sense he's going to wait until it's too late before he really gets to work. When he does try, wine and poor living are going to be his weakness, what ate away at his strength. He'll die in some gutter like all the other poor useless bums.

I only hope that you will utilize some of the intelligence

that you innately possess to try to articulate your situation to the world.

Steady Ray writes:

Dear Jonathan, 3 June 1964

I called your father yesterday to find out if he had made arrangements for you to get back. He feels strongly that it would be better for you to stay in Florida or perhaps go to South America or Hong Kong. He says he could get you a job in Hong Kong through a friend. Your father said that the sheriffs in four counties are looking for you, in connection with your car. I believe the charges have to do with permitting an unlicensed person to operate and the unpaid insurance. Your father said he lost his own license for three weeks over it and has paid $95 in parking tickets. He still does not have the car back and is not very happy about the situation. The Florida authorities notified the Massachusetts authorities and you will not be able to get a license here.

Next point: you always have more trouble when you are in Boston. You are not able to handle alcohol, and living with your friends here will not help if you want to change.

Finally, your father is selling his house, he hopes within a few days, and he will not be able to provide a home for you.

This is a summary of what your father said. He may

well be right that your best bet is to get a job in Florida or Hong Kong. I think he will help you if you decide to stay there, but he will not help you if you come back.

He thinks:

These letters are classics. I will include them in my prison novel. Every letter I receive while doing time will become part of my novel. I will write one word after another and then follow them like a rope out of my cell. Like a chain. Follow the chain of words back to my life.

the time of your life

The Pine Street Inn occupies an entire city block in Boston's South End. When it moved here in the early 1980s the neighborhood was verging on derelict, even though it's minutes from downtown. White flight in the '60s and '70s, combined with an economic practice known as "redlining," where certain sections of the city (read: *black*) were deemed not worthy of investment by the banks, left every third building vacant. The building that became Pine Street is a landmark, a replica of a Sienese tower, marking the entrance into Boston as you drive north on I-93. The tower was used by firemen for a hundred years to practice jumping from a burning building into a net below. Then it became a shelter.

Across from Pine Street, across East Berkeley, looms the Medieval Manor, which describes itself as a "theatre-restaurant." It opened, coincidentally, the same year the Pine Street Inn moved from its original location, on the real Pine Street, to this abandoned fire station on Harrison Avenue. The Medieval Manor, in its brochure, invites one to "step back hundreds of years into a bawdy, rollicking romp through the Middle Ages." You sit at long tables as "guests of the king," while "the minstrel, jester, oaf and wenches respond to the Lord of the Manor's every whim." While taking in the fun you are offered a "sumptuous, seven-course banquet, eaten without fork, knife, or spoon." The Medieval Manor promises to be "the time of your life." Occasionally, when dinner is being served at Pine Street, a well-dressed party of four appears at our front door, obviously having taken a wrong turn. They ask, timidly, if this is the Medieval Manor, and sometimes I say *yes*, and direct them inside.

chet's last call

Most have been in one war or another—Vietnam, mostly—for some it's true and some just believe it's true. Many have been married, many have been in prison. One man speaks through a hole in his throat. Several are blind, many deaf or near deaf. The junkies have holes in their arms that won't heal. A cotton wick needs to be inserted daily, to drain the pus, and most days they forget to have it done. The epileptics need their meds or they seize—if they drink on their meds they seize worse. Men come through the door with limps and canes, with walkers, crutches, in wheelchairs, and crawling. Some are carried in, draped between two friends, feet dragging behind. One has a glass eye he keeps losing. One has FUCK YOU tattooed on the inside of his lower lip. A few have tears tattooed on their cheeks, which means they've killed someone. Some have scars from the corners of their mouths to their ears, which means they squealed. Many fingers are gone, or half gone, to heavy machinery or knife fights. Some earlobes have been nibbled off by rats. One guy was set on fire—now the burn scars rise up his neck like flames. A few of the old guys have hernias—their stomachs have fallen into their testicles, which now hang enormously between their legs. Kenny has had the same cough for five years, so he cannot sleep upstairs. At one point David's teeth were giving him trouble, so he got a book on dentistry from the library and began to learn on himself. He opens his mouth and shows us, how he'd pulled out the infected tooth with pliers, superglued tiny nails in its place.

That first summer twenty or thirty guys could be sprawled out on the benches and floor of the Brown Lobby. We put a cap on the number we will allow in after nine, send the rest back into the night. As the nights get colder more men show up, and a temperature is agreed upon, maybe forty-five degrees, if it gets below that we won't turn anyone away. The lobbies will be open and the men can wander in anytime. Still, some freeze to death outside, those that can't make it back, those that forget there's someplace to go. As fall becomes winter the numbers sleeping in each lobby increase, until by January there are a hundred, a hundred and fifty men sprawled out. Clusterfucked, now there's nowhere to even put your foot—guys stake out corners, tabletops, benches, any square of open floor, and still more come, without anywhere to fall but on top of someone else, who yell and kick and punch the intruder off. Some end up playing cards and smoking beneath the gloom of an exit sign or in the shaft of light coming from the open door of the piss-soaked bathroom. Some wrap their bodies around their possessions and feign sleep. Some pace and mutter, bend to pick butts off the tile, their fingers orange with nicotine. Some piss themselves in their sleep, and the piss spreads out, soaking those unfortunate enough to be in proximity. The weekend supervisor calls himself "Captain Yusef," and he calls the 3-to-11 the "Can-Do Shift."

After work we go out drinking, to the Rat or the Middle East or to Chet's Last Call, to hear the Minutemen or the Pixies, the Del Fuegos or Galaxie 500. Motorhead or Flesh For Lulu. Or just to drink, to lean into each other and shout over the noise, to put our lips to each other's ears, to see how it feels to be that close, another's voice vibrating inside our brains, barely understood but enough. Enough to drive to her apartment after closing time and stay. And then the next afternoon we're both back in the Brown Lobby, listening to the reading of the log. Only now I'd been in her room or she'd been in mine and we know more about each other, we'd seen each other naked or felt the other's nakedness in the darkness and we're both sheepish but charged up by it all and we know we'll go out drinking again after the shift only maybe this time alone or maybe just go straight to her apartment.

• • •

Often I feel like a glorified security guard, often a guest is asked to take a walk because there isn't time to deal with him any other way. And if a guest begins to "escalate," to "go off" *(Look! here comes a walking fire!)*, it threatens the whole building, *poof*, up in flames. Some days it feels like an unending play, a play that began from an idea, the idea of bending down to someone struggling, but that idea kept expanding, like some theory of the universe, until it grew so large that it will be impossible to ever stage. It has become nearly the size of air, or water. A map the size of the world.

It could have just been a job, a paycheck, relatively well-paying for unskilled labor. For some of my co-workers it was, some make a career of less. But I didn't think working with the homeless would be my career. I left several times, for a month or six, only to return, start again, back in the Brown Lobby. I didn't care so much about the money, I had other ways to make money. But I kept returning. At the shelter no one asks where you come from or why you ended up there. The woman I went home with didn't ask why I wasn't trying for something more—a nice car, a real apartment. No matter what I'd say it'd only be half believed anyway. After eight hours her clothes and her hair smelled just like mine. *Everyone's here for a reason*, Joy says, looking at a well-dressed, seemingly put-together guy who claims to be temporarily in a tight spot. She gives him a bed, and by the end of the week the police carry him in, legless and swinging.

two

fire

(1960s) I crawl toward my father's face as we lay on the grass beside a whitewalled tire—a snapshot, an artifact—evidence that at some point, at least once, I was an infant in his arms. The father as ship, as vessel, holding the child afloat. But there was a parallel father as well—the drunk, the con, the paranoid. The father as ship, but taking on water, going down.

When I was six months old my mother gathered us up and left. The truck came while Jonathan was at work and moved us, back to Scituate, one town over. *It's a complete mystery to me why she'd leave. I wasn't drinking, I never drank, not when I was working.* This is his version. She never spoke about that day, not to me. What I remember is that every six months for the first five years of my life we moved, but all within the same town, like we each had one foot nailed to the sidewalk. For a while we stayed on the couch of a woman my mother worked with at a restaurant. This woman's husband lived in a wheelchair, the house all ramped and railed. We slept upstairs, in a hallway, between rooms, out of the way. We were getting on our feet, looking for a place. My mother's parents lived in the same town, she must have left us with one or the other, some nights, just us kids. Our mother wouldn't have stayed with them, not too often. Twenty, twenty-one, she wanted to make it on her own. Not even a high school diploma, she held two or three jobs, in bars and restaurants, in convenience stores. A certificate from hairdressing school, but the only hair she cut was ours, my brother's, mine. Bottle-blond sometimes, she wore a wig sometimes. Once she got her own room she'd line the wigs up on styrofoam heads on the thrift store bureau she'd painted blue. Until then we rented rooms, we rented houses, we crashed with co-workers, with friends, each a rathole, a sty, each a step down. I couldn't help out, my hands useless, not sized for anything in that world. I played with a little stuffed monkey ("Jocko"—expensive, imported, my father charged it to my grandfather, mailed it to me on Christmas), I entertained her as best I could. I'd explain the games I invented, the fort I'd built out of blankets and chairs, how the cat was now my prisoner. "Whatd'ya want me to do," she'd say, "stand on my head and spit nickels?" When I misplaced a mitten or a Matchbox she'd barely look up from whatever she was doing, just matter-of-factly point out "If it was up your ass you'd know where it was." I loved these expressions, playful and surreal.

Five years of this, of piecing together lousy jobs, of roaming, and she had enough. She took a job at the bank, as a teller, so we'd have insurance (*bluecrossblueshield*), so she could get a loan, a mortgage. She could still work nights and weekends in bars, in restaurants. The Bell Buoy. Pier 44. The Ebb Tide, with its unintentionally tragic name. For a while she woke up at five to open the bakery at the supermarket, where she made donuts. This was the only real supermarket in town, having drawn the lifeblood (*bigfisheatlittlefish*) from the smaller markets. I remember it being built on the muddy field that the tenements once occupied. A friend had lived in one of those decrepit buildings—the yellow trucks came one day and knocked them all down. Each evening after the workers left I'd creep around the machines and mud. A small outbuilding was left standing and inside were boxes filled with skeleton keys (a key to a skeleton? or was the key itself a bone?). I took some home and the next evening this building too was gone, bulldozed under.

The bank gave her a loan to buy a two-thousand-dollar ruin, a complete wreck of a house. Nightly the raccoons came to our ramshackle porch and raided the garbage, which was submerged in the yard beneath a lid that flipped open when you stepped on it. We'd watch them from the kitchen with the lights out, amazed at how organized they were, a team—one holding open the lid, another reaching into the pail and passing out the bones and scraps to a line of hungry bandits. The lookout would raise a paw and hiss if we came to the door.

Unless a boyfriend was sleeping over she would bring my brother and me to the supermarket rather than leave us in that drafty house to wake up alone. We'd wander the empty aisles while she opened the bakery. It was unspoken, but we could eat anything we wanted, as long as we hid the evidence. At least that's how I understood our agreement. An entire supermarket. Like a television game show. Aisle of cracker, aisle of chocolate. A few years later I would walk in with the silver coins I stole from the coffee can in her bedroom, coins she'd hoarded from the bank, from tips, and use them to buy candy bars, until one day a cashier asked if I really wanted to use a rare Flying Liberty silver dollar to pay for a Heath bar. Soon after I began shoplifting, deciding it was wrong to take money from my mother. I hit all the stores she had worked—the convenience store, the newsstand, I even had my eye on the bank. I found a loose grate that led into a crawlspace and to the bank's basement. I was skinny, I had a plan. In the supermarket I mirrored what I had done just a few years earlier as my mother was busy making donuts in the still-dark morning, only now I did it in daylight. I was maybe all of eight. I'd wander in, put plums in my pockets, Twinkies, walk out. We got no allowance, and this was where the food was. The good food. I had been feeding myself there as long as I knew. Soon I didn't even bother to see if I was being watched. I ate the plums as I wandered, left the pits on the shelves beside boxes of cereal, beside the faces of smiling athletes. I'd go to the bakery, look past the glass cabinet at the donut machine, I'd remember standing on a chair watching the yellowy dough extrude into the hot oil, watching the donuts form, roiling in the agony of becoming. My mother would set us up at the formica lunch counter on the spinning stools and give us juice, milk, hot donuts. I would take the little packages of jelly and fill my pockets, the vast parking lot slowly coming out of the darkness through the plate-glass windows behind us. Occasionally a carpenter would come and rap on the window, hoping to be let in, to be allowed an early donut. Occasionally my mother would unlock the door, let him in.

Within a few months the house caught fire—the raccoons toppled a smoldering grill left on the back porch. My brother and I were asleep upstairs when our mother came in with Vernon, her boyfriend at the time, and lifted us, still wrapped in blankets, to carry us through the smoky house. The fire station sat directly across the street, I remember running up the stairs, busting in on the firemen's card game. The firemen barely looked up from their hands, gestured to the alarm box on the wall, told us to pull it. Only then did they throw their cards down, jump into their boots and slide down the pole to the waiting truck. They drove past the house first, then returned, dragged the hoses into the backyard, put out the blaze.

It turned out not to be such a bad thing, as my mother got some insurance money and had the whole house renovated. Vernon was a carpenter, did all the work. He was also married, so this was a way for him to spend more time with her without arousing suspicion.

I got stopped one day as I was leaving the supermarket, a half-eaten candy bar in my hand. The manager brought me into a little room elevated above the registers that had two-way mirrors on four sides, just like on television. I realized he sat up there on the lookout for people like me. I felt sick. He asked what I was doing and I said I didn't know. He asked where my mother was and I said at work. He asked me for the number and I said he couldn't call her there, that there was no phone. I might have even started to cry. He asked if I knew that what I was doing was wrong. Yes yes, I said. After an hour he let me go. He told me he'd have his eye on me, that he wouldn't forget my face. I never told my mother, even when, years later, she was pressuring me to get a job there, bagging groceries, stacking shelves, anything.

funeral, unattended

(1970) Weekend mornings, after or before my paper route, my mother, still in her bathrobe, drives me to the Harbor, sends me in to get her coffee while she waits in the car. *Cream-no-sugar,* I tell the woman behind the counter, the code my mother taught me, and she nods comprehension. This is the same coffee shop my mother worked in as a girl, where she met my father, though she never tells me this. As she pulls away I tear a little "v" in the lid for her. We drive past St. Mary's—the lot filling up early, a funeral, high mass. Offhandedly she says, *That's your grandfather's funeral.* At first I'm confused, sickened—*Dead?* But I quickly figure out it's not the grandfather I know, not the one I see all the time, the one on First Cliff, though I'd never considered I had another grandfather until that moment. *Of course,* my *father's* father, he'd also be my grandfather, though I never met him. We must have walked past each other on Front Street countless times, I suddenly realized, stood in line together at the one supermarket in town. My mother must have known what he looked like, but she never pointed him out, never mentioned him at all. It was complicated enough for me to keep track of her own parents, the grandparents I knew, divorced and living in the same town. My brother and I were warned to never mention one to the other, even as we drove from breakfast at Grandma's to lunch at Grandpa's, never to say where we were headed or where we'd just been. And now this other grandfather pops up, dead. He must have lived in the house on Second Cliff, I reckoned, we would pass it on our way to the real grandfather, my mother's father. I knew it was the house my father grew up in, it must have been pointed out to me at one time, but I never went inside. I'd merely glance toward it as we passed, imagine someone at a window, watching me. It was near the water but not on the water, nicer than our house on Third Cliff but not as nice as my grandfather's house on First Cliff.

First second third. Three two one. Elevator, going down.

My father wouldn't have been at his father's funeral that day any more than I would have—he wouldn't have dared the Breen boys and more jail time. I don't know if this second unattended funeral occurs after my father's second marriage breaks up, or even how he got married again with a warrant hanging over him. This was when computers were the size of rooms, not something to hold in your hand. Easier to get lost in a room. Maybe you could just drift north into another state, maybe the courts weren't as aggressive as they've become in tracking down deadbeat fathers, with their posters on subway walls, a picture along with his name and how much he owes.

(As it turns out, my father wasn't in hiding at all. He was living on Cape Cod, writing theater reviews for the local newspaper. Not hard to find. In the past year he named Richard Gere the best young actor on the Cape for his work in *Rosencrantz and Guildenstern Are Dead* at the Provincetown Playhouse.)

An hour or so later that same day I pass the church again, this time on my bicycle—the funeral just ending, a long black line of cars leaving the parking lot, headlights on, snaking their way to the graveyard. I'm riding beside my best friend, and I tell him, in the same offhand tone my mother had used, *That's my grandfather's funeral*, and he looks at me as if I'm insane.

pear

By the time I'm nine I know the world is a dangerous place. I've heard whispers about razor blades in apples, about Charlie Manson and his family. But no one is offering any clear information. Lately I've been studying horror movies on tv my favorites being *The Creature Double Feature* on Saturday afternoons. But even better is when my mother's latest boyfriend takes my brother and me to see zombie and mayhem movies at the drive-in—*Scream and Scream Again, Bloody Mama*—the more gruesome the better.

One night, walking through the Harbor at dusk with my grandmother, where we'd gone to buy yarn for her crewelwork, we stop at the musty bookshop run by Isabel and Rose, the spinster sisters. I thumb through a new edition of *Dr. Jekyll and Mr. Hyde* while my grandmother scans the murder/romances. She likes her books fat and lurid. I've never bought a book before, but for some reason I have to have this one. Under a streetlight outside I try to read the first page, but know instantly I'm over my head—I can decipher maybe half of it. When I get home I try again, then put it aside, knowing I'll be able to read it in a couple years, if I apply myself in third grade. I'll pick it up again in fifth grade and read it through in one night. That same year I'll memorize Poe's "The Raven," and draw coffins and bloody curved daggers in my notebooks. I want to be a writer, a horror writer. This is before I learn that my father considers himself a poet. I've only met him once that I can remember, the day he appeared in my grandmother's driveway with his second wife and my half-sister. *This is your sister*, he said, *say hi*. He looked like the Cowardly Lion, his wife looked like Cher. My half-sister was a swaddled infant, indistinguishable from her blanket. *Hi*, I said.

There'd always been books around our house—my mother and brother were voracious, compulsive readers. Henry Miller's *Sexus* was hidden in my mother's lingerie drawer, alongside her gun and painkillers. She bought the gun the year before to protect herself, but she never said from what. The painkillers were for her migraines, which kept her in bed some days, all day. A family story was that my brother was found reading the newspaper as a toddler, before he'd uttered a word, and to see him, all those years, with a sci-fi book hidden in his lap at the dinner table, his head bowed, it seemed possible. In my grandmother's attic were stacks of books salvaged from her marriage, only accessible by tightroping along the joists between the pink insulation. Forbidden and dangerous, I spent hours up there, poring through these treasures, looking for answers.

In the early 1970s, when I was eleven or twelve, my fascination with horror led me to the occult. The new bookstore in town had an entire section devoted to Anton LaVey and Alistair Crowley—real live warlocks, with shaved heads and scary beards. I'd sit on the floor reading them for hours. One afternoon I looked up and realized I was alone, that the cashier had locked up, gone to lunch, forgotten me. The door opened from the inside, I looked up and down the street, looked back at the register, gleaming and stuffed with cash, decided it was a sacred place, that I wouldn't take anything, because I wanted to be able to return, and after the supermarket I knew how hard it was to go back once you crossed a line.

Within a few months I moved on to mysteries. I preferred Sherlock Holmes to Agatha Christie, because in his world even the tiniest bit of dust was a clue. I convinced a friend that the best way to spend our summer afternoons was to write our own. We collaborated on a story about a murder set in Scotland and Egypt, the two most exotic locales we could imagine. In a couple years I moved on to Vonnegut, and I convinced another friend, Warren, to collaborate on a science fiction novel, to which we added pages daily. By the time I was sixteen and my father wrote me for the first time and I learned that he called himself a writer, I was already on my way, though perhaps part of me latched on to the chance to outdo him.

The summer I bought *Jekyll and Hyde* a distant cousin I'd never seen before or since appeared at my grandmother's with some other vague relatives one Sunday. Corey was a little older and had no fingers on his right hand, just little knobs where they should be. Not even a thumb. I knew not to stare, offered to take this cousin for a walk. I was a good kid. We circled the house, I glanced at his hand when he wasn't looking, thought how hard it must be—how did he work a button, hold a spoon? Why didn't he wear a glove? I didn't mind walking with him, we wouldn't run into anyone I knew, not on my grandmother's lawn. Already I knew where to position myself in relation to those less fortunate—not to stare, not to treat them any differently, not to even mention what's right there in front of us. I'm compassionate, kind, considerate, brave, somewhat clean—a walking, talking Boy Scout oath, whatever, fine by me, just as long as I'm not confused with the freak. Each year they lined us up in the elementary school cafeteria, to be measured and weighed, and though I'm chronically skinny at least I'm always average height, thank God for that. Between my mother's rotating cast of boyfriends, and being nominally Protestant in an Irish Catholic stronghold, and the food stamps, and the frayed clothes, I'm already teetering painfully close to not fitting in, anywhere.

As we wandered my grandmother's yard I showed him the hose, how you could hit the upper windows with its spray, I showed him the path into the woods, and how I shimmied up the gutter pipe to stake out the roof. This might have been a mistake, because I realized too late that he'd never be able to follow me. I led him to my grandmother's pear tree, which she bought and planted herself just a few years earlier. I had helped dig the hole, held it upright while she tamped the dirt back down. A spindly thing, slow-growing, with just one small hard pear, the first, dangling from a branch. We were told to let this pear grow, my grandmother checked it every day. I told Corey how proud she was of her lone pear, and he stared at me straight and defiant, like he was angry with me for some ungodly inscrutable reason, he stared and reached his hand out to this pear, forcing me to look right at it, my mouth dropping open a little. Then he smiled and gripped it with his palm, pulled it free. He threw it into the street, then turned and walked back into the house.

turner's special blend

Twice in the 1970s Scituate will be written up in *Time* magazine as the second most alcohol-consuming town, city or r.f.d. zone in the United States. A sidebar, no explanation, folded into a larger article on the scourge of sniffing glue or drunk driving. The first is some seaside Steinbeck hole in California no one's ever heard of. In Scituate every other business in the small string of stores we call the Harbor is either a bar or a package store, "package" being puritan code for "liquor." From an early age you cannot help but wander the aisles, gaze eye-level into the amber. The mothers, though drinkers themselves, warn their children of the dangers, the risks. My mother says it's in our family, says it will destroy my muscle tone, says she will throw me out of the house. On drives through the neighboring towns she points out the bars my grandfather can no longer enter—that one for swinging on a chandelier, that one for throwing a drink in the owner's face. She tells the story of learning to drive one snowy night in Montana, underage, her father sloshed in the backseat with a drinking buddy, instructing her to just keep it between the rock face and the drop off. Alcohol is the river we sit on the banks of, contemplating. Sometimes we watch ourselves float past, sometimes we watch ourselves sink. My grandmother, the one divorced from this grandfather before I was born, the woman who looks after my brother and me when my mother's at work or on a date, calls ahead to the package store for her half gallon of Turner's Special Blend, sends me in to pick it up. An electric eye bongs as you break a light beam upon entering, I take to jumping over it to surprise the man behind the counter. Dimly lit, aisle of amber, aisle of clear, Turner's is cavernous, a crypt. Each real bottle has its own promotional bottle—plastic, dusty, oversized—lined up on a shelf along the back wall. The iconic Jim Beam, a massive Jack Daniel's. When my grandmother comes to dinner at our house she always carries her own jar of Turner's Special Blend. She knows how much she needs and doesn't want to be caught short. My brother remembers her at Christmas one year, an especially weepy time for her, when she put her hands around his neck and murmured, *My little angel, you wouldn't be so hard to kill.* And though he knew it was only the whiskey talking, he also knew that the whiskey talked daily. In fifth grade I write a report that I spent the weekend skiing in "Vermouth" with my grandfather, that "Vermouth" was a beautiful state. My teacher did not correct this—maybe we were all skiing in a state of Vermouth.

practical joke

(1971) Travis, just back from Vietnam, is renovating the house next door. The war's an unending muddle. My mother bakes a blueberry pie, puts it in the window to cool, invites him over for a piece. Thirty-one, divorced ten years now, she makes a good pie. Travis is twenty-one and still looks like a Marine—his USMC tattoo, his fatigues—albeit freaky, bright-eyed, his hair going wild. Not a hippie, but drifting toward hippiedom. Trigger-hippie, you might call him, as he's armed to the teeth, having smuggled out his M-16 and various sidearms. They begin seeing each other and, as per usual, he begins renovating our house. My mother likes a man who's good with his hands. Skipping school one day, I'm lingering around the house alone when he pulls into the driveway, lets himself in to work on a dead outlet. I hide in my closet, hear him talk to my dog as he works, and what he says sounds insane. He tells my dog that in 'Nam he ate better-looking dogs, that

over there a dog would never get so fat, that all dogs knew enough to run the other way from him instead of rolling on their backs, waiting for the knife to slip in. He tells my dog about the villages he burned and the people he killed and that not all of them were soldiers. About bulldozing a tunnel and later finding out it was filled with kids. Through the cracked closet door I can see him holding my dog's ears and crying and I don't dare breathe. A few months later my mother stands me in the kitchen to tell me she's going to marry him. *That's a mistake*, I say. She nods that she knows but says she'll marry him just the same, and she does, and they're happy, for a while. He's fun to have around, in a frenzied sort of way. If we want to go fishing he takes us down to the Harbor, tells us to wait on the loading dock and goes off to hot-wire someone else's boat. We go out for the afternoon, catch a few fish, and he drops us off again. We knew the boat was stolen, even though he said it was a friend's. We knew there'd be trouble if we were caught but we went anyway. His impunity thrills me, I mistake it for fearlessness, though years later he will admit to being afraid all the time. When he decides to put an addition on our house he takes me down to the lumberyard and I see how he pays for a couple sheets of plywood and a few two-by-fours, how he takes the slip out to the yard and backs up to a stack of plywood and has me get on the other side of it so we can load the whole pile onto his truck, until the springs sag. We jump in the cab and he slams it into drive and with the first jerk forward all the plywood slides out onto the ground. We get out and reload it, his entire body now coiled energy, waving off an offer of help from the guy who works there. That weekend we double the size of my mother's cottage, the second and last house she'd buy, all of us and a few of his friends furiously hammering, desperate to finish quickly because Travis never bothered to get a permit. The last thing we do that Sunday night is paint the whole thing yellow, so it will blend in with the rest of the house. It will take two years to get around to shingling it, and only then when the yellow is peeling off in sheets.

In Vietnam he'd been a mine-sweeper, the guy who cleared the path, made it safe to put your foot down. Usually he was good at it, but sometimes he'd screw up, and when he did someone was blown to pieces. After being in-country for a year he signed on for another hitch, but caught some shrapnel a few months into it and was shipped home. In the States he became a color guard in Washington, standing at white-gloved attention at high-level events. But he'd landed back in the "world" with a short fuse, and when a car full of hippies honked at him at a traffic light that had turned from red to green Travis got out and pistol-whipped the driver, pulled him right through the car's window. Half an hour later, when the police found him, he was in a fast-food joint eating a burger, having forgotten what he'd done. He got off, but then Kent State happened and they ordered him into the basement of the Pentagon, "full combat gear, the whole nine yards." He refused. He knew he'd be sent to college campuses, and was terrified that he'd have to kill more kids. They locked him up in Bethesda for six months, shot him full of thorazine, gave him an honorable discharge, cut him loose. A few months later he was at our dinner table.

I liked to play what were called "practical jokes." I had a spoon with a hinge, a dribble glass, a severed rubber hand. I'd leave booby traps around our house, usually a piece of thread strung across a doorway as a tripwire, one end tied to a broom or the racks from the oven, anything that would fall and make a racket. I don't think I knew that Travis had spent his time in Vietnam checking for tripwires—I don't know if knowing would have stopped me. I would set the trap and maybe it would catch someone and maybe it wouldn't. One night Travis took the racks and tucked them between my bottom sheet and the mattress. I came in later that night and crawled into bed. Why I didn't notice the racks right off I can't say, but hours later I awoke from dreams of torture.

Midafternoon one Saturday Travis comes home after digging sea clams with a buddy. Leaning on pitchforks knee-deep at low tide, they'd each managed to kill a case of beer before noon. He dumps the clams in the sink and tells my brother and me to circle around, he wants to show us his photo album. For the first few pages he's a teenager, cocky beside hot rods, girls sitting on the hoods, one with her arm draped over his shoulders. The next page shows him at boot camp, Parris Island—crewcut, sudden adult. The next shows Vietnamese women dancing topless on tables, and on the next page a village is on fire. Corpses next, pages of corpses, bodies along a dirt road, a face with no eyes. As the stories of what he'd done unreel from inside him, my brother stands up and walks into his room, back to his wall of science fiction. I look at the photos, at Travis, look in his eyes as he speaks, somehow I'd learned to do that, like a tree learns to swallow barbed wire.

Years later, when I track him down, he shows me another photo, one I hadn't seen or don't remember—him on a dusty road outside Da Nang, a peace sign dangling from his neck. The reason he signed up for a second hitch, he tells me, was so that he could go into villages ahead of his unit, ostensibly to check for land mines and booby traps, but once there he'd warn the villagers to run, because if they didn't he knew there was a good chance they'd be killed by his advancing soldiers. Then he'd set off a couple rounds of C-4, radio in that it was still hot, smoke a joint, watch the villagers flee.

The night he showed us his photo album, after the house went quiet, I crept into the kitchen for a glass of water, the sink still full of sea clams, forgotten. Under the fluorescent hum they'd opened their shells and were waving their feet, each as thick and long as my forearm. A box of snakes, some draped onto the countertop, some trying to pull themselves out.

slow-motion car wreck

(1972) Portsmouth, New Hampshire (*More bars per square inch than any city in America,* my father will inform me later, *and all the women like to drink and fuck*). My father's crashing with friends, working occasionally as a longshoreman. "Longshoreman" sounds more romantic, more solid, than what he actually is. "Wharf-rat" is a better term. A photograph that appears in a local newspaper shows my father standing beside his friends Tommy ("Tommy the Terror") and Scotty, dressed the part—black knit watchcap, black wool sweater with buttons along one shoulder, jeans. A pair of leather gloves in his back pocket, a steel hook with a perpendicular wooden handle. The costume to go with the job. The caption under the photo cites the three of them as local artists who work the docks. In Portsmouth he often uses the alias "Sheridan Snow," perhaps to avoid my mother's warrant. He has business cards printed up, which highlight his penchant for alliteration—

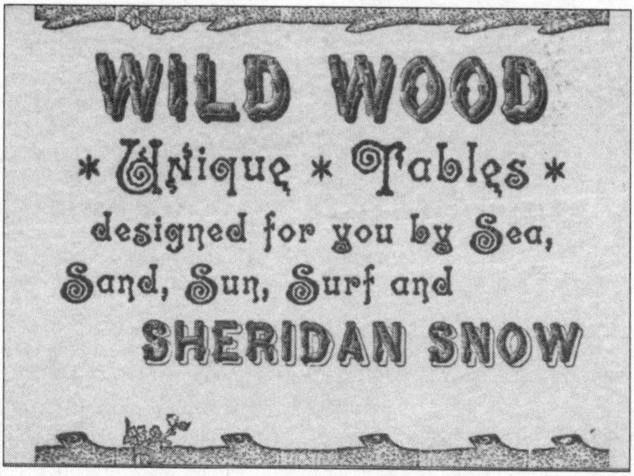
WILD WOOD
* Unique * Tables *
designed for you by Sea,
Sand, Sun, Surf and
SHERIDAN SNOW

This career involves salvaging a chunk of driftwood from the beach, putting legs on it and selling it as a side table. Many people in America invent careers like this in the early 1970s (What color *is* your parachute?). A few years earlier he'd stalk Beacon Hill in a flowing black cape, and then for a few years he wore one of those two-way Sherlock Holmes hats, to highlight his eccentric, poetic side. Later, when he robs banks, he will try to pass as a country gentleman, in town buying antiques. He will carry a Nikon camera around his neck, wear a tweed jacket (*I was always classically dressed, even in Levi's*). As a longshoreman he shows up looking the part of an "old salt," tells long-winded, mildly entertaining stories, but by all accounts a laggard, next to worthless once the boat docked. Years later I track Scotty down—*Jonathan*

created blustery characters to protect himself from being hurt. He was a great absorber of others' personalities. He would lift phrases and gestures from those around him, make them his own. He was like a jigsaw puzzle of different people.

Portsmouth's a small city. The dockworkers go to the galleries for free wine and to feel like artists. The gallery owners like to have them around, to add energy, wildness. They go out to the bars together afterward, end up in someone's apartment, make a night of it. Scotty shows up late and Jonathan's already made a scene, thrown up on someone's shoes, passed out on the coat pile. After two drinks a cloud will come over him and he'll be another person, not nearly as fun as the Jonathan of one drink. Even so, Scotty likes him, in spite of his bravado, his bluster. Especially the moments before the second drink, before the cloud. Just twenty, Scotty has "trouble" with his own father, another drinker. Jonathan's twice Scotty's age, a father figure, of sorts. Jonathan tells Scotty stories of his brushes with the law, his escapades, he lists all the businesses he has run—the car dealerships, the encyclopedia franchise, the theater space—and gleefully recounts how each collapsed. Clearly a bad influence, this pseudo-dad, and that's what's attractive. Jonathan's been at the art game for a long time now, he likes to drop names, hint at the influence he can muster (*Does the name Kurt Vonnegut mean anything to you?*). A newspaper clipping he flashes around shows him sitting at the feet of Shirley MacLaine during a Democratic fundraiser for McGovern. My father makes sure Scotty sees this dog-eared photo.

As the winter ends, Jonathan finesses a place to sleep and steady pay in exchange for painting a house the upcoming summer in Cambridge. Jonathan proposes that he and Scotty become partners, *fifty-fifty*. The owners, a couple he met at an art opening, will be in Sweden for the summer. Free rent, easy work, steady cash, my father plans to rewrite his novel in the evenings and on weekends. Scotty, wary, knows Jonathan always tries to get something for nothing, always tries to get over. But he imagines they'll put in a few good hours each day, make their way through. A house is a finite project, after all. The worst that could happen is what always happens—that Scotty will work harder.

The job has a charge account at the hardware store—paint, brushes, scrapers, drop cloths. Jonathan charges his coveralls—white, denim, professional. If he has someplace to be later in the day he wears them over one of the Brooks Brothers suits he'd charged to my grandfather ten years earlier (*As president of a company I had to look the part*). He likes to keep a brush and scraper in his back pocket, even if he doesn't use them all that much. The first morning Scotty wakes up at seven and Jonathan's already up and drinking coffee, wearing his spotless coveralls. They sit at the kitchen table in the pleasant sun, suffused with good fortune. Mid-May, the owners won't be back until

September, no urgency, summer spread out before them. They can work half days if they choose. They can take three-day weekends. They can stretch it out. Scotty follows my father's lead, says he isn't worried. The owners left five hundred to start off, when they need more it'll be wired. Sounds fine. Scotty says he wouldn't mind quitting early some days, getting into the studio, keeping up with his sculptures. *Yes*, my father agrees, *that's what's important. Anyone could paint this house—they chose us because we're artists. In a few years they'll be able to point to this house and say, Jonathan Flynn painted that. That's worth something to people like this.*

They talk briefly about how to begin. The bushes need to be wrapped in tarps, pulled away from the house. The ladders laid out, ratcheted up into the eaves, the scraping begun. The scraping, followed by the puttying, followed by the priming—the preparation, they agree, this takes time. Scotty puts his coffee cup in the sink and pulls his paper cap over his eyes. My father reaches for the bottle of Johnnie Walker that has been centered on the table the whole time. *A drink to our good fortune*, he proposes, pouring a shot into his cup. The scotch, Scotty will later learn, is charged to the owners as well.

Every morning this is how it will play out—first coffee, a piece of toast, maybe a shot. Then Scotty will climb the ladder and continue scraping where he left off the day before. Jonathan circles below, the paintbrush in his back pocket, surveying, pondering, taking stock, pointing to spots Scotty's missed. Jonathan prefers to stay off the ladders, focusing his energies on the porch. By ten or so

Jonathan says he's making a run to the hardware store, doesn't return until nightfall. Shattered. It doesn't really matter—they're keeping track of their own hours. Still, within a week Scotty begins quitting at noon. Then he starts skipping days.

By mid-August Scotty's vanished. My father circles the unpainted house. Three months and not even the scraping's done. The porch has been primed, as high as he can reach, and now he must start in with the ladders. He doesn't like ladders. *That low-life*, he mutters, leaving him in the lurch, after all he'd done. *Sorry-assed kid.* The owners are due back in three weeks. Yesterday Jonathan had to tell the husband, by phone, that it might not be done in time. This made the husband bullshit—he'd been wiring Jonathan five hundred every month, always heard glowing reports, *fine fine*, and now it's still undone? Jonathan's cut off from the money, if he wants the balance he'd better finish.

At this point Jonathan realizes that he's been too conscientious. All that scraping and priming was just so Scotty would feel needed. No one will notice the eaves anyway, no one will climb a ladder and look that close. As long as it gets a fresh once-over. Jonathan sets the ladder, brings a scraper for a quick scrape, just the big stuff. A paper bucket half full with the final coat. No time for primer, not anymore.

A little hungover, maybe even still drunk from the night before, he climbs. Maybe a little hair of the dog, why not?—forty-four, son of near-aristocracy, father of three, soon-to-be-famous author, forced to creep around roofs in the sun, to work beside morons, for goons. As he falls he thinks, *If you are hurt they will come with their ambulances, they will put you in bed and feed you, they will let you rest.* Or maybe that's just what I have thought, the times I've fallen.

He's found unconscious on the walkway. He was on the ladder above the back porch and instead of resetting it he leaned over too far, lost his balance, the ladder kicked out, dropped him. When he comes to in the hospital later that day he blames Scotty for everything—for abandoning him, for taking the money, for charging the scotch, for being a fuckup. There might be a head injury, impossible to tell, the extent of the damage unpredictable. The house is left unfinished, a blossom of white on the flagstone just inside the gate.

dreamwold

(1972) I get drunk for the first time when I'm twelve, at a place called Dreamwold. This baptism in beer takes place outdoors, in daylight, at an Octoberfest. My preteen friends and I find unattended pitchers and we empty them. Then we find more. Dreamwold is the fantasy village built by Scituate's most famous son, a man named Lawson, the "Copper King," a turn-of-the-century robber baron, long dead, the estate broken up into private homes and institutions. I went to kindergarten in one of Dreamwold's outbuildings. There still exists somewhere a photograph of me walking through Dreamwold with a book on my head for a class in "posture."

That December, just before Christmas, Travis tells me to go out and warm up the truck. It's midnight, a school night. We drive down to the Harbor, coast to a stop beside the chain-link fence around St. Mary's field, kill the headlights. Town's asleep, snow falls. A dim light shines from within the trailer guarding the trees the Knights of Columbus sell. Travis tells me to wait, vaults the fence, leaves black footprints straight to the trees. A car slows, passes. Within minutes he's bounding back, dragging two perfect spruces behind. He tosses them over the fence, I wrestle one into the back of the truck while he one-arms the other. *Twenty bucks is too much for a tree*, he mutters, then laughs as we pull away. *As a kid we'd go into the woods with an ax*, he snorts, *take whatever we wanted.* He cracks open a beer, and for the first time offers me one.

the take

(1974) Early February. Brandishing weapons, the Symbionese Liberation Army (SLA) kidnap Patricia Campbell Hearst as she's watching television with her boyfriend, Steven Weed. The SLA force Hearst into the parking garage and into the trunk of a waiting car. The SLA does not take Weed. I am barely fourteen at this point, "weed" is what I call marijuana. I keep my weed hidden in a book I found in my grandmother's attic and hollowed out, *The Stories of Saki*, which was good but not good enough to save the book from my razor. I have a paper route, and I read the story as I trudge through snow at dawn, mesmerized by the kidnapped heiress, by the idea of an invisible army, by the man named "Weed" useless to stop them.

The ransom note for Hearst comes in the form of a tape recording sent to San Francisco radio station KPFA. In it the SLA demands that Hearst's father, the newspaper baron, give every "Californian in need" seventy dollars' worth of "quality" food. One feast, one last supper, and then she will be freed. After brief deliberations Hearst's father complies. Packages containing two turkey hindquarters, two cans of tomato juice, two cans of meat, and a box of saltine crackers are handed out to hundreds of people at several food distribution points. Two million dollars' worth of quality food.

My father, along with the rest of the country, reads about the kidnapped heiress. In some ways he's also an heir, but to a fortune he will never see. His father died four years earlier and left him one dollar, in this way guaranteeing that the will cannot be disputed. Last May the "Plumbers" broke into the Watergate Hotel for the first time, word that Nixon may have ordered the break-in is seeping out. I stand under streetlights in the middle of my route, reading about Patty, unable to stop reading about her. Everyone now calls her simply "Patty."

After the food is distributed Patty is not returned. All that remains is Weed, who tells the tale over and over, pulling aside the curtain of his hair to show where he took the blow. Without Patty he is briefly a star. Weeks pass, our attention flags, then the image of Patty transformed appears—rifle in her lap, the Symbionese Liberation Army insignia behind her, snakes coming out of her beret—heiress as Medusa, gone over to the other side. Now she is "Tania." A tape recording of her voice says, "This is my choice," and the shrink talking head and the police specialist talking head and the crisis expert talking head all say it is likely she's been brainwashed, likely she's doing this in order to survive, that she's reached a state of transference, which is complex and unpredictable and likely to influence her future actions. But to me it seems obvious—to risk so much for one meal, who wouldn't be charmed?

During these months many newspapers are sold, subscriptions rise, home delivery desired. I read about her every day between houses, I grow up as I read about her. Weed still occasionally looks pleadingly out from below a headline, though by now no one believes she will return to him. Within weeks Tania is photographed by security cameras holding a gun while the Hibernia Bank is robbed. The roiling interest ignites into a frenzy. The SLA is funding a worldwide revolution. I drop a folded paper onto a porch.

A year before his fall from the ladder my father sent his novel, or some version of it, to Viking Press and received a hand-signed rejection letter in response. He will xerox this letter for years to come and mail it out again—to friends, to Ted Kennedy, eventually to me—apparently to prove that he is, or was, "known." *Kurt Vonnegut told me to try Viking. I wanted to stay with Little, Brown, but Vonnegut insisted.* My father puts the rejection letter aside, picks up a newspaper, reads the headlines. He sees her face, the beret, the gun. The grainy surveillance photo, the getaway, the money. Lifted from obscurity to sensation, a level of fame that a writer of his talent deserves falls into her lap. *Huck Finn*, *Catcher in the Rye*, his novel the equal of these masterpieces, but who would kidnap him, where would they send the ransom note, who would even notice if he was gone? A few months later my father walks into a bank, passes his first forged check. Never shy in front of a camera, he allows himself to be photographed. This first time he even uses his real name, Jonathan Robinson Flynn. Setting himself up for a fall, laying his own end. In subsequent forays he will use an alias, his favorite being "Millard Fillmore," the president who abolished debtor's prison.

If you ask him how he got into the checking business, my father will tell you that Dippy-do Doyle and Suitcase Fiddler heard about his head injury and came looking for him. Doyle, in this version, spends his days playing tennis and orchestrating scams—the brains, apparently, behind a few small-time local hoods. Doyle arranges a meeting at the Dorchester HoJo's on the Southeast Expressway. Does my father read about Watergate while waiting? About Patty? Is he drinking buddies with Doyle? Has he boasted about his small-time exploits, his nerve, his willingness to do anything? Doyle and Suitcase arrive with a check made out to my father for $8,800, drawn on the John Hancock Insurance Company. Doyle says he arranged for it because of my father's accident. My father knows it's shady but can't resist going along. Suitcase drives him to the Prudential Bank in downtown Boston, just as Doyle ordered, and my father opens an account with the check. On days when my father is the dupe, not the mastermind, he will say, *I looked at the check, I had no doubt—I'm him, I'm Flynn. Thus began two and a half years in the checking business.* My father will say that by the time he passed the second check he knew it was illegal, but he was "already cooked" after the first one. Asked why he didn't go to the police, he'll say that Doyle knew about his kids and threatened to blow our heads off if he didn't go along. In one version Suitcase Fiddler is the driver, a low-life hood who robbed banks by gunpoint in Canada but now merely drives. He admires my father for never using a gun. In another version Suitcase is a "paper-hanger," a master, the one who forges the checks, a *true artist.* The three of them continue to meet at HoJo's over the next couple years, now Suitcase drives my father straight there after each job. Doyle takes the count, gives everyone their cut. My father claims he never got more than twenty percent, an amount which still irks him, considering he took all the risk—*If I had a loaded Magnum I'd walk up to Dippy-do Doyle right now and put it to his head.*

Patty's an heiress, I have a route. All our money comes from newspapers. I earn so much per paper, very little, all told. My real money comes in the form of tips, left in envelopes between the doors. On Sunday I leave the envelopes, write how much they owe on the outside, always hoping for more. Eventually I even take to putting a little plus sign after what they owe, as a hint. I am saving my money to buy my mother a new car. The current model is a Dodge Dart, the same color as our refrigerator, avocado green, it coughs and sputters in the driveway before it warms up. Summer shuffles into fall. Still gone, our heiress. Experts draw lines on the photograph of Patty in the Hibernia Bank, lines along where her gun was aiming to show it was aiming at no one. From this they determine that the gun was unloaded, though it could also mean that at that moment her mind strayed briefly from its purpose. Or maybe when robbing a bank it is enough to simply brandish a gun, generally, in the direction of the money. Another expert draws a line from one SLA member's gun, to prove that this gun was aimed at Patty the entire time, that she was, in fact, a prisoner like the rest, the tellers and the customers face-down on the floor, hands behind their heads. Lines tracing the possible connections between the players, possible paths of possible bullets, Patty's face the center of the world. Christmas is the season of tips, of real tips, of stuffed envelopes. An occasional twenty. I keep track, know how much I take in. "The Take," I call it.

My mother arrives one day to the bank she has worked at for the past ten years to find a photograph of my father on an FBI wanted poster. It warns her and all bank tellers to call the police immediately if you see him, or have seen him, or have any information as to his whereabouts. My mother brings this poster home to show my brother what kind of man our father is, but she doesn't show it to me.

I've become a fuckup, high every day. It says he's stolen thousands of dollars. She hasn't seen a penny.

Later we'll see a shoot-out, a house in Watts where Patty may or may not be. The police bomb it anyway and it burns to the ground on national tv and only the next day do they search the rubble and say she wasn't there. They find teeth and none of the teeth are hers. Months of silence follow, then it ends quietly. Patty has been hiding out with her two remaining comrades, who, seemingly out of character, jog every morning. Running dogs. The FBI stops them at the end of their workout, when they are the most winded, unable to run any farther. When they batter in the door Patty is in the kitchen, watching television. Walter Cronkite. He hasn't uttered her name in weeks but he will tonight.

red sox

(1975) A helicopter lifts out of the embassy, people cling to the landing struts, we see some fall. This is how the undeclared war ends. Travis moves out as we watch the helicopters on the evening news. Shortly thereafter my mother, brother and I begin a summer of watching baseball on television. That we hadn't given a damn about the Red Sox until then, not really, doesn't matter. We need to toughen up.

All in all it's good Travis is leaving. After building the master bedroom his second act had been the cultivation of marijuana in our very public backyard. The marijuana plants towered ridiculous and gangly above the lesser tomatoes in our tiny garden, and I was sure the neighbors would turn us in. One afternoon I pulled up all the plants, shaved off their roots with an x-acto knife, stuck them back into the ground. Years later my brother admitted to having poured poison on each one, perhaps on the same afternoon, a hundredth-monkey kind of afternoon. Either way, they withered and were gone. Within a year, though, I was rummaging through Travis's roach stash, cleaning his pipe with a straightened paper clip, searching out anything to smoke. By the time Saigon falls I'm drinking whatever liquor I can get my hands on, believing, in spite of all evidence to the contrary, that it will get me laid. I cling to this sodden belief as my mother's marriage to Travis collapses in on itself, grinding to its necessary halt.

That summer she cuts off all her hair, becomes a vegetarian, and drops way too much weight, to hover in the ghostly realm, the realm of vapor and shade. Hollow-eyed, spooked. My brother sits down to dinner with her, shovels in the offered vegetables and grains, but I'm annoyed I have to buy my own meat. By now she's taking pills for her migraines, pills to wake up. Thirty-five and her second marriage has ended as badly as the first. To me Travis had been a reckless older buddy, scary-fun. As a husband he'd been a nightmare. After two years in Vietnam he'd barely fit into our mickey mouse cottage, our badly converted summer shack. They were together from the time I was eleven until I was fifteen, and each year he lived with us our house felt smaller and smaller, in spite of the additions. They slept together for the first couple years in the room he'd built, then he began sleeping on a cot set up in that same room, then he began sleeping at a house he was renovating, unrolling his Marine sleeping bag on the floor of the job site. Then he was gone.

The Red Sox started out that spring bristling with promise, but everyone knew they would break our hearts. *Don't get too excited, it's not going to last*—this is the mantra of the Red Sox fan, the mantra of our Irish Catholic town. Don't hope for much in this life and you won't be disappointed. Save hope for the afterlife.

That spring into summer Travis would return, unannounced, take something he'd left behind—his primer-coated MG from the driveway; a photograph of a mountain from their bedroom, laminated onto a board he'd "distressed" with a blowtorch and a hammer. Slowly he emptied the garage of broken Skilsaws and pornography, leaving behind half-filled cans of paint. Unnerving, his presence still thick around us, my mother would look up from dinner and ask, *Where're the wine glasses?* and we'd know he'd been standing in that spot by the shelf just hours before, when the house was empty for the day. Since he'd done the renovations it was useless to try to lock him out—the windows all salvaged, lockless.

Part of watching the Red Sox together was to hunker down, circle the wagons, show a unified front. Travis kept coming back and we needed to fortify against him. But the greater (if unspoken) part for my brother and me was to be close to our mother, to keep an eye on her. It was clear she was slipping away from us, from this world. My brother understood this first, I think, or I just didn't want to understand it. We'd huddle in her bedroom, transfixed, as men who had a clear sense of purpose strode up to the plate to face down our newfound heroes. Bill "Spaceman" Lee—who advocated the reform of marijuana laws and had spoken out against the war in Vietnam. Luis Tiant—the overweight Cuban exile—whose tics and gestures were weirder than those of any human being we'd ever seen. His mid-windup pivot could last so long that it was impossible to hold your breath while he stared into the infield. He waggled and ducked and twisted and toppled and sneered and menaced and paused and, as one commentator noticed, looked like he was trying to kick off his left shoe. There was something about his body, how all of this struggle led to so many perfect throws, that gave us hope. He didn't make it look easy.

I'm fifteen, an age when most kids are breaking from their parents, spending more time with their friends, developing a secret language only they can understand. But now my mother, brother and I are developing our own common language, talking about Fred Lynn and Bernie Carbo over dinner, over our newfound couscous and curries. We know the strengths and weaknesses of each player, how they'd done against the A's last time around, who to watch out for, who was a hitter, who'd made what incredible catch. I'd been raised to be independent, cooked for myself since I could reach the stove, never had an allowance, left to my own bad devices for as long as memory. My mother had made it clear that she wouldn't be around forever—*If something happens to me* . . . , she'd say. To look into her face for too long only brought up dread. To stare as one into the television on a hot Saturday afternoon, to glimpse the world outside still going on, unfolding with or without us, to feel part of something larger, something that made it to the newspapers every day, that people seemed excited about, something to get caught up in and carried along by—Tiant would be pitching next Saturday, maybe reason enough to stick around, if just to see how it turned out, if just to see him smoke the bastards.

Then the improbable happened—the Red Sox kept winning. Carlton Fisk stood at the plate and the entire Eastern Seaboard held its breath. A big man, "Pudge" leaned into his swing, effortlessly he could knock it out of the park, we'd seen it before, it was in him. We didn't breathe.

In the end they broke our hearts, but not before getting us almost to Thanksgiving. Sprawled in her bedroom, my mother propped up with pillows, I'm on my belly beside her, my brother in the la-z-boy. It's all history now, something about the sixth game of the Series against the Reds, how Pudge hammers one at the last possible moment, bottom of the twelfth, how it hangs over the foul line for an eternity, how he stops halfway to first and jumps in the air, swinging his arms to the right to force it fair. I remember perfectly, the way his body moved, jumping up on his toes, a series of little bunny-hops, his big hands pushing the air like a desperate Zeus, how everyone at the game or watching on tv does the same, damn near screams, *Come on*, it's that important, to win this one game, to let us all move to the next.

chronic bafflement disorder

(1976) My father claims he didn't understand about cameras, didn't realize he was filmed at every window, that after a while they knew him, had his picture from every angle, knew his height, his eye color, his clothes. They had his name, it was just a matter of time. On a desolate back highway outside of Miami, hitchhiking his way back north to do another job, he is stopped by a young policeman. The cop takes his ID, calls it in, returns with his gun drawn. *Put your hands behind your back*, the young policeman says, and once again my father feels time closing off, his hands now behind him, now everything's behind him. Before this was chance, possibility, limitless. But that was the second before the teeth of the handcuffs bit into his given minutes. The policeman can now be more friendly, can hold him gently by the arm, guide him into the cruiser, *Come with me*, though it isn't a request. Into a cell, a holding tank, the bars slide shut, the cycle complete. My father now belongs solely to the world of time, time inside against time outside.

Years later he will say, *My name came up on the computer. I didn't even know about computers, and the cop came back all rattled and nervous and whimpers, "Can you please put your hands behind your back." It was up to me to calm him down, that's how rattled he was to have captured me.* Penniless again when he's caught, but pleased to learn he made it to a wanted poster, pleased that even my mother has once again been forced to consider his grainy face, smiling down upon her. Yet, sadly, he doesn't make headlines. Not like Patty.

At Patty's trial there are conflicting diagnoses. One is "Chronic Bafflement Disorder"—"She was simulating behavior, but was later convinced that she was not lying but acting reactively in fear for her life. She had no mental disease or defect and did it because she was rebellious, extremely independent, intelligent and well-educated; she was not mentally competent and her part in the bank robbery was due to the fact she was upset by her relationship with her boyfriend and she had a subtle hostility toward her parents and the establishment. . . ."

The Symbionese Liberation Army, which claimed to be a cell of a worldwide revolutionary movement, turns out to be a handful of radicals, now all dead or imprisoned.

Only after my father is apprehended and sentenced will my mother tell me what he has done.

Your father's in prison, she says.

Oh yeah, I say.

Interstate transportation of stolen securities, she says.

Hmm, I say.

Interstate transportation of stolen securities—I imagine an eighteen-wheeler, but I can't picture "securities." I don't ask her to elaborate. I never express any interest in my father, mostly because it seems to hurt my mother to even utter his name.

a survey

In school they take a survey about drug and alcohol use—

Do you drink:
a: to be social.
b: because you like the taste.
c: with meals.
d: to get drunk.

Without hesitation I answer *d*: I drink to get drunk. I like being drunk, feel more myself when outside myself. By the time I'm seventeen my mother and I drink together sometimes, and sometimes she shows me the quote she keeps in her wallet—"Never trust anyone who doesn't drink." Those who don't drink have something to hide, an awful secret that will slip out if they were ever to get drunk. By drinking together we prove we have nothing to hide.

Once my friends and I get our driver's licenses, we drive our parents' cars to an abandoned sand pit every night and drink. "The Pits" we call it, a bit of wasteland formerly used by the Concrete Pipe Corporation, now ghostly and apocalyptic, especially after a six-pack. The Monday morning ritual in Scituate becomes learning who had totaled their car over the weekend—wrapped it around what tree, driven off which pier. At one bash a local hoodlum handcuffs me to the door of my mother's car, fishing in my pockets for her keys, threatening to take me for a little drag, before giving up and drifting back into the shadows. My friends wander over, examine the cuffs, shrug, reel back to the center of the party, a stump set ablaze with gasoline.

One of these friends learned to drive by lifting his passed-out father from the driveway and into the family car to take him to detox. A long circular driveway, his house one of Lawson's mansions, by then in disrepair. When he got off the school bus he could see his father sprawled out. His mother said, *I give up*, handed my friend the address and the keys. My friend wasn't old enough to drive but he learned. He tells the story now as if he were speaking of raking the leaves.

near-desert

Prisons are near-deserts of time, though the days, like everywhere, have a rhythm. The sun rises, dreams tumble ever faster through the convict's mind, a buzzer sounds, eyelids flicker, a gradual brightening outside, sudden day within. The big light in the big house snaps on. The bars, the shackles, the walls—even the lightbulb in its own little cage above—all suffused with time.

In theory you cannot die in prison unless you've been sentenced to death, the law is specific on this point. You are to be kept alive but limited, this is the punishment. It's even safer in a prison hospital—it's their job to keep you alive. My father has problems with his legs, phlebitis, which killed his sister, and which Nixon also suffers from, so everyone's heard of phlebitis. This means he will be transferred from prison hospital to prison hospital, with the junkies and the loonies and the terminal cases, and not stuck in with the general population. To separate himself even further he identifies as Jewish. He claims that during the war his mother had converted, to *front-pew Catholicism*, in order to hide her Jewish ancestry. In the federal prison system there are very few Jews, he reasons, so it's to his advantage to be identified as one, to become a member of a minority, to be separated from the masses of Irish and black prisoners. Though he had been an altar boy for ten years, and if asked he would describe himself as Russian and Irish, part of him still felt Jewish, if only to explain why he felt so unconnected to everyone. In prison he becomes secretary of the Jewish Federal Prisoners' Association, publishes some doggerel in the newsletter.

Still, he must stay on top of things. His lawyer used a defense of mental impairment at his trial, based on his fall from the ladder—he was not in his right mind when he walked into those banks. It helped at his sentencing—the judge was lenient—but it will not help him now, awaiting diagnosis. Now he must make it clear that although he was not then in charge of his faculties, now he is. In one hospital my father is told his legs have to be amputated, but he refuses the knife. *Real butchers*, he says. *I would have looked like Toulouse-Lautrec, hacked off just below the knees.* Permission is needed, even in prison, unless he is deemed incompetent, which is a real possibility—a doctor could read his transcripts, judgment could come down, he could wake up strapped to his bed, it's what happens in the wards. But he's lucky—moved from Missouri to Kentucky, from Connecticut to Ohio, he rides out his time in hospitals, keeps his legs.

rule 35

During his two years behind bars my father claims to have been shuttled between twenty different federal prisons and hospitals, in fourteen different states. He refers to this often, the number of prisons, the number of states, to prove he has been subjected to "cruel and unusual punishment." Those are the words he uses in his letters to the judge who sentenced him. Judge W. Arthur Garrity, well-known at this time for overseeing school desegregation in Boston, receives a flurry of letters over a span of two months, sometimes two a day, mostly pleas to consider "Rule 35," which will apparently force him to reduce my father's sentence. In these letters my father also documents clear-cut examples of being treated cruelly and unusually. In one prison he is forced to work running an elevator, with no monthly pay, when his shoulder, right hand, and both legs are "completely destroyed." He sends a medical report to the judge at one point listing these crippling ailments, a report that has no doctor's name or hospital attached to it. It is typed out on a manual typewriter, using unusual medical jargon. "Both legs," it states: "total case of lethal phlebitis." "Lethal phlebitis" is the term my father always uses to describe his legs, to make it clear that he could drop dead at any moment. He describes the federal prison, variously, as "a massive death house," a "federal farce," and "a zoo." He makes it clear that he intends "a full, complete suit" against at least two of these prisons once he is released. He reiterates that he "had a choice in cashing the checks," but he made "the wrong choice." He pleads coercion, memory loss, his fingers broken by Doyle as threats. He refers to promises made and broken by federal prosecutors, insists that he would never do something so stupid again. He signs his letters variously "As ever"; "With respect and regard for the truth"; "Many thanks for your consideration"; "With deep respect to you always, your Honor"; and, simply, "I need my human rights."

Dear Judge Garrity, 13 August 1977

Time, here, costs a man more than a part of his life, it robs him of his skills, his ability to cope with society in a civilized manner, and most importantly, his essential human dignity.

This County Jail thrives on conditions that make degeneration probable and reform unlikely.

My incarceration here violates, clearly, my constitutional rights. There is <u>no</u> medical treatment here, at all.

None. I <u>do</u> have lethal phlebitis. The sanitary conditions are vile. Cavemen could live cleaner lives than inmates can here. In my cage I have <u>no</u> toilet, <u>no</u> sink, no water at all—what I do have is an inmate as a roommate who is openly gay.

My essential human dignity is being destroyed here. And this is our nation's two hundred and first birthday. What I see, and what Little, Brown & Co. are receiving from me, is my clear view of America's Birthday Blues.

As ever—Jonathan R. Flynn, #23361-175

In prison movies the men move slowly, carefully, weighted down. Some plan is always being whispered, someone is about to be shivved, a tunnel spooned out of a wall. The screws twitch their clubs, their cattle prods. The first letter I ever receive from my father is when I'm sixteen, after he's been locked up for a few months—*Tell me of yourself—I regret our mutual loss—perhaps—soon—in our future—we can regain our lost knowledge of each other.* After thirty letters Judge Garrity rules against Rule 35, and my father stays in prison for another year.

barefoot motorcycle

(1978) The pavement drifts past inches below my bare feet, my soles hardened over, but still I must focus—doing sixty on a motorcycle is quantitatively different from, say, riding a bicycle. I can't allow my mind to wander into what will happen if I put a foot down at this speed. *Focus*, I yell up to my brain, as it drifts into the happy-go-lucky stratosphere of this and that. But you have to touch down to earth once in a while, if there are stoplights, intersections, traffic. You have to force yourself to remember your feet, but not to obsess. To allow whatever song's coursing through your addled happy brain to fade into background noise, to not forget the danger but also not become paralyzed. A difficult balancing act on a CB350, a near-perfect machine, the pistons all lined up and firing between my legs, the asphalt unspooling below like sandpaper, leading me back to my one pair of shoes, forgotten in Quincy. It's midafternoon and hot and I've already

gotten high a few times, which makes the day pleasantly endless. Can this be the same sun, the same back road, that Mary and I drove just this morning in her mom's car? We've just graduated high school, no plans for college, it seems enough to ride around on my motorcycle with Mary's arms around me. Mary's my first girlfriend, *Darkness on the Edge of Town* has just come out, and Springsteen's bleak Catholicism resonates in my circle. He's playing the Garden later in the summer and I'd mistakenly left my only shoes, a ratty pair of sneakers, perched on a useless behemoth air conditioner where we'd gone to buy tickets. The ticket counter was at the far end of a stuffy hallway and there'd been a line and Mary and I sat on the cooler floor, pulling ourselves toward the window as the line allowed. The floor was polished concrete, an aggregate of marble flecks floating in a white heaven, and I must have lost track. I'm fast becoming the one who leaves things behind, who blows a rod and pulls into the breakdown lane and unscrews the plates and walks. Who puts his stuff in your basement and never returns. Who steps out onto a sidewalk in a small city, into the stifling air, without his shoes, without remembering he was even wearing shoes, or ever wore shoes.

The choice was to buy new sneakers or to shoot forty minutes back north before the window closed. Some part of me must have been aware of the inherent danger of riding a motorcycle barefoot, but not enough to give up on my only sneakers.

• • •

I'd spent the month before hitchhiking Europe with my friend Doug. While I was away my father was released from prison, and at some point my brother mentioned something to my mother about him, so she set up a meeting, even though my brother didn't want that. She picked my father up at the subway in Quincy and drove the two of them to Peggotty Beach, and they sat side by side, father and son, facing the waves while my mother smoked cigarettes in her car. My father did all the talking, never asked my brother about himself, and afterward my brother never wanted to see him again.

Coming off the backroads, about to make my way onto the highway, a cop pulls up behind me at a light. I never liked that, a cop car directly behind me. I usually walked away owing money, or worse, literally walked away, my vehicle impounded. A couple times already I'd even gone handcuffed to the station in the backseat of the cruiser. When I first bought the motorcycle I didn't have enough money left to register and insure it, so I rummaged around for an old plate, changed a 2 to an 8 with red nail polish. This lasted maybe a week before a cop pulled me over, incredulous, asked me if I knew that what I had done was akin to forgery.

The traffic light turns green and the cop lights go on behind me and I look over my shoulder and he points to a parking lot beside a liquor store I'd been to quite often on the way to and from the city. I know what to do—pull over, keep my sunglasses on, my hands on the handlebars, look contrite yet calm. The cop takes his time, asks for my license and registration, meanders back to the cruiser, punches my info into the computer or phones it in, I don't really know what he does for so long in that car, maybe he's reading a magazine or cleaning his gun, while my feet blister in the sun. After a short eternity he comes back shaking his head, *Well, there's nothing in my book about needing to wear shoes, but I'm gonna give you a ticket anyway just for being stupid.* I shake my head at my own obvious stupidity, consider against telling the story of the forgotten sneakers, thank him, *Thank you, sir.*

Within a month, a week before the Springsteen concert, I will drive that same motorcycle off a winding country road at night, coming home from a movie with Mary, where we'd split a pint of peppermint schnapps and made out. Mary broke her wrist (or, more accurately, I broke her wrist) and I lost my spleen, ruptured it when I went over the handlebars. I jumped up immediately and went for the bike, until I heard Mary, whom I'd somehow forgotten, moan. I was full of confused adrenaline, unaware that my lungs were already being crushed by blood flowing where it should never be.

the fact foundation of america

The first letter I got from my father was handwritten on prison stationery, but once he is released the letterhead appears, the creamy envelopes. The letterhead shows an open book beside the name of his dummy corporation—the Fact Foundation of America, Inc.—listing an address he has never occupied, a private post-office box, the kind you pay for by the month, on Beacon Hill, a "high-class" address, good for a nonprofit-type think tank, which seems to be the image he's striving for. The name of the corporation is centered, with a phone number below the address that will connect you to no one. On the right, beneath the open book, his name is listed as "President." President, founder, and sole member, I will later learn. A quill pierces the book like an arrow through a heart. A quote in the upper left from Benjamin Disraeli (1804–1881): "To be conscious that you are ignorant of the facts is a great step toward knowledge." All I can think is that this is the foundation of a larger scam, one that never panned out, like those half-completed houses you sometimes pass, skeleton walls and a concrete base, the plastic torn and blowing. On Fact Foundation letterhead he sends a note to the soon-to-be-released Patty Hearst. Hearst replies:

Dear Mr. Flynn, Oct. 10, 1978

Thank you for your kindness in letting me hear from you.

To know that you are concerned enough about my welfare and the recent ruling of the court to take the time to write has helped me a great deal. Your thoughtfulness and understanding are very much appreciated.

I send you my prayers and best wishes.

Sincerely,

Patricia Hearst

My father has sent me this letter from Patty Hearst a dozen times, each beginning "Dear Mr. Flynn," each exactly the same, none of them meant for me. The year on the top is always wrong, always fading further into the past, the signature that closes the letter breaking up, from being photocopied too often, a copy of a copy of a copy. On the bottom of one my father writes, *If you don't think a letter from Patty Hearst is heavy—you're gone.*

snapshot

To hell in a handbasket—this is how my grandmother described my future with a knowing wink. After I'd already totaled two cars, my mother sat me down and asked what I planned to do with my life. Seventeen, clearly on the wrong path, I thought for a moment and answered, *Crime.* As tears well up in my mother's eyes I tried to explain—*White-collar, victimless.* She walked out of the room.

A year later, the morning after the motorcycle accident, my mother is strangling me in the ICU, muttering, *You little shit*, the heart monitor wildly peaking, a nurse coming in to drag her off. After I've spent the night in surgery, after I drove off the road, after I ditched the bike to avoid hitting a stone wall. After I waved the first two cars on, insisting I was all right, pumped up with adrenaline, not wanting to believe Mary's wrist was broken. After finally accepting a lift and checking her into the hospital, after calling my mother to say everything was fine, a small accident, No, no need to come down. After I forgot to hang up the phone, after I knocked all the magazines off the waiting room table, suddenly overcome, I just needed to lie down for a second. After I rose up, minutes later, some part of me knowing something was wrong, by then I was seeing triple. After I staggered down the hall to the admissions desk, I think I need to be looked at, I managed, my eyes already gone yellow. I sang the theme song from Winnie-the-Pooh to Mary, waiting to get her wrist set, as we lay side by side on our gurneys, a curtain between us, both still tipsy from the schnapps, begging the nurses for more painkillers, laughing, as the blood from my broken spleen, unnoticed, drowned me from within. When I woke up that morning after going under the knife I can remember my brother halfheartedly pulling my mother off me as the nurse rushed in. Or perhaps he was egging her on.

A few months before the motorcycle accident I had been with Mary at my house. An April night, my mother bartending, not due home until one or two. If my mother was away on a Saturday night Mary was in my bed. That night, after we came up for air, we were drinking whiskey in the kitchen, and Mary opened a notepad to write something down. In the pad she found a letter my mother had written, a suicide note, undated, but referring to the time after Travis had left the house, the summer of the Red Sox, maybe three years before. I read it, and told Mary, told myself, that it must have been from that time, a hard time for us all, but she had gotten through it, and everything now was better. I made this story up on the spot, I had to tell myself something. We killed the bottle of whiskey, and I tore the note out of the notebook and took it into the yard and burned it, four pages in all, and never mentioned a word of it to my mother. But from then on I kept a closer eye on her, and within four months (*Seek, seek for him, / Lest his ungoverned rage dissolve the life / That wants the means to end it*) I drove my motorcycle into a wall.

the ashmont arms

(1978) The day he's released from Danbury, the prison where he finishes out his time, my father takes a series of buses straight to Ray and Clare's house outside of Boston. The first thing he does, after two years without a real drink, aside from the occasional swallow of home-made prison wine ("pruno"), is get drunk. He tags along to a local party that night and ends up rolling Ray in a rug, standing him in a corner. It's good to be free. There are women at the party, some he knows from before, some he doesn't. The next day the hostess asks Ray if he knew Jonathan was an ex-con, that he'd just been released that day. Ray assures her that he isn't violent, that he tends to get drunk is all. Ray and Clare by this time have two children, both girls, nineteen and sixteen. The girls remember Jonathan from before he was put away, and they hadn't liked him much then. Cross-eyed. Unpredictable. *Disreputable is*

an understatement, Ray admits—*Wives couldn't stand him, he was the drunken slob who tries to make your daughter.*

Still, the ex-con's an old friend, and once again he's shown up penniless. Clare's cousin Margaret owns a few rooming houses in Dorchester. Margaret has nine kids of her own but she has a soft spot for broken-down men and knows how to handle them and, more importantly, how to get rid of them if they get out of hand. Her buildings are ramshackle three- or four-deckers, three apartments on each floor, a hot plate and a sink with hot and cold running water in each. Shared bathrooms. Fine for the guys who end up there—marginal, somewhat or full-blown alcoholic, depending on the time of month or day, partly employed or just collecting one type of check or another to keep afloat. Margaret's in it to make money, but she understands that sometimes she'll get burned—Catholic charity meets the free market. If a guy's on a bender, sliding downhill fast and unable to get out of it, locked in his room 24/7, incontinent, she will stop by, knock, look around the room, tell him she's going to leave for a couple hours and that when she comes back she wants him shaved and dressed and she'll take him to detox. If he can sober up for those twenty-eight days she will hold his room, she says, but if she has to put him out his room will be gone and he'll never come back. Half the time it would work. The really bad ones would say, *Put one foot inside the door and I call the cops.* These were the ones who would stew all day thinking about one thing—how best to drink in comparative safety. Drunk but not crazy, they knew the law, and drunkenness, in and of itself, was no longer a crime. If she had to she would wait for this type to pass out, wrap his belongings up in a bedsheet and stash them in another room, take the keys off his sleeping body, drag the body by the ankles into the hallway, call the cops. *No, no, I never seen him before, must have just snuck in to sleep one off,* and they'd haul him away. Margaret understood how to deal with drunks, in part because she'd struggled with her own drinking over the years. She knew there was a point where it was useless to reason.

In comparison to the rest Jonathan looks pretty good. Margaret knows him from parties at Ray and Clare's over the years, and offers him a room in the house on Beale Street, rent-free in exchange for managing the place. Managing consists of keeping the bathrooms clean and collecting the rent, calling her in case anything breaks down or falls in. Once beautiful, this house, with a curved mahogany staircase, a statue of the blessed Virgin in a niche between floors, though the neighborhood itself has fallen on hard times. The Ashmont subway stop is nearby, and the trains screech and rattle at five A.M.

Luther rents one room on the top floor. Four hundred pounds, in and out of institutions his whole life for one psychotic break or another, Luther assures Margaret that he doesn't lose his temper anymore, that whenever he gets close he just takes out his nails and hammers them into the floor. Across from him is Alan, an amateur boxer, punch-drunk, jabbing and ducking his way up the stairs. On the floor below is Baxter—a real "bottom-of-the-barrel redneck type"—drinks the cheapest beer, tapes racist messages to his door. *Jonathan looks like a first-class liberal next to him.* In the beginning Jonathan and Baxter get along, throw back a few in the evenings, but soon they have a falling out—it's said that Jonathan walloped Baxter, and that Baxter's son came over and beat Jonathan good. Jonathan isn't drinking heavily at this time, he hands over the rent along with a neat list of all the things he bought for the house, cleans the bathrooms, keeps his place tidy. He's driving a cab and putting money away. So Margaret has to get rid of Baxter.

Margaret tells me all this years later. At the time I know almost nothing about my father, nor do I care. Lots of people would be good for long periods of time, Margaret says, then pick up a drink and it was over. At first it seemed Jonathan could drink moderately, but within a few months he starts going downhill. He stops handing over the rent, stops answering her calls, avoids Margaret. Other things occupy her, she lets it slide. One month, three. Five. She blames herself, she should have been paying more attention—*You don't have the right to put temptation in front of people.* Even so, eventually she takes him to court. It was hard otherwise to get his attention. He presents a list to the magistrate of the housing court, detailing, among other expenses, two thousand dollars for toilet paper.

Maybe it's at the Ashmont Arms, as he calls it, with

Luther banging nails into the floor above his head, that Jonathan concocts the Fact Foundation of America (*One of my masterpieces—everybody loves it!*). A clearinghouse of facts, the place the world will turn to if they want to know the truth. Maybe he used some of the rent money he collected to have the letterhead designed, to have it printed on the heavy-weight bond. Maybe there *is* a stash somewhere, under a pile in his room, or maybe under the same palm tree where he claims to have buried the money from the bank jobs, a cache of facts that he will one day sell back to the universe.

thirteen random facts

Fact: In 1866 Alfred Nobel invents dynamite.

Fact: In 1882 Hiram Maxim invents the machine gun.

Fact: In the 1948 Scituate High School Yearbook (*Chimes*) my father lists himself as: vice president (three years); in the Key Club; vice president of the Key Club; treasurer of the Student Council; class editor of *Chimes*; sports editor of *Chimes*; in the Glee Club; on the football team (one year); manager of the football team (three years); and in the Senior Class play.

Fact: My father looks small and clean-cut in his yearbook photos—frail, even, especially beside his best friend Ron Patterson, the class president.

Fact: After high school my father attends a preparatory school, then one semester of Boston College, which he flunks. He then pretends to attend the following semester, so he will continue to be funded by his father.

Fact: When I am born my father puts a notice in the local newspaper: "TWIN BOYS, Nicholas Joseph and Edmund Thomas, were born Tuesday . . ." though this is not true. My ghost twin is named after my two grandfathers, Edmund and Thomas, as a way of taunting them, as if to say, *Did you really believe I would name a son after you?*

Fact: In the late 1960s my father remarries and fathers a daughter, the half-sister I met just that once. He names her Anastasia, after the Romanov Anastasia, the same reasoning behind naming me Nicholas. My father, some days, claims to be a descendant, on his mother's side, of the missing Czarina.

Fact: A man named Igor shot the Romanovs. Few people claim to be descended from him.

Fact: My father also claims to be a direct descendant, on his father's side, of the "first king of Ireland."

Fact: The name Flynn comes from the Irish word *flan*, which translated roughly as "ruddy" or "red-faced." The name Flynn, it seems, derives from a general term for a commoner, a bog-dweller, those distinctly outside the castle walls. More akin to "hey, you" than "my good lord."

Fact: In 1839 Dostoyevsky witnessed a mob of peasants attacking his father. In some versions they poured vodka down his throat until he died.

Fact: I can witness my father pouring vodka down his own throat any day of the week. My role is to play the son, though I often feel like a mob of peasants.

Fact: In 1878 Benjamin Disraeli said: *You are not listening now, but one day you will hear me.*

fish pier
(the two types of college)

(1979) An endless haze, waiting for yet another boat to appear on the horizon, the work in and of itself nothing to look forward to, the boredom nearly unbearable. The boats can dock as late as ten at night, which means we'll work until two, three. We've been at it since morning—lolling around, getting high, hiding out—until finally the captain radios in that he's passing the last buoy. The pier boss finds us, shakes us out of our hiding places, assigns jobs—two lumpers with pitchforks in the hold, knee-deep in slime and ice, shoveling fish into a basket; another on deck above, a gloved hand on the line, feeding the basket through the hatch; another on the pier manning the winch, tipping the overflowing basket onto the culling table; another two at the table, sorting round from flat; then a couple on the two-wheelers, slamming an empty box onto the scale, waiting until the cullers slide the fish

in, then icing the box, nailing down the lid. The captain writes the weight on the lid with a wax pencil, marks it in his book, we swing another box on top, stacking them four high, eight hundred pounds of fish total, then haul it all off to the walk-in freezer. I started that August, working the two-wheeler, a year to the day after I drove my motorcycle off the road, and after three months I'm bored silly, mostly from the endless waiting.

It had taken the better part of the year to recover from the motorcycle accident. In the weeks after my spleen was removed I spent my days before the television or outside in the sun, in either a chemical or a marijuana haze, depending on what my friends brought me. I lost a lot of weight, hovering below one-twenty for a while. Near the end of August my brother was readying to return to college for the fall and I'd forgotten to apply. He was getting the house ready for the winter, working in the crawl space, fiddling with the furnace. As he passed me on his way out to the garage, he muttered, *Why don't you get out of that fuckin' chair, help out?*

> I'm recovering, I reminded him, why don't you fuck off.
>
> What'd you say? he demanded.
>
> Deaf fuck, I said.

As I turned my head away he coldcocked me, scraping a handful of keys from my jawbone midway down my neck. He walked out as I pressed my hand to the wound.

• • •

It was true I needed a job, needed to do something, get some direction. Most of my friends were starting college, town was emptying. A few weeks later I began working for a cleaning company, a franchise with bright yellow vans. I was given a set of light blue polyester shirts with my first name embroidered over the pocket, sent into strangers' houses with buckets, solvents and rags. I was unable to leave my hometown. I wanted to stay close to Mary. I wanted to keep an eye on my mother.

Once I started working my mother decided I should pay rent—three hundred a month plus food and utilities. Phil, one of the friends I'd gotten drunk with at Dreamwold years before, would come home some weekends from school and we'd drive to boatyards and get high. On one of those nights we decided to live on a boat the upcoming summer. We found a thirty-one foot Trojan for a few hundred dollars, a ruin that everyone said would never float again. It took three months to fix her up, inventing a version of carpentry as we went along, and we launched her into the North River that June. After a year of meat and beer I'd gained back most of my weight.

My mother's back together with an old boyfriend, Liam, who this time around is working at the fish pier in Plymouth. Ten years earlier, when they'd first been together, I thought Liam looked like Tom Jones, but then each of her boyfriends reminded me of someone on television. Liam's now in the business of smuggling drugs. It isn't hard to figure out. He disappears for two or three months at a time down to South America on "fishing trips." Not since *Moby-Dick* did anyone fish that long. I ask my mother if he's a drug smuggler, and she denies it in such a way (*What makes you say that?*) that I know it's true. That summer I tell her I'm bored with cleaning, that I want to work with Liam at the pier. I don't say it but I see myself working my way up the "Organization," making a run to Colombia. Simple mathematics. It could finance college, if I ever go, and if not it would still be better than any of the jobs in restaurants and banks I see my mother drag herself to day after day. It is, as far as I can see, the only way out. Besides, I have nothing against marijuana. My mother, though clearly torn, sets it up. Liam drives me for my first day of work and introduces me around. On the way down he tells me that I'll hear a lot of bullshit around the pier, not to believe it all, to just keep it to myself, and I understand.

Tony, Liam's best friend, owns the pier. A year earlier the Mob had rented it out for the weekend. Late at night they docked a boat laden with marijuana and unloaded it. Tony and Liam had been running together since schooldays on Winter Hill, a tough part of Somerville. As kids they'd stolen cars, then graduated to heavy equipment—earth movers, backhoes, cherry pickers—and set themselves up in the construction business as low-level tough guys. Owning the pier was the latest venture, but the only illegal activity they had come up with so far was bringing in mercury-tainted swordfish from Canada, which was banned in the U.S. and so brought a decent price on the black market. The weekend they rented out the pier to the Mob, Tony and Liam sat in a car and watched what was happening, deciding right then and there to enter the big time. Red and the Goon, two henchmen from the Winter Hill days, were with them. Armed with shotguns (easy to keep in the trunk of a car, you could be a hunter), they kicked open their doors, four doors opening at once like in a twentieth-century western, walked up to the head mobster, sitting in his own car overseeing the unloading, and kidnapped him. They brought him to the fish house and held him there at gunpoint for two days, demanding a million dollars. As unlikely as it seems, they got it, and overnight took over the business of bringing drugs into the East Coast. Tony owned the pier, the boats, the trucks, the drivers, the mechanics, the legit business front, and he'd just proven himself fearless. Liam's girlfriend (my mother) worked in a bank, which eased the flow of thousands of dollars daily. "Laundering," it's called.

Within a year Tony's gang is awash in cash. Liam made two successful runs, more were planned. They let go of the other, lesser criminal activities and focus on smuggling. Charismatic and generous, Tony's charm allows him to avoid capture over the next few years, as he has a few cops and a judge in his pocket. I begin unloading fishing boats under the watchful eye of the DEA, who camp out full-time on surrounding rooftops, filming.

• • •

The pier boss, Dex, sleeps in his car, and his car never moves. Parked facing the harbor, overlooking the pier, he shoots up, drifts off. The pier is in an abandoned industrial yard, near where the Pilgrims landed. Dex isn't dumb, he's been to a few semesters of college—real college, not the "college" everyone else gets sentenced to. Maybe in his mid-thirties but he looks ancient—the teeth, junkie teeth, few and fewer, and he doesn't seem to care. He sleeps in the clothes he wears to unload the boats, caked with gurry and fish slime, he sleeps a lot. We all stink of fish, but Dex has given up on any pretense of even trying to clean up. Waiting for a boat to appear on the horizon, we hammer together fish boxes, "coopering," it's called, and for those few hours we call ourselves "coopers." As the fall drags on, fewer and fewer boats come in, so we cooper more and more. By the end of October we have hundreds of boxes, stacked taller than a man. I spend my time building elaborate mazes from the stacks of boxes, with hidden paths leading to a central room I disappear into to get high, read, sleep. Most of the job consists of learning how to hide, of how to appear busy, of killing time. In this way it's a continuation of my twelve years of public school. Hiding seems the point of everything.

I'm going nowhere, and not very fast. The monotony of being perpetually high and trying to look busy is worse than cleaning houses, so I decide to quit, but before I can I'm taken aside by Keith, the electrician. Known as the "Professor," Keith knows my mother, always asks after her. He takes me out to lunch and offers me a job as his apprentice. Officially Keith's the electrician for the boats, for the fish house, and he looks the part—wears a tool belt, messes with boxes sprouting medusas of parti-colored wire—but it's a front. High up in the Organization, he maintains the radios that keep in touch with boats that aren't going out for fish, the type of boat that Liam goes out on. He calls the radio the "Mothership." Working for Keith means that I'm moving up the ladder. On the surface I'm learning a trade, which I need, and at the same time I'm being ushered into the big time, the big money. This is good, this is the plan—electricity can be my front.

One of my first jobs is to spend a week in Tony's trucking yard, burning documents behind the building in a steel drum. Keith checks up on me once a day, to make sure I'm pulverizing even the ash, scattering it. I know I'm being filmed as I do this, Keith points out the telephone worker strapped to the pole directly across from the yard, waves to him. But no one ever approaches me, and in three days all the records are dust. It's some kind of test, to see if I can handle the conceptually illegal before being offered a shot at the real. I'm then moved back to the fish pier, to rewire the boats in ways that had nothing to do with fish, simply making them comfortable for longer trips. Boats still come in, fish are unloaded and in the fillet house fish are cut and packed and shipped out. But no one believes this is the real money. After that weekend, with the kidnapping and the tough-guy stance, Tony never uses the pier again, not for drugs. The drug boats now unload in Portland, Maine, a washed-up port at this point in its history, off the map. Red and the Goon haul the marijuana down from Maine in eighteen-wheelers. Sometimes, if it's the season, they stash it in a load of Christmas trees. This all comes out later. At the time I just know, along with the FBI and the DEA, that something's happening.

Sometimes Keith sets me up in the morning hanging fluorescent lights in the fillet house, then disappears for the day. He expects me to hang maybe one light a day, if that—as long as I'm set up to look like I'm working. Some have real jobs—the cutters, the drivers—and my pristine status draws some resentment. One morning Joey, just released from prison after ten years for killing his wife's lover with a shotgun, comes up to me with a shovelful of ice as I'm on a ladder, contemplating a box full of wire. Keith insists I work with the power on, says I can't be an electrician if I'm afraid of electricity. I've been shocked countless times, showered with sparks, held screwdrivers as they melted in my hand. Joey looks up at me and smiles, dumps the ice into Keith's toolbox, then stands there with the shovel over his shoulder. I look at him, at the ice, shrug. I'll spend the day drying off Keith's tools.

• • •

Everyone who works for Tony is broken down in some way. Almost weekly the local papers allege he's a drug kingpin—to say you're on his payroll isn't something to crow about. But I'm learning a trade and he pays cash. My mother and I are closer at this point than we've ever been. Something about the both of us working for gangsters, the details left unspoken, binds us together. We both hope the money will transform us.

Some days Keith tells me to go to his house, into the bedroom closet, to a shoebox filled with cash, count out five thousand, meet him in a bank parking lot. I begin to understand that this is one way he spends his days—driving from bank to bank, depositing cash, laundering it clean. I imagine soon I'll be tapped to do something only someone on a motorcycle can do (I'd bought a bigger motorcycle after the crash, blaming the wipeout on my smaller bike), something fast and low to the ground. A run.

In January, two weeks before the resumption of classes, I get a letter from the University of Massachusetts, telling me I've been accepted, a full ride—all I have to do is sign my name. I can't even remember applying—maybe it was done during my senior year of high school, in conjunction with the SATs, a cafeteria full of us signing up for the public university, like a Moonie wedding. It turns out that despite the carousing my grades put me in the top ten percent of my class, at a time when higher education is still considered a right. I'm torn about going, in part about leaving my mother alone, in part because I don't want to lose my footing in the Organization. The carpenter, who recently moved out on his wife and two kids so he can sit outside a tent in the state park under a kerosene lamp each night and kill a bucket of beer in peace, just looks at me and rolls his eyes when I mention that I'm thinking of not going. *Don't be an asshole*, he tells me, *you have your whole life to work.*

Two weeks later, hungry to learn after two mind-numbing years, I'm sitting in a classroom, wrapping my brain around *King Lear—Who is it that can tell me who I am? Does Lear walk thus? Speak thus?* I hold on to my job with Keith, going home every other weekend and holidays. If there were an opening on a boat I'd leave school in a heartbeat.

love saves the day

(1981) Emily—fresh-faced, braless—after a year with the gangsters I feel a hundred years old beside her. My first creative writing class I make a point to find a seat near her. Emily's story, about a man who sells cocaine and gets lost in it and ends up dying a very Jack London death in a snowstorm, is better than anything I'm writing, the best thing in the class. We begin talking and decide to go to a party together on Halloween. I show up at her dorm room that night with Doug, the friend I went to Europe with who I eventually followed to Amherst. Sloppy makeup around my eyes, a choirboy robe, I'm the approximation of a ghoul. Doug wears a broken plastic street lamp as a helmet, his body wrapped in a shower curtain, a spontaneous mess. Emily's still transforming herself into a wood sprite. I roll a joint, we pass it. We drink some beer, small talk. Once sufficiently spritelike and sparkly, she takes out a baggie with a large quantity of white powder in it, asks

if we want "to sniff." Doug and I look at each other—the bag holds ten or twenty grams of cocaine, easy, and we've never seen more than a gram at a time, ever. She's eighteen, dating her boss, a twenty-nine-year-old coke dealer and the owner of a music shop in Provincetown. Generous with his drugs, as are most of the older straight men in Provincetown, especially with teenage girls. When I meet him a few months later he takes me aside, tells me to treat her well, and gives me a baggie full of quaaludes, as if they're the keys to his car. Doug and I tend more toward crystal meth, which is cheaper and lasts longer, though teeth-shatteringly unpredictable. But we don't say no. We help ourselves to an unhealthy line or two. I then offer Emily half of my hit of acid—*Love Saves the Day*. It's my second or third time tripping, Emily's first, and she's understandably trepid. Awake all night, at one point I find her touching her reflection in a cruelly lit dorm bathroom, asking if she'll ever be the same. I kiss her then for the first time and whisper, *No*.

We got the acid from Sam. Sam lives in an old camper, the type you pull behind a car—rounded corners, a tiny sink, a table that folds down. He pays a farmer a couple hundred bucks to park it in a field for the winter. It has no heat, no electricity—essentially a bed in a field, dead husks all around it. I never ask where he shits. That winter we all end up living together, through the cold months, in Doug's dorm room. Doug's the only one supposed to be in the room, except for a phantom roommate who never appeared. I'd forgotten to sign up for housing and after a week sleeping in my car Doug offers me the empty bed. Sam comes by for a shower, leaves his toothbrush, a change of clothes. The weather turns. Sam hooks up with a teenage girl who's likely a runaway. One night it makes no sense to send them out into the snow to bicycle back to the camper. They curl up behind our desks, and that's where they sleep for a few months, at least until the girl goes back home.

When Sam isn't sleeping on our floor he'll dress up in a skeleton suit and stand at the trashbarrels in the dining common, a sign taped to the wall behind him giving statistics on world hunger, on how many children have died that day. He'll silently reach into the trashbarrels and pull out the food others toss, eat it with his hands, there in his skeleton suit.

Emily and I stay together for six months, until the school year ends and we drift back to our hometowns. That summer I live on the boat with Phil and work for the gangsters. Once, after having been "missing" for a few weeks, Tony lines all the local misfits who work for him up on his porch. Holding a wad of hundreds, he asks each of us what he owes. For the last couple months I've been wiring the lights around his new swimming pool. When he gets to me I say, *Eight hundred*, which I figure is about right. Tony laughs, shakes his head, looks at the carpenter, rolls his eyes—Eight *hundred*? He reaches out, pinches my cheek, slaps it lightly, still laughing—*Eight fuckin' hundred dollars?*

The carpenter shrugs. *The fuckin' kid doesn't think I'll kill him*, Tony mutters, then peels off eight bills.

That November, back at school, Emily's now with someone else, and one night we're all at a party at his apartment. Emily's telling a story about a friend of her family's, an eccentric guy who comes to their house for Christmas and Thanksgiving. I'm half listening, eavesdropping from another conversation. Emily's generally soft-spoken, but telling this story animates her. This guy approaches a woman in a bar and begins chatting her up. After a while the woman says, *You don't even know who I am, do you?* And he, thinking she might be famous, says, *Should I?* She answers, *Well, you should, you bastard, you married me.*

The story seems somehow packaged, unlikely, the punch line about being so out of it you try to pick up your ex-wife too wacky. Emily's telling the story, in part, as a cautionary tale, of the fate that awaits us as would-be writers—this guy calls himself a poet. When Emily says the man's name I listen harder. When she says he's a failed writer I down more of my beer. This eccentric friend had related the story of encountering his ex-wife around her family's dinner table. Her family had laughed, entertained by their friend's outrageousness. One of his parlor tricks over the years had been to read aloud the love letters women had written him. They remembered the young wife, asked about her, but this was all he knew, this random encounter. I watch Emily's face. She said he drank too much, that he'd spent time in federal prison, had fallen off a ladder onto his head, that his memory was gone. He claimed to have written a novel but no one had ever seen it. She says the name of the novel—*The Button Man.*

The party moves to other stories, its white noise washes over me. I sit back in my armchair, look at each face, try to piece it together. Emily and I had gotten together over a year before, had stayed together for a while, were still close. And now my father, who I don't think about much at all, aside from the infrequent letter, turns out to be a close friend of Emily's family. Her parents, I will later learn, are Ray and Clare, whose names I've never heard before, though they remember me. After a few minutes I tap Emily's shoulder. *That guy you were talking about*, I say, *that's my father.* I'm known to not always speak the truth, but still she stares at me in horror. *I'm serious*, I say.

family friend

No one would notice Jonathan wandering upstairs as Ray and Clare's annual New Year's party rages below. Maybe he's looking for a free bathroom, maybe a little air, a place to clear his head. All night he'd tried to down a glass of water between drinks, pace himself. He stands before the sink and checks his eyes in the mirror. How long can he hold his own gaze? Does he look as loaded as he feels? Tonight the mirror is unkind, makes his face so haggard. But his cheeks have the flush that always comes, makes him look rugged, his hair slightly mussed. *A party, for chrissakes, let's get to it.* He can hear the girls singing below, angels calling him. He wakes up with his cheek pressed to the tile floor. *Must've dozed off.* The party below is winding down. He moves through the house, he knows the girls' rooms. He will just stop by to tuck them in, to say how much he enjoyed their song, but his heart's beating so loudly.

• • •

Jonathan had lived with Ray and Clare, off and on, for years. Even if not invited he would appear, drive his cab from Boston to Ipswich, forty-five minutes away. Ray would always welcome him, got a kick out of his hijinks. If Jonathan had money he was generous, especially as far as liquor was concerned. He'd arrive with a couple bottles, put them on the table with a flourish, drinks all around. I learn all this from Emily. More often than not, as the years passed, he'd arrive penniless. More and more of his things were kept in their basement, or in boxes left with other friends. In this way he could travel light, have a change of clothes waiting, a razor, a toothbrush, a book to replace the one he'd finished. In Ipswich he kept a suit at the dry cleaner's, used it as his storage. He'd drop off the one he was wearing, change into the clean one right there. They knew him at the dry cleaner's, he left Ray and Clare's phone number, they would call Clare sometimes—*I'm not sure where he is or when he's coming back*, she'd say. But he always came back, eventually, to pick up his suit, to clean himself up, to stay a few days—always optimistic, the work on his novel always going well. At one point Ray even set up a room for him, with a desk and a typewriter, so he'd have a place to write. Emily remembers him coming by for Christmas one year, he called that morning, had nowhere else to go. Emily, the youngest, barely ten, but she could see that Jonathan was trying very, very hard to be appropriate. As the girls got older it seemed less and less of a good idea to leave them alone with him. If they got close he growled. If you left him alone in the house too long he'd get into the liquor and drain it. The girls would come home from school to find him passed out on the floor. Or worse. One Fourth of July Clare baked an elaborate cake, something for after the fireworks. In the middle of the afternoon Emily came in from the barbecue to find Jonathan passed out on the couch, a hole gouged in the center of the cake, chocolate smeared on his face, his hands, the couch itself. *Is this man ever going to leave?* Emily wondered.

The night I found out that Emily knew my father, knew him better than I ever would, we went back to her room. I don't know what she said to her boyfriend, or if we told our friends, but she wanted to show me her record collection, the albums she'd pilfered from her basement, some that had my father's name on the cover. I recognized his handwriting from his letters, his unmistakable scrawl. We'd danced to his Zorba the Greek album at parties, I'd even put it on, but had never noticed my father's name on Zorba's face, his arms raised, a kick-step.

o christmas tree

(1982) Thanksgiving. Back home for the long weekend for the holiday and for a friend's wedding, I accidentally leave my notebook in the bathroom. In it I had begun a story about a woman who works two jobs and tries to fit in a couple hours between each to be with her kids. This woman wants her kids in the kitchen with her while she cooks, wants them to tell her about their days. The kids sit on the counter while she chops carrots. I didn't get to the part where it becomes clear that those moments they had together between her jobs were precious. I hadn't gotten that far. My mother must have read it while I was at the reception, and while I'm downing shots my mother begins her suicide note. She begins by writing how she has just finished reading my notebook, about how perceptive I am. Two weeks later she finishes the note, when I'm back up at school, getting ready for exams. After swallowing a fistful of painkillers she goes for a walk along Peggotty

Beach. An hour later she comes back home, groggy. "I was unable to throw myself in the ocean," she writes, the handwriting more erratic as the painkillers seep into every cell, shutting out lights in empty rooms. On the last page of her four-page note she writes how she loves me and my brother and her father, before a voice comes into her head—*Why don't you use the gun?* These are the last words she will write.

The day after she shot herself I'm shown this note at my grandfather's kitchen table. Two friends had driven me home from Amherst the night before. My step-grandmother tries to console me, says the note shows my mother had been deranged in some way, not in her right head, but I know it was the drugs taking over her mind, the overdose that made her hand tremble, the letter almost unreadable by the end. My brother and I find fifty thousand dollars in her safe-deposit box the next day and this same grandmother points out that my mother had always been frugal, that she must have saved it over the years. I explain that it's drug money, money she'd skimmed off her laundering favors—her cut, so to speak, blindingly clear. The money itself is troubling. The story I'd told myself was that she'd been tired of working so hard, tired of being poor, yet here was fifty thousand dollars, squirreled away, doing nothing.

Two weeks later Emily and I drag a Christmas tree into my grandmother's living room. It's a year since we found out who we were, and we've been together ever since. My grandmother reaches up to embrace me, whispers loud enough for Emily to hear, *Did you swipe it, Nicky?* After Travis left I'd continued to pick up our tree at midnight from St. Mary's, but until this moment I didn't know my grandmother knew, all those years. My mother's barely ash. I'm twenty-two.

I swiped the tree after reading a self-help book that said not to make any life changes after a major trauma, to keep doing what you'd always done. I would have gone back to work for the gangsters, but the gangsters had all been arrested. Everything had fallen apart over the past year, after they'd begun flying cocaine in, and started using it, and got sloppy. Even my mother began using, leaving cut straws in her glove compartment, I'd find them when I was home from school, split them open to lick out the bitter residue. And now this car is mine, the first new car she'd ever owned, a Subaru wagon. I park it and never drive it again.

I reappear at school at the end of January, hollowed out by it all, but I don't know where else to be. I return to my room off-campus, in a house with four "radical" women, my friends, who taught me, finally, how to be a vegetarian. I enroll for classes, show up on time, but I can't seem to focus on the second half of Shakespeare, the comedies. Or on eating. And I can't stop crying. At one point a few weeks into the semester I find myself slumming in the

Frost Library at Amherst College, reading Faulkner in one of those comfortable Ivy League chairs, and after a while I realize I haven't turned the page in over an hour. I focus on a sentence, a word, and get hung up—each seems to have its own set of problems, its own code, until at some point I understand that I'm holding the book upside down. I right it, but even then my mind gets entangled, a sentence comes at me like a truck without a driver, bearing down—*It wasn't any woman that got her into what she don't even call trouble*—I try to get out of its way, I turn it over and over, but it's more an echo than a piece of something larger. My eyes go to the period and back to the first word, it means something more than I can unlock. *Wasn't any woman . . . got her into what . . . she don't even call . . .* I know then it will be impossible for me to finish school.

In an overlit room, standing before one of several windows, like in a bank, a registrar informs me that in order to withdraw without flunking I need to have an extenuating circumstance. I whisper that my mother just killed herself, but maybe this woman's hard of hearing, she squints and shakes her head as if she doesn't understand, so I repeat it, but still she doesn't understand, so I say it again, and again, each time a little louder, until I nearly scream it.

Only a shrink can get me out of school without failing this late in the semester. The health plan allows ten visits, one per week. The doctor's about my age, perhaps slightly older, his face untroubled, eager. A resident, working off his required hours at the university clinic. At our first meeting we look across his desk at each other for a long time, until he asks me how I'm doing. My chart, which I'd filled out a few minutes earlier in the waiting room, lies in front of him. I know he can read that my mother has recently taken her life. How am I *doing*? He nods. I smile and turn the question over in my mind. I begin to point out that it isn't really the right question, but start to laugh before I can finish, and keep on laughing, a laughter that builds on itself. How *am* I doing? He might as well ask, *Would you like more pebbles in your shoes?* or *Besides that, Mrs. Lincoln, how'd you like the play?* I'm laughing like a goddamn hyena at this point, and each time I look at his face, now clearly riddled with concern, now aware that he's perhaps in over his head, confronted by a truly deranged person, a madman, it makes me laugh harder, falling-off-my-chair laughter, painful, side-splitting laughter, gasping for mercy, tears streaming down my cheeks, only fueled more with each glance he makes toward the doorknob. Afraid of *me*? I can barely put one foot in front of the other, I read books upside down without knowing it, for chrissakes. At the end of our session he says I can come as often as I like, every day if I want. I imagine I must have finished at least the ten sessions, for eventually I leave school without failing, though I remember not another moment with him.

evol

I drop out that spring, return to Scituate to get the Trojan ready for the water. As soon as it's afloat, though, it begins to feel small. On a boat that size the tables lower to become bunks, the cushions become mattresses. Phil's mother had died a few months after mine. Cancer. He'd gotten to say goodbye but he also had to watch as she vanished. As a teenager I'd spent days on end with his family, and his mother had been one of my personal saints, always made it known I was welcome, even after I totaled their family car one drunken night.

Phil and I try to have fun that summer but it's strained. Nothing means anything—we can't drink enough or get high enough, not anymore. By July we decide, in an uncharacteristically American impulse, that a bigger boat's the answer, one we can live on through the winter. We'll tie it to a dock Phil found in Boston. This way we can keep living together.

• • •

The boat we find is a vintage Chris-Craft—forty-two feet stem to stern, twelve-foot beam, double-planked mahogany. Twin-screw. Yacht. Originally owned by a judge. Christened *Catherine*. Asking three thousand dollars. Out of the water eight years when we find her, a faded jewel, nearly forgotten in a boatyard in Scituate, on the North River, the boatyard itself tucked away, not visible from the street, its sign overgrown with brambles.

That August we sell the Trojan, buy the bigger Chris-Craft. Within a month, realizing how much work has to get done before the weather turns, I quit my job building greenhouses with the carpenter, both of us refugees from the gangster roundup, and begin working full-time to pull the Chris-Craft back into shape. The boat was built in 1939, the same year my mother was born, and if I stand on the deck and look north I can almost see the spot off Third Cliff where we'd scattered her ashes.

Every waking hour from September until December I spend in the boatyard, scrambling up and down ladders, punctuated by runs to the hardware store, to marine supply stores, to stores that specialize in fasteners. Before we came along the previous owner had begun fiberglassing the cabin, and it makes sense to finish the work. We need a string of clear days in order for the wood to be dry enough to take the resin, and October's weather along the North

River doesn't always cooperate. As we poke at the wood we realize that in certain key places much of it's punky, needing to be replaced. The entire hull wants refastening, especially below the waterline. Buying the screws to do this is akin to buying drugs—we drive into Boston's South End, to Allied Nut and Bolt, and pass a hundred or two hundred dollars to a man behind bulletproof plexiglas in exchange for a couple tiny packages of silicone bronze screws, things of beauty that promise to last longer than all of us. As the days grow shorter we discover a gap in the hull you can put your fist through, along the chine, that line where the freeboard meets the hull. Somehow in going over the boat we'd missed it. The owner of the boatyard tell us, without great optimism, what we might try. He lends us four hydraulic jacks and we line them up along the chine, using a plank to distribute the pressure, then slowly crank them up until we can eyeball the line of the hull back into shape. Most days I find myself working alone, as Phil held on to his job, perhaps not as desperate to see her float again, perhaps not feeling quite so homeless. Eating oatmeal for breakfast, skipping lunch, smoking more and more dope, I'm determined to get her in the water before mid-December, the one-year anniversary of my mother's death.

Many friends come down for a day or two to help. Emily puts in hour upon heroic hour. We find some wooden letters from an old fruit stand and spell out the word *EVOL* on the stern—the title of a Sonic Youth album and "love" spelled backward. By early December she's ready. We put rollers under the cradle, inch the cradle onto a train track, the track leading down an incline to the lip of the river, a steel cable connecting the cradle to a pulley. Once at the water's edge we have an hour to wait for the tide to float her free. We know that after eight years the seams will weep for days, that she will have to be closely watched until the planks swell tight. As soon as river water touches the dry wood it finds its way into the bilge, weighing her down. At flood high tide there isn't enough water to lift her, and tomorrow the flood tide will be a foot lower. We stand on the cradle trying to rock her, but she's already too full of water. A nail is sticking up from the cradle, I press my sneaker into it, to bend it over, to make it safe, and instead drive it deep into my heel. The steel cable's holding us tight, and as the tide begins to recede the owner of the boatyard gets an axe and cuts it. My sock fills with blood as *EVOL* drifts free.

shelter

We land in Boston just before the ice comes, near the anniversary of my mother's death. We dock at a marina in Fort Point Channel, home to a small community of live-aboards. That first winter we invent ways to keep warm—plastic on the windows, styrofoam insulation under the floors, three to a bed. Our water comes from a hose, and the hose often freezes. A small woodstove overheats the cabin by sucking all the oxygen out, forcing us to open the doors, to lay flat on the floor, lightheaded and gasping, tormented by suffocation dreams, desperate to be closer to the last pockets of air, until the fire goes out and the cold pours in and we awake shivering. We hang old tires over the sides to keep the ice in the channel from lifting the boat into the air and crushing the hull. Eventually we take to wandering around with electric blankets draped over our shoulders, the extension cord dragging absurdly behind.

• • •

That first winter Ray and Clare will now and then ask Emily to invite me up to their house in Ipswich for a family dinner. *Sure*, I say, *I'll be there*, and then not show. Emily tells me after the first time that it was better I hadn't gone, that Jonathan had come, that her parents had wanted us to meet, that it hadn't been pretty. I find it best to arrive unannounced, to be erratic, to keep them guessing. I've had enough surprises, it's better if I'm the one doing the surprising.

I'm driving a 1963 Chevy pickup, a behemoth, the paint a faded green patina, the color copper turns, duct tape around the wheel wells, the nose already stove in by an eighteen-wheeler when I bought it. A few tons of steel, my armor, a do-I-look-like-I-give-a-fuck-about-the-paint-job? type of truck, a do-I-look-like-I-have-enough-insurance? type of truck. Given a wide berth, if I want to change lanes I put on my blinker and ease into the lane, whether the BMW makes room for me or not. A truck that demands politeness. If I'm going somewhere I don't really want to go, like dinner at Ray and Clare's, the truck will invariably die on me, quit moving, stubborn mule. Nothing can hurt me in that truck.

Not that anything's wrong with these dinners—the food invariably high-end, the town gentile, lily-white. One could see it as a respite from living in downtown Boston. But I always feel on display. Each glass of wine I throw back feels measured. Here, for the first time in my life, I'm Jonathan's son. That they want the reunion to take place under their eyes, around their dinner table, with Emily by my side, feels wrong. Perverse. Their intentions may be nothing but generous but it doesn't feel that way. It feels like a freak show, and I choose not to be one of the freaks. Ray asks, *Have you heard from Jonathan? He asks about you all the time.* I say, *I got a few letters. You should get in touch with him*, Ray says, *he's getting old, he's harmless now. I will*, I say, *I'll stop by and see him.* Ray tells me that my father lives in a rooming house on Beacon Hill, I take the address, fold it into my pocket, and on the drive back to Boston toss it out the window. Years later Clare will tell me that Jonathan would never mention my brother or me at all, that it seemed to her that we just weren't that important to him. She tells me this with a mixture of revulsion and respect—*At least he wasn't a maudlin drunk*, she will say, *the type who solicits your pity with talk of* O my lost sons. . . .

Phil has a job with an architectural firm a ten-minute walk from the dock. I work doing carpentry, carving a townhouse on Commonwealth Avenue into condos, replacing six-inch molding with drywall, which leaves a nasty taste in my throat. By the end of February I'm laid off (*hallelujah*), so I drift down to Nicaragua for a couple months to meet up with Emily, who's studying Spanish. We want to be near the Sandinistas, their revolution a glimmer of hope in the world, just as a few years later the fall of the Berlin Wall will be another glimmer. We come back to Boston and the boat as summer begins.

Just aft of us tourists pose hour upon hour to be photographed on the deck of the Boston Tea Party Ship, holding aloft a styrofoam bale wrapped in burlap, TEA stenciled on the outside, ready to toss it into the filthy water. At sunset we hang out on our aft deck drinking bottle after bottle of red wine as a thousand revolutions get played out behind us. The bale is tied to a rope so it can be hauled back on deck, to await the next camera, but it often breaks free and drifts over to us. A punked-out girl named Giselle lives on a boat next to ours and works at a homeless shelter. The Pine Street Inn. It sounds at least as worthwhile as how I'm spending my time. Real estate in Boston is moving from an overheated phase into a long rancid boil, and more and more homeless people are appearing on the streets daily. It's impossible for them not to tug at one's consciousness. You say you want a revolution? Giselle says I can probably fill in at the shelter if I'm interested.

three

chronicle of disaster and the absurd

(1984) August. A year and a half after my mother dies I'm sitting in a change of shift meeting at the Pine Street Inn. Three in the afternoon, ten, twelve workers straggle into the empty Yellow Lobby to sit on benches in a loose circle and listen to the reading of the Main Log. In two hours these same benches will be filled with homeless men. Most of the workers sip coffee, many smoke, all seem to be only half listening. Each afternoon the 3-to-11 shift will show up in time to hear the 7-to-3 read the log. Ritualistic, those going off to those coming on. Now I know that my father lives in a room on Beacon Hill, maybe twenty blocks west, Ray keeps telling me to visit. My father's on my radar, but most of the time I shut it off.

10:20—Two or three proselytizers from an unnamed religious group infiltrated the yard today and some of our guests were seen lined up on their knees on the sidewalk for some sort of ceremony. This is to be discouraged, as we have a captive and vulnerable audience who are easily influenced.

Chronicle of the lost, chronicle of disaster and the absurd, a near-forgotten document of American history—the Main Log of the Pine Street Inn Men's Unit. What's written in the log is nearly always the same, variations on a few themes—someone falls, further down or further apart, a new guest arrives, someone moves on. The reading lasts anywhere from five minutes to half an hour, depending on the kind of day it's been. There are barrings to be voted on, notes about a guest decompensating, another who's talking about checking into detox. The men, still outside for the day, are just starting to line up in the yard for their beds. A few are inside, waiting to get into the clinic, or to talk with a counselor. One seems frozen sitting upright, his forehead glued to the table.

At about 12:30 this afternoon I observed Jack Styles performing certain sexual acts on Bobo Jenkins. While there's a time and a place for everything I don't feel 12:30 in the afternoon is the time, nor the Brown Lobby bathroom the place. Because of Jack's behavior and obvious disregard for P.S.I. rules and his agitation of the other guests, I'm bringing Jack up for barring.

OFN Bobo for his part in the above.

Everyone's acting out continually, in one way or another, whether sitting in a corner with a coat pulled over his head or giddily lit one night after weeks of calm. A guest does have to go the extra mile in order to get noticed above the din. He has to make a significant scene in the midst of an unending scene. Jack is described as "b/m, 6'0", brown skinned, very active libido." The vote goes against barring him. Bobo, for some reason, is not even considered for barring, merely put out for the night (OFN). Maybe to be on the receiving end of a blow job is seen akin to being on the receiving end of a punch, though it never seemed that way to me.

Timers for lights fail, locks jam, radios refuse to transmit. All this is written up, *ATTENTION MAINTENANCE*, theoretically to be attended to the next day, soon.

In a few days the Department of Mental Health will give us a way to "pink paper" psychotic guests on weekends. This means that if someone goes berserk we can sign a form which will commit him to a locked ward until Monday morning, when a doctor can evaluate. The police, theoretically, will transport. Then Solomon Carter Fuller, the psych hospital, decides to admit no more patients. A woman died after being left in seclusion unattended for twenty-three hours straight and it's all over the papers.

Ambulance 911 called for a man with cuts on face and head, claiming to have been hit by a car twice on East Berkeley Street. Melvin loses his wallet and $90. Another new guest, Emmett—at least the tenth this month—hearing voices, doubles over in pain at loud noises. Willie puts his fist through a window when refused a cup of coffee. Rene comes to the door with a knife wound to his left hand. Anton reports being robbed by four barrees around the corner at five A.M. Danny's bleeding profusely from the face. Ultraviolet lights are installed in an effort to curb the spread of contagious tuberculosis. The bomb squad responds to a call they received at their headquarters. Alphonse, found with a utility knife while getting treated for scabies, is barred automatically. A woman calls regarding her missing brother, asks us to have him call her if he shows up. Another man calls for *his* brother, who left a suicide note at home, so he's calling everywhere. Riddell keeps falling asleep with lit cigarettes and setting his coat on fire. Nick Hitler, on a rampage, spits in another guest's face. An unidentified male found facedown on Washington Street—fell on some broken glass and bled to death.

• • •

Another quiet night on the 3-to-11 shift, Lucero writes at nine. At ten Ben Craig, another new guest, comes to the door, spacey and disoriented. Later, as we direct him to a bed, he insists we give him his "real bed."

crowbar

(1984) Christmas. I've been working at the shelter for five months—it has begun to enter my bloodstream. Volunteers wrap donated gifts—hats, gloves, socks, cigarettes—to be handed out to the guests on Christmas Eve. Parker's gift, a pair of red pajamas, delight him, though they pose a dilemma—to take a bed all are required to trade their clothes for a flimsy white johnny, but as the line of men snakes up the staircase, one is now in red. How do you tell a homeless man that he cannot use the gift you have just given him? We might as well have wrapped up a toaster for him, or a gift certificate to have his carpets cleaned. Parker wears the red pajamas every night for two weeks, and he wears them all day as well, under his clothes, as long johns. Until the night I notice a small envelope in his top pocket, and it turns out to have ten joints inside. I confiscate the pajamas, give him back his street clothes, send him out into the cold night. But I let him keep the marijuana. How I came to this punishment I cannot now say. Some would have barred him for the drugs, some might have ignored it. Almost all would have taken the pajamas, though, as they had begun to smell.

That spring Phil and I decide to move the boat to Provincetown, a village of artists, fishermen and sexual outlaws at the tip of Cape Cod, a hundred and twenty miles overland from Boston, a fuck-you finger of sand sticking into the Atlantic. Emily's parents have a summer house there, which we can crash in occasionally if the harbor gets too rough. After two years in Fort Point Channel we want to float in water we can swim in. Besides, as real estate along the Boston waterfront continues to heat up, our "landlord" has turned ugly. Boats cut loose, gunplay at midnight. We vanish one May morning before sunup, drop anchor in Provincetown Harbor three hours later, a quarter mile offshore. Phil returns to Boston, to his job, his girlfriend. I drive to the city every other week, to work a night or two at Pine Street, to see Emily.

In Provincetown I row a tin skiff each morning to shore, row back out at night. If the tide is low I drag the rowboat out over the flats, pants rolled up around my calves, shoes left on the dock. I don't know what my feet are touching and I grow to not care. At high tide it's easy—the skiff's floating above the eelgrass and tiny crabs and muck, I just step in and push off, aim the bow toward where I know the boat awaits, pull at the oars. A few times a day I row back and forth, unless I spend the whole day on the boat, which I often do, if I have enough food, if I have nowhere to be. And if the next day's also empty I won't go to shore then either, until days pass without setting foot on land. Emily's parents can watch me with binoculars, if they choose, and if I smoke enough pot I can almost see them in their picture window, bringing me into focus.

The days I go into Boston I leave Richard, a new pal, to keep an eye on things—to see if the waterline's sitting heavy, if the pump's working. Richard, a sculptor, landed in Provincetown from New York a few months earlier to escape a heroin habit that had gotten out of hand, sick as a dog when we met. We both work at the Moors Restaurant—a "garbage job," as Richard puts it. Richard, part of New York's downtown club scene, claims to have made Keith Haring sleep on his couch, spurning his advances. He still has a loft in the shadows of the World Trade Center, and we will eventually go there for weekends sometimes.

Before we become tight Richard will swim out to the boat after midnight, after the bars close, to work off some excess energy, too shy to pull himself on board, shivering in the dinghy until he catches his breath or gets too cold, and then he'll head back shoreward. The next day he mentions it—*I swam out to your boat last night. You should have come aboard*, I say. He swims out with a waterproof plastic case from Marine Specialties dangling from his neck, a dry cigarette and a lighter inside. By August Richard's leaving cigarettes on board, and sometimes staying over. On an August night we dive from the top deck and as we enter the ocean our bodies are completely lit up by phosphorescence, like underwater superheroes.

The boat will be anchored in Provincetown Harbor for the next seven summers. Some years I'll live on her alone, some years with a friend. For long stretches it's my only real home, which fuels my desperation to keep it afloat. "The ocean's always looking for a way into your boat," a Coast Guard pamphlet warns. With other boaters you exchange stories of breachings and near-sinkings and total losses. You tell about storms and how they'd been fought or ridden out or succumbed to. I know one whose boat sprung a plank while being towed, and while jamming some towels into the breach his hand passed clean through the hull, pinning his arm, the ocean rushing in. He had to time the roll of the waves to pull free. I know fishermen who rode out hurricanes with their bow to the storm, the wind sandblasting their eyes until all their blood vessels burst. When they tell the story the no-longer-whites of their eyes shine crimson. I walk the streets studying the tops of trees to measure the wind; I know the tides without looking; I dive on my anchors every other day and reset them in the sand; I see the cabins need paint and try to make more time. All of it fills me so I don't have to dwell on what's really in my brain—a palmfull of pills, a gunshot wound, a splintered chair. A nightgown left heavy with blood.

Summer becomes fall. That time still passes, ignoring my mother's absence, somehow overwhelms me. Going into my second year at the shelter I'm discovering unknown reserves of bad energy inside me that need to be tapped. Provincetown's good for that—the so-called last resort, the end of the world, jumping-off point to oblivion. Provincetown can absorb nearly anything, nearly anyone who can't fit in elsewhere, no such thing as too freaky, too lost, not here. By late October the police make their annual post-summer sweep through town, rounding up the most obvious drug peddlers, the walking wreckage, the ones who'd been flush all summer on tourist hungers and now find themselves eating the profits, the product, spending all they'd accumulated. Summer's over, the police murmur, buy a bus ticket or check into jail.

By November I'm caught unawares. As the town emptied I'd stayed on, unsure what to do next. I'd never hauled the boat out of the water, I didn't have a plan. Late in the season and still a quarter mile offshore—no telephone, no electricity, a propane stove, a radio powered by AA batteries, somehow reluctant to move back onto land, feeling that land itself is a temporary state, a transition. Living on the water quiets my mind. What can I pass through now on my way to more water? Another Christmas at the shelter? I gaze at the shoreline—all those houses, each window lit, families inside, whole lives unfolding—convince myself that I'm not a part of it, that the lives behind each window have nothing to do with my life. The boat has become supreme isolation, chosen isolation, holding myself apart from the world, which I only dimly understand anyway. I can sit on the aft deck and never be surprised by anything again—no phone will ever ring, no one will knock that I haven't seen coming for a quarter mile. That I can go to sleep any night and wake up having broken loose—a failed knot, a line frayed, the anchor dragged—that I can drift out of sight of land makes a twisted sense, in line with my internal weather. When everything has proven tenuous one can either move toward permanence or move toward impermanence. The boat's sublimely impermanent. Some mornings the fog's so thick that I exist only in a tight globe of clearing, beyond which is all foghorn and unknown.

Though the boat weighs in at sixteen tons I've underestimated how difficult it will be to haul her for the winter. Not only to take her out, but to find a home for her on land. In subsequent years I'll know to haul her earlier, by the end of September at the latest, before the season of nor'easters and emptiness. I'll know to enlist the help of friends, people who know these waters, know boats. But this first time I'm green, naïve, dumb. I've waited too long. I need someone to tow my boat to shore, where a truck will meet her at the ramp, back a forked trailer around the hull and lift her into the air on hydraulic pads. The man who operates this trailer is named Steve, able to thread the beamiest boat down the narrowest street, between telephone pole and stray parked car. But I haven't yet met Steve, or seen what he can do. I first need to meet Crowbar, who perhaps owns the only boat still in the water so late in the season. I get his name from someone at the Old Colony Tap, who swears he's due back any minute. After a fruitless hour and a couple Rolling Rocks ("rock 'n rolls," he calls them) this friend of Crowbar's offers that he might just know where he's hiding, if I want to take a drive. I have nothing to lose. I get in his station wagon, and we set out slowly, his muffler grumbling, our exhaust stitching together the couple dozen streets that connect Bradford with Commercial. We stop at a house on Mechanic Street, two other guys pile in. We circle a joint silently. Then we stop at Perry's, where it seems clear I should buy beer for everyone in exchange for this favor I'm being offered. Crowbar isn't at the next house we stop at, or the next. The driver pulls up, tells us to watch the car and disappears for what feels like a long time. He comes out shaking his head, passes around some valium. The sun's low by now, the shadows cold and long, the car moving slower and slower, and with each house Crowbar's farther and farther away. At one a woman comes out to the car and tells us he just left, but we forget to ask her where he was headed. While waiting outside a house on Nickerson some sort of argument breaks out and the two guys in the back kick open their doors, storm off in different directions. Dark now, darkness falling suddenly this time of year, and I become aware that the car is parked, and I'm alone in it, and I'm not sure which house the driver has disappeared into this time, or how long he's been gone. Dead-low tide, the boat still chained through the salty ink to the sand. I'll row out later, check the lines, the pump, maybe even spend one more night.

morocco

(1986) Bicycle past police lights twisting the blue from the night, past a man setting a box on fire to make a pot of tea. Lean forward enough and it's as if you're floating, as if there's no machine supporting you, the earth spinning an inch below your feet. Blur your eyes and sing a little song to yourself to keep upright—the song keyed to the rhythm of pedaling. Skim over the dark earth, arms spread, the sign of the cross, *Look, Ma, no hands*, crucified by the air, crucified by the night. Who doesn't want to just disappear, at some point in the day, in a year, to just step off the map and float?

After considerable struggle I managed to get the boat on land, then I flew to Amsterdam to meet Emily, who'd been traveling Europe for a couple months already. I needed to get away from the shelter for a winter—the last night at work I'd been scratched in the face by one of the psychotic guests that I had such a good rapport with. He drew blood, just a drop.

Within a month Emily and I find an apartment in Paris, and I find a typewriter in the closet, set myself up to look like a writer. The sublet turns out to be somewhat illegal, the former tenant trying to make some money by passing us the key. Within two weeks the landlord discovers us and wants us out. But we'd paid two months up front and so we stay, even after the heat and electricity are shut off—eating by candlelight, collecting boxes to burn in the fireplace. When it's time to go, Emily flies back to America and I drift south, to Salamanca, then Lisbon, then farther, taking a boat to Tangier. I don't plan to stay long, to get high or buy drugs, but by midnight of my first day I'm stumbling through a medieval maze back to my hotel room in Chefchouen, trying to conceal fifty grams of unprocessed hashish under my t-shirt, a grapefruit-sized ball of bright green pollen.

In Morocco I learn to buy cigarettes, to split one open by licking the side, to empty the tobacco onto my open palm, to break off a chunk of hash and balance it in the center, to take a lighter to it until it softens, to blend it all together and roll it into a very heavy joint and smoke it before getting out of bed in the morning. One and you're ambulatory, it dulls the knife edge of the day. Glide into the market, you can still talk when you're high, you can always look. Pointy yellow slippers. A multicolored hat. The hashish dulls and simultaneously focuses, reduces the day to a pinpoint, to a voice inside laughing, a board strapped to your back to keep you standing—all you are now is high. Two joints and the doors close, you don't have to go out today. Who would you see if you did?

I'm reading Duras and Bowles and Beckett—dark, absurd, strangely comforting. I've been working in the shelter for a couple years, I want to see how close to the edge I can come without falling. Two weeks later I find myself in an alley in a town called Mogador, buying opium from Mohammed and his friend. Just a little. The alley dead-ends at a wall. Mohammed unfolds a knife to shave off a gram (*what kind of opium needs a knife to cut it?*), then he turns this knife (*goddammit, why is there always a knife?*) toward me, touches my chest with the blade, asks softly if I'm sure I don't have any more money on me, just a little.

I've already been punched by police in Lisbon for taking a photograph of the wrong people. In a few days the police in Mogador will pick me up for speaking with a veiled woman. I'll have to spend a day in jail while they decided my fate, the hashish and the opium back in my hotel room, in the drawer with my passport. By the time I make my way to the border of Mauritania, to the edge of the Sahara, I see no end to being lost. You can spend your entire life simply falling in that direction. It isn't a station you reach but just the general state of going down. Once you make it back, if you make it back, you will stand before your long-lost friends but in some essential way they will no longer know you.

summer of suits

I drag myself back from Morocco, finally, and make my way back to America. Emily's now seeing someone else, and I have no place to live. I go back to work at the shelter, because I miss it, because I need a job. A newcomer, a woman who works the Cage, tells me she's leaving her apartment in the North End, and maybe I can move in. Incredibly small but ridiculously cheap—two hundred and fifty dollars a month allows you to lie in bed and contemplate the refrigerator. It's May, the boat's on land in Provincetown, and I agree to let Emily fix her up and live on her for the summer. By now Phil's given up on living on the water, and I decide to spend most of my time in Boston, working. Slowly, over the course of the next few months, warily, Emily and I move back toward each other.

• • •

The landlord of the North End apartment is an elegant Italian named Luca, and the day he hands me the key, as he's passing it into my hand, he tells me, slowly and deliberately, *And you know . . . this is the North End . . . and that means . . . no blacks.* I'm touching the key to my new apartment, and I don't have any place else to live, but my hand jerks back as if burnt.

Well, that's no good, I say.

I know, I know, it's a terrible thing, he backpedals, but it's not me, it's the neighborhood.

I take the key, a devil's bargain. I'll be gone within six months.

A few days later Luca tells me about some clothes he has in his basement, clothes he'd like to donate to the homeless. Work with the homeless for any length of time and you learn that everyone has a trashbag of old clothes they would like to donate to the cause. Many will call you "noble" for the way you are "sacrificing." They will thank you, say that they couldn't do it but are glad you can. Even the mayor will show up, always just before Christmas, and declare that the work you are doing is the hardest and the most important in the city. Luca knows I have a pickup, he wonders if I can go down into his basement with him someday, we can load the clothes together. Sure, I say, but it will take me nearly two years to get back to him. It's not high on my list, another trashbag full of moldy castoffs. When he tells me about the clothes he also asks my opinion about the homeless, about the reasons, why there seems to be more and more. This is another conversation I will often have with people, for I am now an expert. They're all drunks, right? If you give money to panhandlers they're just going to drink more, right? These people don't want to live inside, they don't want to work, this is the life they prefer, right? It becomes clear to me that I'm supposed to console those asking these questions, that they need me to say something that will make them feel better, confirm that there's nothing for them to do, that the problem is as inscrutable as Africa. Or perhaps they are afraid that homelessness seems more and more to be a fluid state, and they would prefer it to be something one is born into, like India and their Untouchables. Sometimes I point out that eighty percent of the homeless are invisible, like the proverbial iceberg, that when I walk through the city now every other person I see is someone I know from the shelter, but if you didn't know you'd think they were on their lunch break, enjoying a little sun. *Who's your favorite bum?* one girl asks, when she hears I work at Pine Street. I find her and her friend on Boston Common, chatting with Warren, another of the friends I got drunk with at Dreamwold all those years ago, the same Warren I wrote sci-fi with a few years later. He blew into Boston a few weeks earlier, appeared at my door penniless and needing a place to crash, as he will every four years or so for my entire life. These two girls see the same guys every day around Kenmore Square, and they go back and forth as to which is their favorite. *Do you know Karl*, she asks me, *the one with the broken guitar?* Even this girl has a bag of old clothes, asks if I can come by sometime.

Most of the people I hang with at this point work in the shelter. I'm also killing time with Ivan, a poet in his late thirties, though he hasn't published much, if anything, and I've never read a word. Dark-skinned, tight dreads, solid, Ivan weighs in at over two hundred pounds. I'll have him over to my apartment in the North End often, and we'll get high, and when we emerge into the hallway Luca will always be there, changing a lightbulb, though I never see him any other time, except when the rent's due. Someone in the neighborhood made an emergency call—*Black man loose in your building!* Ivan and I float down the stairs, Luca looks at us wide-eyed, unable to comprehend how life has gotten so out of control. Ivan and I are negotiating with another landlord to rent an entire building in the Combat Zone, an abandoned strip joint that Ivan tracked down the owner of, and we all meet regularly to hammer out an agreement. We know this new landlord is Mafia, we read about him in the papers, but he treats us all right, and the building is perfect. This strip joint, Good Times, was shut down maybe ten years before by the FBI. The prostitutes literally dragged johns out of their cars as they cruised past. They found that Harvard student in the doorway one morning, stabbed dead. After I'm living there a year or so, Liam, my mother's gangster boyfriend, tells me that it was the bar he and his boys would frequent when in Boston. He even took my mother there a few times. When we first go inside there are still drink glasses lined up, gold lamé hanging from the walls, a list of the girls who'd be performing that night—Crystal, Amber, Cindi—taped to the dressing room door. Good Times—the sign still hanging above the gate when Ivan and I move in. Ivan takes the top floor, Richard and I take the one below, and we will find tenants for the other two. Just before we move in Richard is diagnosed HIV-positive, he shows me the test results in my truck, parked in the North End. I am devastated but (*lord help me*) I also feel self-conscious—two men crying in a pickup.

By this point my brother and I have sold the house we grew up in, which is just as well, as I never spent another night there, was never able to, after my mother died. Even to this day driving into Scituate takes some effort, a willful distancing from myself. My body pushes itself away from the steering wheel as I drive, as if it wants to crawl into the backseat and curl up forever. I go to Scituate now only to see my grandfather, and before night falls I'm back in my car. We had a yard sale, paid off the mortgage, and put whatever furniture was left into storage, where it will stay for years, sixty dollars a month split between my brother and I, until he moves all he wants out and I keep paying. Both grandmothers, my mother's mother and her father's second wife, die within three years of my mother. Only men are left—my brother, my grandfather and me. My brother has become an artist, a painter, supporting himself with carpentry. He lives alone in Somerville in a building he and a hundred other artists bought and converted into live/work studios. The three of us begin having lunch together in the North End once a month. I have some money in the bank now but I don't know what to do with it. "Blood money," I call it, and it just sits there.

Working the Brown Lobby I notice a young guy who starts showing up for dinner, standing just on the edge of everything, holding his plate in one hand, eating and eyeing the room. He doesn't look like he belongs, mostly because of his shoes, very high-end. The leather's been cut away to reveal two steel toes. A reporter, I think, doing a lousy job of being undercover. I try to draw him out. *Nice shoes*, I say. *I just bought them today*, he replies. I want to encourage him not to get used to the food, to warn him that a shelter is a form of quicksand, but the conversation goes nowhere. The next few times I see him I leave him alone. He doesn't sleep upstairs, he only eats and then goes.

A year later one floor's still vacant in the Good Times building. A couple guys come by to look at it—Jasper and Sean—drove out from Indiana together the year before. A few months earlier Richard, Ivan and I had a party, a blowout on all five floors, a couple bands, dim lighting, and the Indiana boys had come. I've been trying to get my friends to move in but the building's still very raw and everyone's afraid of the Combat Zone. Young and full of energy, Jasper and Sean are trying to be artists, taking classes. They bring dope, we hit it off. We have them come back a few times, just to get a sense of them, and on the third visit I notice the shoes. Jasper's the guy from the shelter.

> I know you, I say, you eat at Pine Street.
>
> Yeah, sometimes, he says with a shrug, when I'm out of money.
>
> Those shoes. You bought them the day I met you.
>
> Cost me a hundred and sixty bucks, Jasper says, my entire unemployment check. I was broke for a while after that.

Damn nice shoes. A few months later Jasper will sell them to me for forty dollars to help him pay the rent.

It'll take me a couple years to get back to Luca and his trashbags of clothes. I've passed the apartment on to Warren, so I'm still over there fairly regularly, and I see Luca now and then. I make a date to come by the next Sunday with the truck. Jasper comes with me. Luca leads us into the basement, to several racks of suits and women's dresses, wrapped in clear plastic, with the tags still pinned to them. Luca, turns out, had been a tailor in the fifties and early sixties, and these were the clothes that people hadn't picked up. Beautiful, from my favorite era of men's fashion, sleek and tapered. Jasper and I load them all into the truck, along with the racks, and bring them to the building, deciding along the way that we should really each take a suit for ourselves, since we've never owned one, and maybe give one to each of our friends. Gowns for the women, and even a couple furs. Back in the loft we set up the racks and try on the suits, settling on a subtle plaid for me, a gray sharkskin for Jasper. Richard takes the vicuna. We get high, and spend that afternoon, and it turns into the entire summer, walking around the Combat Zone in our suits, and all our friends are in suits, we walk into Foley's like a gang of Mods, in our beautiful vintage suits.

silver key

The guy in number 5 left just yesterday, flaked out, disappeared. Talk he had family in Florida, a brother maybe, left his door open and just kept walking, left the key in the lock. Never even got his key deposit back, probably kicking himself now, twenty bucks, pissed away.

The key to my father's room on Beacon Hill is still in his pocket, but the sheriff's stopped by, handed him his walking papers. February, not a great time to be out on the street, but he cannot go back to his room, not easily, not without a hassle. A few weeks ago he threatened the new landlords (*goddamn queers*) and now they want him out.

I sat on the edge of my bed, stared at the closed door. Pondered it. Waited for the knob to turn. Beyond that door were the queers and the city. One toilet in the hall, they come up behind you while you're pissing. One toilet for five rooms.

The queers always knew, the knock always came, the door-knob jiggled. I knew Victor, the room next door, had him in for a drink. The only oldtimer left, here when I got here, held the door like a gentleman. Brought him his papers when he couldn't get up. The queers didn't own it then, it was the old woman, Malloy, then the queers. I never asked for anything, paid my rent every week, kept to myself. You knew they could hear everything. I'd see Victor in the hall and we'd just nod. Even the walls seemed thinner, like I could push my fingers right through them, like they were just paper, nothing beyond. How could I know? Outside was so close—passing sirens, footfalls.

Some nights he sneaks in after midnight. The next day he can't leave until the hallway's silent. More and more lately he doesn't even bother, just drives all night. While piloting his taxi he scans the city for places he can sleep out rough, if it comes to that. An experience, grist for the mill.

*Early in the morning I come back, after my shift, the city still dreaming. First the four steps up, then the gold key in the heavy door, then the hallway, past Victor's, past the toilet, then the silver key to my door. Some mornings I'd be so worn out I'd just pass right through the doors and be in bed. Some days I'd wake up and not know if it was morning or night. The clock read seven—*A.M. *or* P.M.*, it didn't say.*

Over the years my father's spent a night or two at the Salvation Army. Slept in the Greyhound station on more than one night, upright in a plastic chair, feeding coins into a tiny television bolted to the armrest. Between places, was all, scoping out the next thing. He still has friends, he can make a few calls. Twenty years earlier he finessed a suite at the Ritz for six months. He'd been selling encyclopedias door-to-door without much luck (*Broads'd answer the door in their nightgowns and say, "No, my husband ain't here, come on in for a drink"*), sleeping on a friend's roof on Beacon Hill, and one night in a downpour he ducked into the lobby of the Ritz. *Encyclopedia Americana's relocating to Boston*, he told the desk clerk. *Room service, the works*, he boasts.

> *Light filtering through the leaves outside, shadows of leaves on the shade, a murmur somewhere in the walls. It made more sense to unscrew the doors and lay them on their side, to park the taxi beside my bed, to fill the tub with ice, to close my ears with newspaper. I called my son from the payphone in the hall, told him to bring his truck, he could have whatever he wanted, that the queers wouldn't get their paws on a thing. He'd never seen the inside of his father's room, never saw the picture of his mother beside my bed, me holding him in my arms at the door on Pinkney Street. He'll come with his truck and we'll move somewhere, another room, or maybe to Maine, with a barn.*

inside out

(1987) I've been working at the shelter for three years at this point, an old-timer, working less or not at all during the summers when living on the boat. Three years is a lifetime at the shelter. The Cage became Housing became the Floor. Now full-time, a counselor, sometimes even the supervisor—I have risen to the top. I'm not thinking of my father much at this point. I get a letter occasionally but sometimes I don't open it for weeks.

Until one day, out of nowhere, my father telephones—*Get over here with your truck*. The first time I've heard his voice on the phone, the first time I've ever spoken to him, really, beyond that "Hi" when I was eight. *I'm sitting behind my door with a shotgun*, he now says, *waiting for the knob to turn.*

I go to the address he gave, bring my truck. I ask Emily and Doug to come with me, as witnesses, as backup, as support. I didn't know when he said shotgun if there would be a shotgun. I took him at his word. *I want you to have everything,* he said. All my life I have been what is known as accident prone—broken nose, broken arm, broken knees, broken spleen, broken teeth, broken fingers, broken cheekbone, broken ribs. While doing construction—drilling concrete, cutting pipe—three times steel slivers became lodged in my eyes, and three times removed. Your eyes are covered with scars, the doctor said, any more and you won't be able to see. In context what was a drunk sitting behind a door with a shotgun? But when we get to his building I go in alone, because if there is a shotgun I don't want a crowd of us in the hallway. I knock on his door, but from the side, as I'd seen tv cops do. I don't touch the knob until he barks, *Who is it?* and I identify myself.

I find him sitting naked in a galvanized tin tub in the center of his room, bathing and drinking straight vodka from a silver chalice, like some demented king from in the Middle Ages. As I push the door open wider, still standing off to one side, still thinking of the shotgun, he rises from his bath and stands before me, naked. His breasts sag, suds funnel off his cock. *Thanks for coming,* he says, *I'll be with you in a minute.* I try to look him only in the face as I stagger backward and out into the dim hallway. *Take your time,* I mumble, my brain racing. Why was he naked? Why had he risen as I opened the door? Why had I come when he called?

Water can be a symbol of purification, to stand naked before someone a sign of truth, of nothing to hide. A chalice can hold a sacrament, a chalice can hold poison.

Nakedness can be both a threat and an offering. Archimedes lowered himself into a tub and formulated the laws of mass and density. Eureka! Water is the universal solvent! But water also drowns, rivers rise and breach their banks, fields become mud, family photo albums fatten, teacups float from cupboards. Why had I come? The years my father was in prison I could imagine his room—the thick walls, the bars, a slit of blue sky high above his head. Sometimes I imagined a cage, stacked on top of other cages, each with its own man inside. Or a hole in a basement with bars for a ceiling, a screw pacing above, twirling a nightstick. I could place him in a prison, he who had been unplaceable. But that had been ten years earlier, when the letters had started. Ten years of a father built entirely of his own crazy words. When he called I didn't think of not going. If I didn't go to him I would always wonder, if not about him then about his room, this room he was now losing, just to picture it, to hold it in my mind.

When my father calls me back in he's half dressed, buttoning a shirt. *Pleasure to see you, Nicholas. Aside from the circumstances.* I look into his face, try to see myself. I listen briefly as he rants about the new owners, then I go outside and call in Emily and Doug. My father smirks at Emily, never having seen the two of us together, asks about her folks. *How are Steady Ray and Clare de Lune?* He begins to tell Doug *of being forced to listen to the faggots going at it, night and day*, but Doug cuts him off. I glance around his room, crammed with old magazines and what appears to be worthless junk. In the newspaper that morning I'd read that computers can now simulate what cannot be seen, the shape of "nothing," the structure that holds this nothing together—its representation looked like a gaping mouth. *Anything you want, kid, I'm serious.* I glance at a painting, all spatters and drips. *That's a real Pollock, kid, he was a friend. Worth a fortune now. It's yours.*

Half an hour later I give him a few hundred dollars to put his stuff in storage or to find another place, ask only that he not appear at the shelter, that he not fuck up my job. He tells me not to worry. I take the painting, along with a copy of Orwell's *Down and Out in Paris and London.* A few days later my brother will point out that Pollock had misspelled his name when he signed the painting. There was no shotgun.

cloverleaf

The world's so large, each city full of cheap rooms, each room behind a door. Men lie in these rooms, press their bodies into mattresses, pull the shade in the morning, pace wide-eyed at night. Someone always comes along, picks you up. You have to end up somewhere, right? Damn near law of physics.

If not for his cab my father will be outside. *I have plenty of places to go, but no place to be.* Easy to sleep in the cab, his hands tight on the wheel. He's not homeless, not yet, not ready for sleeping on the ground, not sober. Overnight the taxi becomes his room, the city his floor plan. Logan to Kenmore, Beacon Hill to Harvard Square, back to the garage in the Fenway to refuel, the great rotary of being, the cloverleaf of life. The plan is to live out of his cab, lease it twenty-four hours at a time, three back-to-back shifts. Park down by the waterfront, in Southie, in Winthrop, watch the planes take off, stash a bottle under the seat, drive to the storage unit, pick out some clothes to last a few days, eat a sandwich, drive. He still makes money—listening for the dispatcher, ferrying people here and there, driving past black men in suits with their hands in the air. If he has to shit in the middle of the day he goes to the Greyhound station, where no one notices a taxi parked out front for half an hour. A spot reserved for taxis. For a shower he goes to the Y in Charlestown, just over the bridge from the North End. Dunkin' Donuts for breakfast. It's not all fun and games. Cabbies get shot in the head every night, everyone knows they have a pocketful of cash. Between the door and his seat he keeps his spiked club, where his left hand can find it quick—*Bammo, spike to the jugular, lowlife won't know what hit him.*

But one night in late March he forgets to stop drinking—meter on, meter off, blackout, awake. Another overnight in jail, to stand before the judge in the morning. *The police said they found an empty fifth beside me. Said I hit someone or some fucking thing down by the Common. What could I say to that?* A fine must be paid, damage made right, before he steps out into the cold sunshine without his hack license, a free man on probation.

Boston, thankfully, is a small city, walkable. So he walks, up Beacon Hill to his post office box, to check in on the Fact Foundation, then along the mall on Commonwealth to Mass Ave, then down to his storage unit. It's almost one by the time he makes it, by the time he changes into a new shirt it's too far to walk to Charlestown for a shower. Besides, he's hungry, after refusing the powdered eggs they offered him in the cell. He walks back to Beacon Hill, because that's what he knows, stops into the Sevens, orders a bowl of the soup, takes his time eating, reading the paper between spoonfuls, asks for more bread, gets it, asks for a beer and they bring it, spends half of the money in his pocket before he steps out into the dusk.

The start of the first night, the inevitable dark. He wanders over to the library, open until nine on Wednesdays, he knows that. He'll write another letter to Ted Kennedy, let him know what's happened, this new situation. Kennedy will want to know, the poor and the hungry are his constituents, both he and Kennedy care deeply about the poor and the hungry. *We are put on this earth to help other people*, my father's letter begins.

Fifteen minutes before closing a guard asks my father to please make his way to the front doors. He must open his bag at the exit, show the contents to the man behind the desk. He does not look at the man, doesn't say a word. The man puts his hand into my father's bag, moving binders and loose papers, absentmindedly looking for books, his hands closing in on a toothbrush. My father snatches his bag away and storms out. A block west is a Dunkin' Donuts, my father heads straight for it, muttering to himself. *That ape*. Harassment, pure and simple. Tomorrow he'll talk to whoever's in charge, file a formal complaint. His breath visible before him, lucky if it's forty. Dunkin' Donuts closes at eleven, at least this one. The one by the Garden is open all night. A cup of coffee could easily last two hours, especially reading the

Herald. Customers come and go, one bearded guy wanders in, the girl behind the counter gives him a free cup on the condition he takes it outside. She even knows his name, *Eric*, she calls him, and shrugs at my father, as if to say, What else can I do? My father smiles back. Cute girl. Just before eleven she's cleaning up, pouring coffee down the sink, wheeling trays of unsold donuts into the back room. My father folds his paper, thanks her, leaves. He considers asking where she lives, maybe try for a night or two on her couch, but decides against it. Maybe tomorrow night he'll strike up a conversation, explain his situation, how he's between places.

The library's now dark inside, a dim light giving shape to the high-ceilinged lobby, the rest fading into shadow. Trinity Park lies directly across from the library, Trinity Church rising like a medieval thought amidst the glass and steel towers. My father picks a bench facing Boylston. Who can he pretend to be, sitting here, what can he be waiting for, what story will passersby come up with? The park is lit but it's too dark to read. Besides, he's read both the *Globe* and the *Herald* cover to cover. Not yet spring and not quite warm, not yet, but warming. Cabs slowly pass, en route somewhere.

He awakens to a hand in his pocket, yells out. A dreadlocked man hisses, teeters back and forth into the shadow of Trinity, a stiff-legged crackhead walk. My father stands, touches his pockets, unsure what was there, what might be gone, begins to follow the crazy thief, turns and walks quickly in the other direction. The library won't open for six more hours. A bus stop on the corner, he could wait for a bus, but no buses run, not at this hour. He could sit in the kiosk but the crackhead will find him, waiting just out of sight for him to fall asleep again, to run his hands all over him. My father's trying to hold on to a few dollars for morning, for coffee, to buy some time inside, but the crackhead will find it, will take anything, laugh in your face, crazy bastard, even a sandwich, where can you hide anything, what can you hold on to? You might as well wake up each morning shipwrecked on a deserted beach, all your belongings washed away.

If it rains he will remember the kiosk, which does have a roof, three sides out of the weather. But you cannot stretch out on the benches, there are armrests welded on. In the back of the library he sees a discarded blanket—closer he sees it is a man curled up on a grate. Hot, wet air steams up from the grate, warming the man like a dumpling. He's seen this before, bums sprawled out and drinking, but he never actually stood above the blowers, let the hot air seep into his clothes. The air is sucked out of the library, he can hear the dim whir of machinery below him, the excess from the heating system, even on the coldest nights there is too much heat inside, books cooking in superheated rooms, enough to heat the sidewalks, to heat the air outside. When it snows the snow will not stick to the grate—a dark, wet spot in a whiteout. The drunks fall there, driven by cops, by clubs, by the cold. Some inner radar keeps them alive, they stagger through the storm, blind drunk and goofy until they find the steam and then they fall. Like coming upon an oasis in the desert, their bodies melt into the grates, the steam seeps into their coats, into their pores. It's another prison, these blowers, because once you've landed you cannot leave, not if there is nowhere to go, not without a destination, because one step off the blower is cold, hypothermia cold, now that you are sodden. Blankets rise off your body in the fan's heat, hang above your sleep like a dream before sailing off into the slush. Cold nights the guys crowd on, and if you arrive last, if you are on the edge, you could die, roll over a few inches and you're a goner. The blower is a room of heat with no walls. My father stands in this room, invisible man in an invisible room in the invisible city. He sits beside the fallen man, steam rising, warming them.

the piss of god

Sometimes a man falls asleep in the midst of buttoning his jacket, his fingers hanging on to the last button. Sometimes, embedded in hot asphalt, you see a key, shined by the soles of pedestrians' shoes. You check your pockets, suddenly worried. The sidewalk calls, using the trick of gravity to bring you to your knees, to close your eyes, to make you sleep. If there's grass, if you can see it, each blade catches a sliver of streetlight, each blade wants you to hold on. Face-down you swear you can feel the earth spin, hold tight or you'll spin off into outer space. Forget about ceilings, about walls, about doors, about keys. The bread you ate at lunch is already turning to soil inside you, nightsoil now, darkness hovering inside. Soon your flesh will crumble off you, those on their way to work the next morning will pass your whitened skeleton like so many styrofoam cups—bleached, perfect.

If not for the rats you could crawl beneath a bush. A bush. A bench. A bridge. The alliterative universe. Rats too can pass through that needle's eye to enter heaven, as easily as they pass into a box imagined into a house. Houses inside buildings, houses inside tunnels, some exist for only a day, some, miraculously, longer. This box held a refrigerator, the refrigerator is in an apartment, a man is in the box. Tomorrow the box will be flattened and tossed, you've seen the garbagemen stomping them down to fit into the truck. Wake up on the grass, soaking wet. Dew is the piss of God. *Another bullshit night in suck city*, my father mutters.

And then there's the Celtics, losing just across town. Last night Mackie had a la-z-boy set up in Rat Alley, watching a television hotwired into a light pole. My father stepped into Mackie's living room, checked out a couple minutes of play—can these still be called the glory days of Bird? Step out of your room, settle into a discarded recliner—are you inside now or out? Position your chair before your television, take your walk, find your coffee, by morning it all will be gone—no inside no outside, no cardboard box no mansion, no birth no death, no container no contained, a Zen koan, a frikkin riddle. A garbage truck hauled the tv away, another will be put out on the sidewalk tonight. But a la-z-boy, my lord, maybe not again in this lifetime.

countdown

A couple months after he's evicted, a month before he arrives at the shelter, I see my father sleeping on a bench on the Esplanade. No more room, no more cab, all has led to this bench. The first beautiful day of spring, families out for a stroll. He staggers to the edge of the river to piss, his cock wild in his hands. A little girl points. For some reason, each time my mind returns to that day, I remember that little girl.

Every week, it seems, scientists discover a new gene to explain why we act as we do, why we feel sad or why we get fat. Genes, it's now clear, are a mark on the blood, and the mark can be read and the life plotted. Easy as reading a map. This red mark is your father, across a vast sea from you. The scientists say that one day I could stand in the exact spot my father once stood in, hold my body as he did. I could open my mouth and his words would come out. They say it is only a "tendency toward," a warning. They say it is not the future, but a possible future.

I got high not long after seeing him on the Esplanade. I had a pipe I brought back from Morocco the year before, a long painted stem, a brass bowl. I told Richard I saw my father sleeping outside and Richard said, *Your father's a nightmare.*

riddle

One book in my grandmother's attic was a collection of riddles, mostly kids' stuff, lots of those black-and-white-and-red-all-over kind of riddles, but they got more complicated toward the end. It had the Sphinx's riddle to Oedipus, one about albatross soup I never understood and one that I wrestled with for months—

Brothers and sisters I have none,
But that man's father is my father's son.

A sketch showed a man on a sidewalk, pointing vaguely into a crowd. After a year I decided that the guy was looking into a mirror, just to put it out of my mind. Years later I realized I was wrong.

that man's father is my father's son

A man came in this afternoon looking for you, Captain says.

We're sitting in the office, a closet off the Yellow Lobby.

Yeah? I say.

Said he was your father.

Captain's voice is singsong, it rises at the end of each phrase. I'd never noticed before.

He had ID, Captain sings. He wanted a bed.

A bed? I say.

Sort of demanded a bed. Said his son worked here, that his son'd get him a bed.

What do I say to that?

He was sitting right where you are, Captain sings.

Involuntarily I stand up, wipe my hands on my pants.

He said it was only for a few days. He just lost his room.

He lost his room three months ago, I say, gesturing toward the empty chair.

You knew? Captain asks lightly.

I can't blame him for asking, but again I can't think of what to say.

You don't have to stay, Captain sings, low. Take the night.

I saw him by the river a month ago, I start to explain, but it sounds so spacey. On a bench, I say. Asleep. It's like a frikkin opera.

If you want to stay you can, Captain offers.

A little girl pointed, I say, but what does that even mean?

He'll be here at six, Captain says softly. After his job.

I'm not really looking at him. I'll try to look at him.

Day labor, Captain sings. I gave him a work bed—

The phone rings. Captain looks at it. I look at it. Captain picks it up on fourth ring. Don't call an ambulance, Captain says into the phone, he's been like that since noon. Uh-huh. Then call an ambulance. He hangs up the phone. Fuckin Billy, Captain chuckles.

Fuckin Billy. Does he have proof? I ask. Did you see it?

He said he'd bring it. You don't think he's working?

Maybe. I don't know. I don't even know him.

Pause.

You don't have to stay tonight. Go home.

"Go home" has become the refrain, the chorus welling up.

Who else knows?

It came up at change of shift.

The log?

The log.

You wrote in the log that my father showed up looking for a bed?

"New guest."

Pause.

Long pause.

Captain leaves me alone in the office. The needle comes off the record. Take your time, he said, but there was no time. Only so many minutes a counselor can sit outside the fray. I look around the office—Are the walls closing in? Are planets colliding in my brain? Did Captain just sing me a song?

I sat for ten minutes alone in the office, then I went to work. A few hours later my father showed up, made his way to the Cage, presented the bed ticket Captain had given him earlier, disappeared upstairs. No ominous music, no deep chords. He wasn't backlit as the doors blew open, the wind didn't pick up, the earth kept spinning. Just another "new guest"—new ones appeared every day. He raised his arms at the door to be searched, just like everyone else. *Bottles or weapons I have none, but that man's father is my father's son.* It all took a few minutes. Nothing was said.

mayberry rfd

I'd grown up watching Otis, the town drunk on the television show *Mayberry RFD*, who let himself into the jail cell each night with a skeleton key, which he rehung within arm's reach to let himself out in the morning. Each town had a few, at least the towns I knew. A Mugsy. A Mousey. A sign of tolerance. Inevitable. It was said you could get Mousey to hurt someone, to burn down a house, steal a car. All it took was a bottle. His brother taught us at day camp, he led us in singing "500 Miles" on the bus on the way home, and we all knew Mousey, his brother, the lost one—*Lord I can't go back home this-a-way*. Mugsy's kids went to school with me, one was in my class, I'd grown up playing with him. Bombardment. Geronimo. We knew them, knew their families, their struggles were public, a failing acted out daily, daily forgiven. We could pray for them, if we prayed.

When I was fifteen, sixteen, you could get Mugsy to buy for you, you could find him in the parking lot of the package store, and for a couple beers he'd buy you a case. If the cops were around he'd have to get in the car with you, like you were all going to a party together, old buddies, and you'd drop him a few blocks away, and drive off into the liquid night.

My father put on a good front at first. Evicted only recently, he'd lived on his own for years. Outside for only a month or so, broke, but still put-together, lucid, somewhat clean. When he first arrives he has one eye unmoored, having been cross-eyed for years. It floats in his head like a ghost satellite. Gave him an intense look, Ray says. On his legs he wears support stocking, for the phlebitis. But he doesn't appear psychotic, claims he's never been institutionalized, never been on meds, never even been in a detox. Maybe he has traces of a head injury, maybe in prison he'd been locked up in a psych ward for a while, but the doctors made no diagnosis, at least not one he's willing to talk about. The drinking, the fall on the head, all "organic" damage, the psych people say, we can't touch him. A blustering, damaged man, but many are worse off. Where else is he to go?

like it or not

Dear Nick, 6/22/87

Many deep thanks for your recent help. All grist for the mill. 12 or 13 years ago—a title entered my mind—I was a guest of the Harbor Lights—briefly. Had just come in from Palm Beach—waiting for another bank run with the great Dippy-do Doyle. The title—"Down and Out in Boston and Cambridge"—George Orwell's first was "Down and Out in Paris and London"—The past 2 months have brought the title back to me.

Writers, especially poets, are particularly prone to madness. There exists a striking association between creativity and manic depression.

Why are more creative people prone to madness? They have more than average amounts of energies and abilities to see things in a fresh and original way—then because they also have depression, I think they're more in touch with human suffering.

I've really enjoyed—as a writer—my time at the Pine Street Inn. It's been a pure pleasure to merely stand with my back against a wall—watching my son at work. It has been a very, very long 25 years.

Whether you like it or not—you are me. I know.

I thought my last evening at Pine Street—waiting for 8:00 PM to come—I thought if your very beautiful mother were alive and if she could somehow see this scene—her youngest son at work and his Father a resident—in Pine Street—a shelter for the homeless—the beaten—the sad—the losers in life's great game—Jody would have laughed loudly at the entire macabre scene. —I don't get my license back for a month—I am trying other work. It is very, very hard.—

Closing lines—Nick—it is a disgrace that the Pine Street Inn allows cigarette smoking within its walls. A shame. A pure shame. I am an avid non-smoker.

Eno the Beano—27 Putnam—tells me you are into drugs—if so—good luck.

With love and respect, Nicholas—

Your Father, Jonathan.

Even the years before he made his way to the shelter our paths might have crossed. We both did construction, off and on, so perhaps on a job site, leaning on our respective shovels, staring at each other across the ditch we'd created. Since we both considered ourselves writers we might have listened to the same poet at some literary event, breathed the same air. He drove a cab, so I could have been his fare one night, if I ever took cabs. We both drank, so we might have been in the same dive, on the same night, vying for the same waitress's attention. Boston isn't a large city, but still a city of four million, so it wasn't necessary that we would meet. I could have made sure we never did, gone to New York, or San Francisco, or anywhere else on the planet. But I went to Boston, and stayed, and began working at Pine Street, which was and is a village within the greater city, an inverse city, where the majority of the townspeople, not just a few, are drunks or what we used to call idiots.

transparent

Three months now since my father first walked through the shelter door. Tonight he's relatively sober, able to raise his arms for the frisk without attracting undo attention, to move efficiently past the slumbering bodies to the Cage, to check his valuables, sign his name. I watch him from across the lobby, but don't approach. Even without seeing him I can picture each step he takes. Once upstairs he will hand in his bed ticket and receive his hanger, shoebox, wrist tag. Sitting on the bench with the box beside him he'll see himself in the funhouse mirror—his head grossly enlarged, his body birdlike, his hands mickey mouse hands. He'll take his clothes off carefully, hang everything on the numbered hanger, place his shoes and socks in the box. Naked, he'll rise, hand everything over the counter, get his bar of soap and ration of shampoo. Getting on nine, the rush over, the showers empty now except for him. A trough around the perimeter, like a moat, carries the water and dirt and sweat and suds away.

The day my father walked through the doors I became transparent. I couldn't find a way to talk about him with my friends, with my co-workers. Some approached, sideways, crablike, offered support, sympathy, but this was merely fuel for my shame. After a while, with the daily frenzy inside the walls, it just became a fact—That guy's father is a guest here. A newcomer would try to take that in, process it, make it line up with his experience. Maybe his father was missing or a drunk, or had embarrassed him once or twice. Another month would pass, and it became normal. His father sleeps upstairs, like in some parallel home.

Toweled off and in his johnny, my father climbs the next flight of stairs. The days long now, muted daylight filters into the dorms. A live-in staff worker wordlessly aims a flashlight at my father's wrist. They pass between rows of men, some snoring, some staring wide-eyed into the gloom. One mutters an endless monologue, one paces back and forth to the toilets. One stands at a window watching the taillights on the Southeast Expressway, fading sparks.

• • •

One night a co-worker says that I have the worst luck of anyone she's ever met (*We arouse pity by cultivating the most repulsive wounds*). A version of empathy, I suppose, but I don't really want to talk about it. If we go out drinking after work, if I end up spending the night with her, maybe I'll say more, as we talk afterward, as a way to explain something about myself, why I'm the way I am, why I'm in her bed and not Emily's. An affair is a room to disappear into for a few hours, another place to hide. But if asked directly I'll say he's just another drunk, that's what I've always heard, a drunk and a con man, he has nothing to do with me. *I don't know you at all*, she will say, a few months into our affair, *but if you ever want to talk* . . . and I'll smile a skull's smile and one by one the lights will go off inside me.

same again

The usual I say. Blood of Christ I say. Essence. Spirit. Medicine. A hint. A taste. A bump. A snort. I say top shelf. Straight up. Two fingers. A shot. A sip. A nip. I say another round. I say brace yourself. Lift a few. Hoist a few. Work the elbow. Bottoms up. Belly up. Leg up. Set 'em up. Freshen up. What'll it be. Name your poison. Mud in your eye. A jar. A jug. A pony. I say a glass. I say same again. I say all around. I say my good man. I say my drinking buddy. I say git that in ya. Then an ice-breaker. Then a quick one. Then a couple pops. Then a nightcap. Then throw one back. Then knock one down. Working on a scotch and soda I say. Fast & furious I say. Could savage a drink I say. Guzzle I say. Chug. Chug-a-lug. Gulp. Sauce. Mother's milk. Home brew. Everclear. Moonshine. White lightning. Firewater. Antifreeze. Wallbanger. Zombie. Rotgut. Hooch. Relief. Now you're talking I say. Live a little I say. Drain it I say. Kill it I say. Feeling it I say. Slightly crocked. Wobbly. Another dead sailor I say. Breakfast of champions I say. I say candy is dandy but liquor is quicker. I say the beer that made Milwaukee famous. I say Houston, we have a drinking problem. I say the cause of, and solution to, all of life's problems. I say ain't no devil only god when he's drunk. I say god only knows what I'd be without you. I say thirsty. I say parched. I say wet my whistle. I say awful thirst. Dying of thirst. Lap it up. Hook me up. Beam me up. Watering hole. Hole. Knock a few back. Pound a few down. Corner stool. My office. Out with the boys I say. Unwind I say. Nurse one I say. Apply myself I say. Tie one on I say. Make a night of it I say. Dive. Toasted. Glow. A cold one a tall one a frosty I say. One for the road I say. A drinker I say. Two-fisted I say. Never trust a man who doesn't drink I say. Drink any man under the table I say. A good man's failing I say. Then a binge then a spree then a jag then a bout. Coming home on all fours. Rousted. Roustabout. Could use a drink I say. A shot of confidence I say. Steady my nerves I say. Drown my sorrows. I say kill for a drink. I say keep 'em comin'. I say a stiff one. I say fast as possible. I say the long haul. Drink deep drink hard hit the bottle. Two sheets to the wind then. Half-cocked then. Knackered then. Showing it then. Holding up the wall then. Under the influence then. Half in the bag then. A toot. A tear. A blowout. Out of my skull I say. Liquored up. Rip-roaring. Slammed. Fucking jacked. The booze talking. The room spinning. Primed. Feeling no pain. Buzzed. Giddy. Silly. Glazed. Impaired. Intoxicated. Lubricated. Stewed. Tight. Tiddly. Juiced. Plotzed. Potted. Pixilated. Pie-eyed. Cock-eyed. Inebriated. Laminated. Stoned. High. Swimming. Elated. Exalted. Debauched. Rock on. Drunk on. Shine on. Bring it on. Pissed. Then bleary. Then bloodshot. Glassy-eyed. Mud-eyed. Red-nosed. Thick-tongued. Addled. Dizzy then. Groggy. On a bender I say. On a spree. On a drunk. I say off the wagon. I say gone out. I say on a slip. I say in my cups. I say riding the night train. I say the drink. I say the bottle. I say the blood bank. I say drinkie-poo. I say a drink drink. A drink a drunk a drunkard. Swill. Swig. Faced. Shitfaced. Fucked up. Stupefied. Incapacitated. Raging. Seeing double. Shitty. Take the edge off I say. That's better I say. Loaded I say. Wasted. Looped. Lit. Off my ass. Befuddled. Reeling. Tanked. Punch-drunk. Mean drunk. Maintenance drunk. Sloppy drunk happy drunk weepy drunk blind drunk dead drunk. Serious drinker. Hard drinker. Lush. Drink like a fish. Boozer. Booze hound. Absorb. Rummy. Alkie. Sponge. Sip. Sot. Sop. Then muddled. Then maudlin. Then woozy. Then clouded. What day is it? Do you *know* me? Have you *seen* me? When did I *start*? Did I ever *stop*? Slurring. Reeling. Staggering. Overserved they say. Drunk as a skunk they say. Falling down drunk. Crawling down drunk. Drunk & disorderly. I say high tolerance. I say high capacity. I say social lubricant. They say protective custody. Sozzled soused sloshed. Polluted. Blitzed. Shattered. Zonked. Ossified. Annihilated. Fossilized. Stinko. Blotto. Legless. Smashed. Soaked. Screwed. Pickled. Bombed. Stiff. Fried. Oiled. Boiled. Frazzled. Blasted. Plastered. Hammered. Tore up. Ripped up. Ripped. Destroyed. Whittled. Plowed. Overcome. Overtaken. Comatose. Dead to the world. Beyond the beyond. The old K.O. The horrors I say. The heebie-jeebies I say. The beast I say. The dt's. B'jesus & pink elephants. A hummer. A run. A mindbender. Hittin' it kinda hard they say. Go easy they say. Last call they say. Quitting time they say. They say shut off. They say ruckus. They say dry out. Pass out. Lights out. Blackout. Headlong. The bottom. The walking wounded. Saturday night paralysis. Cross-eyed & painless. Petroleum dark. Gone to the world. Gone. Gonzo. Wrecked. Out. Sleep it off. Wake up on the floor. End up in the gutter. Off the stuff. Dry. Dry heaves. Gag. White knuckle. Lightweight I say. Hair of the dog I say. Eye-opener I say. A drop I say. A slug. A taste. A swallow. A pull. Sadder Budweiser I say. Down the hatch I say. I wouldn't say no I say. I say whatever he's having. I say next one's on me. I say match you. I say bottoms up. Put it on my tab. I say one more. I say same again.

the van

(1988) My father's been homeless for almost two years now. I've spent the past summer in Provincetown again, living on the boat, working at the marina, commuting to Boston every couple weeks to work a few shifts at Pine Street. Emily's begun working in the Pine Street clinic—handing out meds, changing dressings, washing feet. My father still has a work bed held for him, our paths cross once in a while, sometimes we'll exchange a few words. He tells me he's in touch with Little, Brown, he tells me Kennedy is working on his case, he tells me he's been robbed. In September I move back to Boston, work a few shifts, realize I can't do it anymore. I can't bear to be in the shelter (*The dirty, repulsive, slimy universe of pain!*), not with him likely to pop up at any moment, my drunken jack-in-the-box. I begin filling in on the Outreach Van more and more. The Van was started the year before as a way to make contact with and offer services to those who, for one reason or another, won't come in to Pine Street, either because they're barred or because the shelter seems its own little hell. Working the Van, I start to believe there's more hope out on the streets than inside the walls. Those who choose to sleep out haven't been as institutionalized—outside there are no lines to wait in, you have to make your own way. The people we see lived in abandoned buildings and train stations, in cardboard boxes and in doorways. The hours are from nine at night until five in the morning, the graveyard shift. After a few weeks I apply for a full-time job on the Van. In this way I will no longer have to see my father at all—he will be in bed when I come on, just waking when I punch out.

My new job requires me to take on clients as a caseworker, to develop relationships with them in order to determine what services might be appropriate—detox, psych, elder housing, a pint of Thunderbird, whatever. Some mornings when I punch out Joe Morgan is lurking around the cars, and one day I ask if he wants to get some breakfast. No one knows how long he's been skulking around Pine Street. Ten years? Twenty? He passes through the doors like another man's shadow, his face pressed to the wall, almost part of the wall, like he's using it to pull himself along. Mumbling and squirrelly, small with large hands, a hooked nose, his graying hair slicked back, Joe Morgan never sleeps in a bed, never lines up with the rest, almost no one has spoken to him in all these years. We walk to a diner in Southie, where he nearly gets us killed by muttering about the "hippies" in the adjacent booth, whom

I would describe as "bikers." We begin having breakfast once a week. As I get to know him I ask the basics—family, Social Security number, last residence, work history. All spotty. The psych people have nothing on him, though he says he took "nerve pills" at one point, and that they helped.

One morning he asks me why I call him Joe, that his name's Martin. Martin Adams. I have no idea where the name Joe Morgan came from, and turns out neither does he. He tells me that when he walks along the streets he can hear his father's voice calling him, *Martin, Martin, Martin*, that he's always moving either away or toward that voice. Now that I know his real name I take him to the Social Security Administration offices to see if they have him in their computers. It turns out he's been getting a disability check for the past twenty years, and that this check's been going to his brother, a middle-class guy living in a nice suburb, who's Martin's payee. In the beginning the brother would drive into Boston, find Martin, buy him a meal, some new clothes, leave him with fifty out of the three-hundred-dollar check. Sometimes even take him home for a few days, wash him up. But after a while the brother came into the city less and less. The checks kept coming, the brother ended up putting an addition on his house, a sunroom off the kitchen. When they sat across from each other in the Brown Lobby, after twelve years without a word, Martin deadpanned, *I haven't seen you around lately, where've you been?*

As fall sets in I begin letting Martin sleep in my studio. After seeing him lurking outside my building one too many damp mornings as I come in from a night on the Van, I invite him in. Put a blanket on the floor as if he were a dog, make him coffee when he wakes up, let him out in the afternoon. Work is seeping into every pore. I take a photograph of him and he asks, *Why do I look so old?*, convinced I have doctored it. Inside, outside, home, homeless, the lines blur. He's as old as my father but he's not my father. At night I drive the Van to abandoned buildings, to stairwells in alleyways, to bridge overhangs. I know the names of the guys who stay in each spot—that Kevin will be at the Horseshoe, that Skid will be on the B.U. blower, that Gabe will be on the Mall, and he will have nailed another sole to one of his shoes, every night he tries to make them even, now teetering on five-inch platforms. Near North Station I squat in a doorway beside Black George, who's been talking detox lately. A friend from New York, just off the train, passes by us on the sidewalk, five steps away. Without thinking I call out his name, *Chris*, and he turns, tentatively, takes a step closer, stops. I'm sitting in the shadows with Black George, wearing a coat I lifted from the clothing room, a bottle between us. The coat won't last me through the night, I'll pass it on to someone who needs it more. *How's it going?* Chris asks, confused.

I've been with Emily for nine years, working at Pine Street the last four. Halloween I spend the night with a friend in the East Village, a woman I've been seeing off and on for years. Emily finds out, confronts me, and I see that I really don't know what I'm doing, that I'm adrift, as the Buddhists say, on a river of forgetfulness. A hungry ghost.

Emily tells me I have to either get into therapy or we're done. I call Lou, a therapist who comes recommended by another friend. An appointment is set for the next week, coincidentally on the anniversary of my mother's death, six years before.

That weekend a friend takes me to a party in the South End, to the loft of the brother of one of the Beastie Boys, or so she claims. Wearing a sweater pulled from Pine Street's clothing room, I feel shabby beside the beautiful people. After an uncomfortable hour I end up in a back room with my friend, smoking crack until daybreak. I've never done it before, and I'll never do it again, but it makes me feel like Superman for fifteen minutes at a time, full of self-confidence and charm, until the hit wears off and each nerve screams for more. Before I take the first lungful the guy with the lighter asks if I know what I'm doing, if I've done it before. He even tells me not to, tells me he hasn't left that pipe for three days. I nod my head like I understand, like there's nothing I don't understand, as I fall back on the couch, my lungs now big with smoke.

the pine street palace

Dear Nick, Friday the 13th, 1989 (January)

What does it feel like to drive a van for Pine Street—scooping bodies off our filthy streets to carry them to the well run Pine Street Palace?—

A gentle-old man—in our fully fucked up clothing line this morning—smiled—as he said to me—behind him—"This place has died since Mr. Sullivan died. This new man is an asshole—he hires assholes and they work like assholes—!"

I fully agree—Up Pine Street! A Palace of Serfs—

Respectfully—Jonathan

This letter comes a few days after another in which he tells me, "I did apply for a job at Pine Street in a letter to Mr. Ring several weeks ago—a job as a counselor—No answer. I have since found out through the grapevine that one must be out of Pine Street one full year before he or she can get a job there.—So it goes. I must struggle on."

One night in late January the counselor working Housing will be unable to rouse my father. Slumped and naked, he will stare at himself in the funhouse mirror, repeating, *But I'm only twenty-eight years old, why do I look like this? What happened to my body?* The counselor, new to the shelter, half believes this man is twenty-eight, half believes the telescoping of thirty years. This counselor will work with me later that night on the Van, and apologize for being late, explain he was with a drunk who kept saying he was twenty-eight, but his body looked forty years older, his body ruined. I knew he was talking about my father even before he said his name. I was the one who was twenty-eight. Within a week this note will appear in the log:

> 6 February 1989
>
> 8:20 Jonathan Flynn responded to a guest's request that he share a can of deodorant with an intense verbal assault toward the other guest on racial and sexual themes. Mr. Flynn would not respond to intervention. In fact he accelerated his verbal assault still on racial and sexual themes, but with more focus on verbal ridicule and perhaps a more colorful group of slurs.
>
> 8:50 The SPO, Chris, Paul, Greg and Brian escorted

Mr. Flynn to the Brown Lobby wrapped in a sheet, as he had refused to dress himself.

I come in to work at nine that night, stopping first to read the log. I see the note about my father, see the way the woman at the desk watches me as I read. Then I pass through the lobby to pick up the Van, to drive it to the back door, to load it with food, coffee, blankets, the nightly stopover before heading out. Passing through the lobby I see my father, upright and ranting, his head lolling from side to side, his naked body wrapped in a sheet. I walk past him, past my co-workers, who had spent the last hour wrestling him down from the showers, who had finally given up trying to get the motherfucker dressed again, grabbed a sheet, wrapped him in it, dragged him down. I'd never seen this before, never seen a man dressed only in a sheet in the Brown Lobby. Roman, almost Imperial.

ham

Noah had grandiose plans to save the world. Noah, it should be remembered, was a disreputable man who heard a voice. The villagers, his neighbors, laughed. Noah, a bit of a drunk, was not taken seriously. The voice said, *By what you make you will save the world.* And so, reluctantly at first, Noah began his life's work, an impossible project, something much larger than himself. But at night Noah was again filled with doubt, and he drank to quiet the voices. The people in his village spoke behind their hands as he passed, touched their caps, smiled. The village was miles from the ocean and Noah was spending his days building a boat—*Made it out of hic-kory barky-barky.*

Noah had three sons—Shem, Ham and Japheth. Ham came upon his father one day, naked and ranting, building his impossible boat in a blackout. God had spoken, God kept speaking, God wouldn't stop speaking. For witnessing his father naked and drunk, Ham and all his offspring became accursed forever, to the end of time.

My father may not hear voices but he also has an impossible project, he's also filled with a force larger than himself. In nearly every letter my father has sent me for the last twenty-five years he tells me his writing is going very, very well. His novel, such as it is, if it is at all, written in blackout and prison, is his ark, the thing that will save him, that will save the world. His single-mindedness impresses most, his fathomless belief in his own greatness, in his powers to transform a failed world, to make it whole again by a word, by a story. That if you stick with your vision long enough you will be redeemed. All this in the face of near-constant evidence to the contrary. The actual circumstances of his life—his alcoholism, the crimes he's committed, his homelessness and decades of poverty—these are mere tests, and what is a faith not tested? Noah needed to gather nails, to sort the animals, to convince his sons. He planed his timber and laid out the ribs. His ark would be bigger than the temple. We all need to create the story that will make sense of our lives, to make sense of the daily tasks. Yet each night the doubts returned, howling through him. Without doubt there can be no faith. At daybreak Noah looked to the darkening sky and vowed to work faster. My father cannot die, he tells me, will not, until his work is completed. But is there a deadline inside him for when he must finish, a day, like Noah, when the rains begin? When the boat, finished or not, begins to rise from the cradle?

Within a week after seeing him wrapped in a bedsheet and ranting, his bare feet in a pool of his own piss, my father has gone down even further, each night coming into the shelter drunker, more abusive, more out of control. He takes a swing at Cookie, calls her a "dyke cunt," but Cookie gives him another chance, merely puts him out for the night—*He's your father, for chrissakes*. But by the end of the week, when I arrive at nine for my shift, my co-workers look at me wearily—they've had another long night battling him. I've chosen to leave him to them, to escape the building, to spend my nights driving the streets. Finally, he is brought up for barring:

> 13 February 1989
>
> Jon was OFN this evening, and when he was told he had to go to the Laundry Room he exploded into anger. He started yelling and screaming racial slurs, lesbian cracks, verbal threats and every swear he could think of toward Dianne and Cookie. He was highly intoxicated, very upset and unmanageable. He was finally escorted by Paul and he was shouting and swearing all the way down the alley. Jon has created problems in housing and this is not his first

outburst at the front door. When he is intoxicated he is extremely hard to handle and its time for BH20 and a rest for the staff.

Stamped in for "BH20 or Bar," meaning if he refuses to go to the thirty-day lockup detox at Bridgewater State Correctional Facility he will be barred for at least two months. He's described as "w/m, 5'7", white hair, slanted eye, gray stubble, 150 lbs." I know my father will never voluntarily check himself back into prison. At the change-of-shift meetings his barring is voted on. I am at one of these meetings. The vote goes nine to bar, one against, and one abstention. I would like to say that I abstained from the voting, but I don't remember if this is true. It is just as likely that I voted to bar my father, in support of my co-workers.

The rains, as we all know, did come. The boat lifted above the drowned world, and the disbelievers perished, and no one was more surprised than Noah. The first right thing he'd done, and it came from obeying a voice only he could hear, which others took as proof of his madness. But what of Ham? It didn't matter if he told anyone about his drunken father or not, if he chided him or tried to dress him, if he lifted his struggling body back into bed, if he took his hand and told him where to place his feet, none of this changed the fact of what he'd seen. It's possible he opened a door innocently, followed the sound of Noah's voice cursing God and the sky, possible he didn't even look, that he turned away before seeing. And it's likely that Noah hadn't noticed the door opening, couldn't have told you who had come in, which son, wouldn't remember anyway. Apparently it's God's call. Ham saw his father drunken and naked, and for this he was cursed, and all of his offspring, and the races that led from these offspring, accursed forever.

four

headlong

All over the city men are falling—*nosedive*, *header*—crabwalking from benches lower and lower until the ground rises up to catch them, until the earth says *stop*, until the sidewalk tilts and the lights go out. From above, with infrared, you can see them, the outlines of bodies dotting the city, falling to their knees, rolling onto their sides, frozen in a pantomime of sleep. Points on a map, an electrified tourist map, the scenic spots lit up, marked. Scan the corners, the edges, the just-out-of-sight, the places men go to piss, any horizontal will do. One of those lights could be my father, but he keeps moving, through the night, finds a stone mattress, dozes off.

fuckin gonuts

setting:

A donut shop, evening.

Marie: I saw your father the other day.

Son: I didn't know you knew my father.

Marie: He didn't look so good.

Son: Maybe it wasn't him.

Marie: Who else would it've been?

Son: I mean maybe you got him confused.

Marie: Confused?

Son: With someone else.

Marie: Who?

Son: Another man.

Marie: Which man?

Son: Someone else. Someone not my father.

Marie: Why would I do that?

Son: I don't know. I didn't know you knew him. Do you know him?

Marie: He's a hard guy not to know.

Son: Maybe it's not him.

Marie: Who else would it be?

Son: A lot of guys.

Marie: He sleeps in the parking garage, right?

Son: Sometimes. Which garage?

Marie: Barlow and Ron were giving him a hard time the other day.

Son: Barlow's garage?

Marie: And that kid who got himself burned—

Son: Kevin?

Marie: He was good-looking, before they set him on fire. You can tell.

(*beat*) Barlow did it.

I don't know, maybe Barlow. Crazy enough, when he's drunk—

(*hisses to manager*) SNAKE!

(*beat*) Buy me a coffee, would you? The manager's putting his eye on me.

(*beat*)

Son: (*standing*)

Marie: Would you hang out with someone who even maybe set you on fire?

Son: You want a donut or something?

(*beat*) I'm going to get a donut. You want one?

(*beat*) I'll get two.

(*beat*) You know anyone named Eno?

Marie: How can you hang out with someone who set you on fire?

Son: Eno the Beano?

Marie: You talk to your old man much? He's not making much sense these days. Like he's been out too long.

(*beat*) What's a beano? Some kind of pill?

Son: You never heard of him?

Marie: I know an Eno. He sells drugs. Wears that nasty hat.

(*beat*) Keeps the drugs in the hat, like he's clever.

(*beat*) Your father into drugs—?

Son: This Eno told my father *I* was into drugs.

Marie: (*beat*) Everyone says that.

Son: I mean, who is this guy?

(*beat*) Everyone says what?

Marie: Well, you are, aren't you?

Son: I don't even know him.

Marie: (*beat*) It snowed last night.

Isn't it early for snow?

(*beat*) I ended up in the garage. The top landing's okay.

(*beat*) Barlow's voice coming up the stairwell. I kept real quiet.

(*offhandedly*) Your old man doesn't look good. Someone should get him inside.

Son: You should get inside.

Marie: You getting more coffee or what?

Son: (*sits down*) I don't even know him.

Marie: He's got those crazy eyes, like one's unscrewed or something.
(*squints into Son's face*) You're lucky you don't look like that.
(*beat*) The manager here's been hassling people lately.
Sticking his nose up my ass.
(*beat*) Like you're going to get hurt if you don't drink more coffee.
You don't even have to do anything.
Could be freezing rain, nuclear winter. Coffee's gone, you're out.

Son: We can still try to get you in somewhere.
(*beat*) You know, it's what we do.

Marie: (*ignores him*) Last Sunday Barlow and Ron were out of booze.
Crazy looking for it.
Only the bootlegger on Sundays. No credit with the bootlegger.
Not for Barlow, not for anyone.
You need cash.
Who has cash, Sunday morning?
(*beat*) Barlow killed a guy.

Son: I heard.

Marie: That's got to be something.
Sixteen years in Walpole.

(*beat*) They shouldn't have let him out, a guy like that.
(*beat*) So Barlow and Ron lure this old man upstairs—

Son: They—?

Marie: —They lure *your* old man upstairs.
Top floor. That empty building beside the garage.
Said they had a bottle.
You know the building, all the windows gone?
No one there on Sunday.
(*beat*) When they get to the top they grab him—
(*beat*) Upside down, five-story drop.
Held him by the ankles. *Upside down.*

Son: They didn't drop him?

Marie: Five stories I heard.
(*beat*) Even took his coat.

Son: (*beat*)

Marie: It *snowed* last night. Slush *every*where.

Son: The Van has coats.

Marie: Last night Barlow was telling the story.
His voice come up the stairwell, like he's whispering in my ear. (*shivers*)
Said next time he'll drop him.
You know the building I mean?

Son: (*beat*) I never noticed.

Marie: He's a freakin psycho, Barlow.

Son: How did they get inside?

Marie: Your old man doesn't look good. He's outside all the time.

(*beat*) The manager kicks you out of this place at nine-fifteen.
Last night he put his face this close to mine. This close.
I had to wipe the spit off.
It doesn't close until nine-thirty. That's what the sign on the door says.
How can he do that? Is that legal?

how's my driving?

(1989) I steer the Van down the Mall dividing the up from the down of Commonwealth Avenue, its walkway littered with statues of the unknown rich—a man in a sailor's hat looking over a bronze sea; a man with one hand in his coat pocket, fingering his coins forever. Past the benches my father haunts, three a.m., the radar begins to hum. What color was his blanket yesterday? Olive drab? Maroon? Last night it snowed, you could follow his footprints from his bench to the church overhang, until the snow filled them. I drive slowly past a blanket shaped like a man—here is a man, shaped like a blanket, shaped like a box, shaped like a bench. Easy to miss. If this is my father, if I leave a sandwich beside his sleeping body, does this become a family meal? Is this bench now our dinner table? Are we inside again? Is this what it means to be holding it together? Am I coping? How's my driving?

It's just Jeff and me tonight, someone didn't show. Shaved head, weight lifter, ex-Marine—Jeff has been working with the homeless since he quit drinking a year ago. His girlfriend didn't follow him into the land of sobriety. This causes Jeff a lot of turmoil. His anger, though, can be an asset on the Van. More than once I see him slam a homeless guy against a wall who'd threatened us. A hands-on kind of counselor, a cowboy, a terminator. It's against policy but there's something refreshing about it, once in a while. Good to have him on your side. Aside from these infrequent outbursts he possesses the gentle demeanor that sometimes trails the newly sober, that deep acceptance that comes with realizing how badly you'd fucked up your life. Yet he's still drifting dangerously down his own river of rage.

I hop the Van over the curb into Boston Common, which isn't legal, but the cops ignore us. On the Common a man's allowed to graze a flock of sheep, goats, cows, whatever, this is in the articles of incorporation from 1634, this is the original purpose for this public land. But that same man, that shepherd, is not allowed to sleep. If the shepherd falls asleep he can be arrested. The sheep may all be asleep but the man must watch them sleep. Russell walks the periphery. Plaid suitcoat, red shirt, polka-dot tie, white shoes. Hard to miss. He's become our favorite person lately (Who *is* your favorite bum?). Tonight he sports a captain's hat. My recent coup was to offer him a stick of gum and have him accept it. This after three years of seeing him sleeping out, three years of him telling us he was just on his way home, only to find him later in a doorway on Newbury.

Dear Nick . . . what does it feel like . . . scooping bodies off our filthy streets . . . to carry them to the well run Pine Street Palace?

I stop the Van beside an unidentifiable form asleep on a bench, offer to watch the radio. Jeff knows why I stay behind, but he doesn't ask about it. I write in the log, 3:05, _____ on a bench, the common by the bandstand. Jeff squats beside the bench, to see if John Doe is breathing, to see if he's hungry, to see if he's covered. *Scooping bodies off our filthy streets.* Who is our John Doe? What *does* this feel like?

25°. Snow builds a monochromatic city. The statues stare over the shapes of sleeping men, whitening. Still not cold enough to drive the hard-core guys inside. Bobbie Blue-Eyes. Jimmy the Hat. Black George. Indian Dave. The blankets that cover them are now also white. Jeff comes back. *It's Paul,* he says, *he just wants another blanket.* I write, "Paul Carney, blanket." Jeff shakes the blanket out—a red sail in a white sea—dusts off what snow he can, drapes the rough wool over the shape of Paul. Paul's shape fills the bench, the blanket becomes a fort. His breath fills the fort, heats it. Words come from Paul's head. A knock on my window—Denis Delaney, his face covered with tar. His knuckle leaves a black kiss on the glass. Always wild, but even for Denis this is another level. I get out, mention the tar. Denis tells me it came from the Lord, *The Lord offered His cup and I drank it, drank its sweetness, to drain the evil out.* The Lord did this because Denis is the devil.

How so? I ask.

I cut people up, he answers.

A new map of the city has been created, several maps, actually, transparent layers, they can be laid one on top of the other. One shows only fire hydrants, another only stoplights, another each school. My map would show the places one could sleep if one was or became or planned to be homeless. It would show each bench, each church step, each bridge, each horizontal, each patch of grass. We ask Paul if he wants to go back to the shelter with us but we know he won't go. *No, no,* he says, *I'm just out here enjoying a little fresh air. I do my best thinking out here.* We got him to talk to a psych doctor once, the doctor asked if he heard things other people don't. *Sure,* Paul answered, *I hear birds in the morning when everyone's sleeping, I hear trees rustling when no one's around.* We convince Denis to come for a ride, I lay a blanket on the seat, give him cigarettes, coffee. I say, *Let's go talk to someone about the Lord.* He stares at the tip of his cigarette, murmurs into it. Oily light, steam rising from cracks in the asphalt, rivers of heat flowing beneath the streets, the center of the earth boiling, heat factories on the edge of the highway, acid rain. We drive slowly to

City, talking calm and low, hoping a psych nurse is on duty, but once we pull in Denis refuses to enter, wanders off between streetlights.

Back downtown we check the alley off Bromfield (*bomb-field*). Best to make a racket walking down Bromfield, sweeping the flashlight in arcs before you to scare away the rats, calling out, *Moses, Moses?* Maybe we have a message for Moses, maybe he's unbarred, maybe some meds await him in the clinic. At the end is a gate you shoulder open that leads to a staircase behind the Orpheum Theater. If we don't find Moses on one of the landings we'll find someone else, huddled in the pissy utter darkness, who either knows Moses or doesn't, who either knows or doesn't know where to find him. Changeable and random. Some guys check into detox for the winter, some burrow deeper under blankets.

Later I'll stand over my father as he sleeps under the church halogen. Impossible light. Jeff stays in the Van, lets me do this alone. Snow dusts his blanket, his eyebrows, the bag tied to his wrist like a tourniquet. Barred now, now nowhere inside for him to go, now every night I could find him. Starlings fill the trees above us—isn't it late for starlings, don't they fly south? His chest rises and falls, tiny cracks in the dusting of snow, miniature avalanches, a distant rumble. The halogen's hum fills the sphere of light I inhabit. I cannot remember a way out of this sphere. He breathes in this hum. I breathe in his hum. If his chest still rises, if his blankets seem adequate, then I won't enter this building he has built. If I step into the lobby of his chest I will sink up to my knees in nothing. I will lose my feet, like traversing a swamp. *We had gardeners and chauffeurs growing up*, he says. *When this is over I'll be sleeping inside the Ritz, where I belong.* I stand on the sidewalk searching my pockets for the key, embedded in the asphalt below my feet. *What does it feel like . . . whose filthy body . . . how far to the palace . . . ?*

fort point
(mountain of shoes)

A mountain of shoes reaches nearly to the ceiling. In another corner a mountain of t-shirts beside a mountain of sweaters. Mountains of pants, suits and underwear rise up one floor above. Tectonic fashion plates colliding. These new mountains loom above where the men sleep. This is the "overflow" shelter, Fort Point, a warehouse just across the highway from Pine Street. The deal to transform it into an "overflow" shelter, to get the men off the floors of Pine Street, was negotiated with the city in 1987. Other shelters have opened as well—the Laundry Room at Boston City Hospital, where you sleep to the sound of dryers tumbling sheets through the night; the Round Church, where you are offered a stiff-backed chair, and if you doze and fall from the chair you are asked to leave; the Armory, where you sleep beside a locked room filled with machine guns and dynamite. By now nearly every church basement in every town in America is lined with at least a handful of folding cots. At dinner with Emily's parents one night Ray will ask me how many homeless there are in America now. A million, I'll estimate, maybe two. Four hundred million people in America, Ray bellows, even two million is an acceptable percentage.

From the start Fort Point is like Australia—an island off the highway, floating on a cloverleaf off I-93, difficult to reach. Those who work there are cowboys, renegades, they make their own rules. Sometimes a guest who's barred from Pine Street is given a second chance at Fort Point. A ten-story warehouse slated for demolition, directly in the path of what will be called the "Big Dig," maybe it will last five years. To invest structurally in Fort Point is silly—to replace broken windows, leaking pipes, or even paint the walls. It takes on the feel of a theater set, the bare minimum to get the men fed, showered and into bed. The food is driven over from Pine Street in the same vans that transport the guys who cannot negotiate the highway, the ones who even if you walk them to the Mobil station on the corner and point to it, *That building right there*, draw a little map, still they walk off in the wrong direction. Truly a temporary shelter, which is perhaps ideal.

Above the men sleeping at the doomed Fort Point ("the Fort") rise the mountains of clothes. A couple of live-in staff workers tear open trashbags of donated cast-offs, toss them into the appropriate mountain, using shovels, rakes, mostly their hands. Another couple of guys are in charge of sizing the shoes and pants, marking the size on a piece of masking tape. A job with no end, for the mountains before them grow faster than they can measure. Finally it's decided that some of these clothes should be sold to the Rag Man, sold by the pound, the money used to buy new socks and underwear. Never enough socks and underwear. The Rag Man sorts through the clothes quickly—anything usable will be put in his buck-a-pound bin, the rest will either be shredded for mattress stuffing or donated to Third World countries as a tax write-off.

My father will end up sleeping at Fort Point even after he's unbarred from Pine Street. Six months outside have filled him with bitterness. Or brought to the surface the bitterness he always carried, and this bitterness is directed toward Pine Street. The months he sleeps at Fort Point I will not see much of him. Within six months he will be barred from there as well, for bringing a bottle of vodka up to his bed one night, after months of going downhill. It's February again, and he is Johnny Bench.

I'm making twelve dollars an hour, plus benefits. Medical, dental, sick days, vacations. The first ten visits to my therapist are covered. That spring, as part of a nationwide protest, tent cities are erected all over America. As shelter workers I suggest we print up t-shirts that read, THE HOMELESS PAY MY RENT, but no one else thinks it's funny. Across from the tent city on Boston Common is an ice-cream shop, Emack and Bolio's. The name comes from two men who stay at the shelter sometimes. As younger men they'd been radio personalities in Ohio, comedy and songs. We all know them. Ten years earlier they were being evicted from their Boston apartment, and a young lawyer took on their case, pro bono. They lost, but the lawyer offered them twenty dollars apiece for the right to use their names for a business he was starting with a friend. Emack and Bolio's. The sign shows two hobos licking cones. Though they ended up being homeless for years on end, the real Emack and Bolio were also offered free ice cream for life.

My first summer at Pine Street I drove a van around Boston to pick up donations one day, mostly clothing. Brooks Brothers was one of my stops, the same Brooks Brothers where my father had charged his suits to my grandfather years before. A well-dressed man directed the van to the alley, where he met me at the side door, holding a box the size of a mid-sized television. He handed me some paperwork, pointed to where I should sign. I glanced it over and noticed the declared value of the box was ten grand. Four suits, each valued at over two thousand dollars. A tax write-off. *Ten grand?* I said, holding the pen. I tried to imagine Beady-Eyed Bill in a two-thousand-dollar suit. The guy looked annoyed. *Ralph always just signs, who the hell are you?*

the bootlegger

The Bootlegger sells one thing—pints of Pastene white port, sweet rotgut, four dollars a pop, no credit, no arguing, his trunk open until the product's gone. Circling the shelter in his beat-up station wagon before dawn, he parks in the shadows between streetlights. We see him there just before the sun comes up as we bring the Van back at the end of the night. No one's ever seen his face, not clearly, and no one knows his name. He lives somewhere in Southie, buys by the case. Even if you bought each individually at a package store it'd only be a dollar fifty per jug. But the package store won't open until eight, and in three hours a lot can happen, none of it good. It's a high-risk business—patrol cars, desperate clientele, darkness—hence the markup. The drunk has to have enough wits about him to put four dollars aside the night before. Some try to stash a bottle before stumbling off to sleep, but then you have to remember where you stashed it—it was dark then and it's still dark—if it's even still where you hid it, with the whole city searching for a sip from eleven to eight, the dead time. Even if you could afford a bar, if your clothes weren't shiny and you didn't stink, the bars close by one. One until eight's a lifetime. If you work it right you blackout by eleven, and the sun blistering your lips wakes you. When the sun's up you can always stem enough for a bottle—a *good morning*, a *beautiful day*, an upturned palm. It's better if they don't see you shake—many don't understand that a sip stops the shaking.

At dawn dew shines off the blacktop. After I write up my notes from the night on the Van I end up leaving the shelter with the men, on their way to the labor pool or to the Bootlegger. I see my father by the Herald Building, half a block ahead of me, near where Martin hears his father calling. Lit doorways, brightening sky, the city beautiful and empty, cleansed by the darkness. I catch up with my father, fall in step, we walk together toward downtown. I ask how he is. He claims not to be drinking, but I don't think he knows what this means. *I'm trying to put some money aside*, he says, *get my life back together.* Then, surprisingly, he asks if I think there's something wrong with him, he's been told he has paranoid delusions, and sometimes he thinks it's true. I ask him if anyone ever diagnosed him, if he's ever seen a psych doctor. *No, no, but I've been told I'm paranoid, that I have delusions.* A house built of cards and now the house is gone. We pass Danny, rising from a grate, wool-wrapped, army wrap, the blanket slides to the ground. What you fear your whole life comes to pass. You end up living toward it, you spend your life running from it but your foot is nailed to the sidewalk. You circle around it until you wear yourself down. As I look at my father I can see, for the first time, how afraid he is, how he's been trying to run for a long time. *Do you think I'm delusional, do you think I'm paranoid?* Yes, yes, and for this I would even drive you to the doctor myself, in my own car, on my own time. But he wants no doctor, won't commit to an appointment, he's late for the slave traders, all the jobs will be taken, all the vans full, he's got to scrape some money together. The bridge goes over the Turnpike here, we split off and I walk the ten blocks home, down the alley, along the wrought iron, a cage around me, a camera watching.

over 100 lbs.?
over 100 miles?

In my father's bag he carries a change of underwear, socks, soap, a toothbrush, a comb. Pens to write with, paper for letters, the forms he needs to prove to whichever agency whatever they need to know. What was your last job? What was your last address? What is your mother's maiden name? A paper bag with handles, reinforced with duct tape, inside a plastic bag, the type they give out at supermarkets. From this bag, in the restroom of the library or the bus station, he can make himself recognizable, to himself, which has become a daily struggle. Outside too many nights and your face begins to change, to alter. You spend time being invisible in public places, trying to look like you are waiting for someone, that you haven't been in that booth, nursing that coffee, not long. You stretch it out, for when it's gone so is your reason for being there.

• • •

At his table in the reading room of the library my father fills out a form from the Department of Health and Human Services. He's trying for a disability check, as it's becoming difficult to even work day labor, sleeping outside every night, difficult to pull himself together from his bag. On this form he lists his previous work experience as "Longshoreman," "Laborer," "Cab Driver." The type of business for each is "unloading ships," "construction," "transportation." The dates he worked each job (month and year required) are "varied" to "varied," "varied" to "varied," "7 days" to "10 years." The days per week are "_____," "_____," and "seven." The rate of pay is "union rate," "union rate," and "tips." In part two he changes his job title from longshoreman to "scallywag," which my dictionary defines as a scamp or rascal. The form asks:

> A. In your job did you:
> - Use machines, tools, or equipment of any kind? yes or no. *no.*
> - Use technical knowledge or skills? *yes.*
> - Do any writing, complete reports, or perform similar duties? *no.*
> - Have supervisory responsibilities? *no.*
>
> B. Describe your basic duties below:
> *Unloading ships from other countries in Portsmouth, N.H.*

Richie Moore was my boss. I lived in Portsmouth N.H. before it became a yuppie town—rents were human—I am a poet—I need a low rent place to live.

C. Circle the number of hours a day spent:

Walking	*8.*
Standing	*0.*
Sitting	*0.*
Bending	*constantly.*

Describe what was lifted, and how far it was carried:
over 100 lbs.? over 100 miles?
(*left unanswered*)

Part III—Remarks

Use this section for any other information you may want to give about your work history, or to provide any other remarks you may want to make to support your disability claim.

Cab driving gave me bursitis—I can't sleep at all.
A lady doctor at MGH told me in writing to stop the cab driving—construction killed my legs—I have lethal phlebitis—lethal—I lost the use of my right hand as a longshoreman—I have a classic deformity of the (unreadable)—*I am also 50% blind—I have visual asquinty—no depth perception at—all—which limits me from 90% of work. My memory was totally destroyed in an assault on my life—*

My father will spend what's left of the night upright on a bench, down near the Ritz. Across from his perch are a thousand windows, each window opens onto a room, the container and the contained. A thousand rooms he's not inside.

king of ireland

At night the city empties of all but the most essential. Each building appears then, jewelry store or bank, separate one from the other, radiant. Stand before each anew. A rock in a river—waves, debris, current, it all passes over. In daylight the wind comes from all directions, a sheet of newspaper blows against your leg, turn your face to the wind. At three A.M. even the wind rests. The headlights of a car rise over the crest by the Steaming Kettle—its sign is the thing itself, an oversized bronze kettle that never empties of steam. The headlights brighten storefronts, newsboxes, Alice, tucked in her doorway, blanket over her head. Alice no longer sleeps in the ATM, no one does anymore, the cops chased them all to the blowers. We now know that Alice had a family once, a husband and a couple kids, and one night she was clipped by a car while broken down on I-93 waiting for a tow truck, and something jarred loose in her head. Organic damage. The police brought a photograph of Beady-Eyed Bill to Pine Street, taken by the bank cameras, asked if we knew him. A still from the goddamn movie of his life. More steam rises from sewer caps, the underlife forcing its presence upon us. And then the car recedes, its music fading down Park to Boylston, until its headlights fall on Brian. Ratcheted up, wired and sleepless, Brian wears three army blankets over his head like layered ponchos, a hole cut in the middle of each, making his slow way up, stopping at a barrel to poke for half a sandwich, half a beer, stopping at each payphone, checking the change slot, knowing that the phones release dimes secretly. If you sit on a bench long enough you can hear them releasing, hear the coin drop, all over the city—a tithe, the part of the field left unharvested.

My father closes his eyes. A siren cuts through Charles Street and his head is briefly all siren. The siren grows smaller, his head grows smaller, until it is the size of a cricket, or the size of the sound a cricket makes—it must be directly under his bench, moving its violin legs. Brian stands before my father, unwrapping a butterscotch drop, untying the cellophane slowly—now my father's head is all cellophane, the whole city's cellophane. My father keeps his eyes shut. Brian passes the golden lozenge into his mouth. He crinkles the wrapper and flicks it into my father's cheek. My father opens one eye.

Whad'ya want?

Want? To offer you a butterscotch drop is all.

What?

Butterscotch.

No thanks.

No?

I'm fine.

Fine? You call this fine, laddie?

Brian rolls the hard candy in his mouth, slurring his words. He fishes another drop from his pocket and holds it in his upturned palm. My father wants to take it, but he knows it will be a trade, and there's nothing he wants to give. He has no gift he wants to offer.

Flynn, isn't it?

You know it's Flynn, my father growls, and every night the same thing, and no, *brother*, I don't have a spot, or a taste, or anything at all to share on this cold cold night.

Ha. Have I asked you for anything, Mr. Flynn? *Lord* Flynn?

Brian offers the butterscotch one last time, shrugs, unwraps it, puts it in his mouth.

In Ireland we ruled, brother, do you remember? In Ireland we were kings. Now look at our kingdom, a kingdom of benches, left to filch candies from storefronts.

A police car slows, passes.

Have you ever sat in a field, brother, end of summer, the grasses pressing up on your backside, maybe a few dandelions and clover, all that's left, and the clouds passing overhead so quickly you can see the shadow coming?

I'm more of an ocean man myself, my father grumbles.

Ah, but it happens on the ocean as well, don't it, if you look into it long enough? The wheel can't help but turn. Some end up on top, some on the bottom. But the wheel keeps turning, turning even now, nothing can stop it. It is in the nature of the wheel to turn, like it is in our nature to drink. So how about it, laddie, brother, piece of my own heart? Are you holding tonight? I can't fathom what would bring you to this particular bench at this particular time of night if you weren't holding a wee taste.

My father has closed his eyes again. He knows Brian, knows that if he brings out his vodka Brian will drain it, he will stand before him and praise the goodness of heaven and tilt his whole body back until the bottle empties into him. And they may be brothers, and they may have been kings, but only Brian will be drunk. And my father will still be on this bench. A sheet of newspaper blows against the bench, lingers, tumbles on, catches against Brian's feet. He picks it up with a flourish.

Look, headline news—"Two Micks Seen Outside Park Street Station." No one has ever seen them apart. Rumor has it they are the same person. Ha. It's all here . . .

Brian stands on the bench, waving his hands at the daffodils that fill the beds behind them,

. . . and not only is every article about us, but the

newspaper itself, the ink, the pulp, it's all us. And these flowers . . .

Brian swandives into the daffodils, lying among the broken stems, arms outstretched, laughing,

. . . these flowers, brother, these clown flowers—

Enough, the cops will come, my father hisses, taking out his bottle.

five

santa lear

Each night, like another night in a long-running play, I wander the empty streets, check on every sprawled man until I find him, tension built into each blanket. Each man has a role—one will be the lunatic king, one will be the fool. One will offer dire warnings, one will plot against us, one will try to help. I am forced to play the son. Most nights our paths cross before dawn, but sometimes months will pass without contact. The stage is done up like the outdoor space of an anonymous American city—broken neon, billboards of happy products, vast, empty. The light is dim, but we can make out figures draped in blankets, on benches, in doorways, beneath bushes. Each night I wander among them, and some I speak with, and for some I leave food. Another blanket. A coat. Any one of them may or may not be my father. Though the audience expects the encounter, they've paid for the encounter, I may not find him. Weeks may pass without a climax. Maybe housed, maybe dead, maybe he has left the city, though that is unlikely. The action flags, the audience lulled by the dull repetition, the same faces, then a new face (*tonight the role of Suzy will be played by Lili Taylor*), which soon becomes once again the same face. The night my father does rise from beneath a blanket, what am I supposed to say? *Hard by here is a hovel?* or *Gracious, my lord, you cannot see your way?*

Out since early February, now it's nearly December, count the months off on your fingers. One freezing night in the past year my father's left foot got frostbitten. In a letter to me he writes, *I am losing my left toes (due to not taking off my shoes at night)*. Piece by piece he's leaving this world (*Accursed fornicator! How are your stumps?*), with no bomb coming to take him whole. I put this letter in the cardboard box with all the rest. Some months he sells blood to pay the rent on his storage unit (*miss one payment at the Happy Hound, your stuff's in the dumpster*). When he tells me this I give him some money, whatever I have on me. Bench boy, box man, rat food, I want him to be a projection from the machine hidden inside my head, I want him to fall from the fifth-story window, I want to unplug the machine. Some nights I imagine running him over with the Van—*your father's dead*, the phone will say, *we're holding him in the morgue*. I've been there, seen the tiny freezer doors stacked to the ceiling, the gurneys draped with sheets, the toes tagged, just like the movies. Where will they hang the tag on my father? Months later I find him, limping. *The doctor wanted to amputate*, he says, *but I walked.*

• • •

Still outside, winter everywhere, snow falls (*Grain upon grain, one by one, and one day, suddenly, there's a heap, a little heap, the impossible heap*), his toes now blackening in his sock.

For the days leading up to Christmas he works for the Salvation Army as a fake Santa—the belted suit, the faux trim, the ringlet beard. Stationed on a sidewalk before a black pot, he rings a bell. I first learn of this when he tells me, one morning at the shelter as I finish the graveyard shift on the Van. I run into him on his way to get into his suit. He even shows me a photograph, and I'll be damned, there he is, one of the downtown Santas. A bell-ringer, my father. Later, walking, I realize I'd never noticed just how many Santas there are, I pass dozens of them, one on every corner, same black pot, same worn suit, but from now on I'll never know if one is my father. The Santa Brigade of the Salvation Army, each face disguised—rosy-cheeked, rosy-eyed, rosy-nosed—each bleating out a bleary, *Ho-ho.* If I look too closely into any one of their faces an eye will wink, or blink, but this doesn't mean it's him. Maybe they all wink, crinkle their eyes, *Ho-ho.* One stands before a Dunkin' Donuts, a pink-glazed monstrosity the size of a truck tire filling the window behind his head.

setting:

A sidewalk outside an urban donut shop. Rush hour. Stage crowded, action frozen. Scratchy Christmas carols play. A slide projection on a scrim of glistening, sick-colored, overlit donuts, ten times normal size. As lights come up slowly the stage clears, leaving five SANTAS *and three* DAUGHTERS. DAUGHTERS, *dressed exactly alike in white aprons and wearing same black wig, bobbed with bangs, stand in a row before the scrim.* SANTA FIVE *surreptitiously chases a dawdling* BUSINESSMAN, *coming up behind him, head low, gesturing wildly, giving him the finger with both hands.* BUSINESSMAN *looks over shoulder uneasily, but* SANTA FIVE *straightens and looks down at feet, at walls, seemingly innocent, until* BUSINESSMAN *turns away.* BUSINESSMAN *exits.* SANTA ONE *squats on floor, holds a bullhorn before a close 'n play, playing Christmas carols, oblivious.* SANTAS TWO *and* THREE *loll together, before a black pot suspended on a wooden tripod, halfheartedly ringing bells, smoking, murmuring to each other, scratching themselves, bleating out an occasional ho-ho.* SANTA FOUR *is passed out on a small mountain of shoes.* SANTA FIVE *now pokes through a trashbarrel, paranoid, glancing around. Heavy snow falls, tapers off.*

Daughter One: Seven days a week this—

Santa One: (*through bullhorn*) Snow on! I will endure, on such a night as this!

Daughter One: (*annoyed*) —is the process.

Santa Two: (*gestures to* SANTA ONE) His wits begin t' unsettle.

Santa Three: Canst thou blame him?

Daughter One: Monday. Day One—plain, the classic donut. God's gift—flour, eggs, milk, butter—good, clean, all-natural ingredients.

Santa One: (*bullhorn*) The ha-ha, the ho-ho.

Daughter Two: (*ignores him*) Those that do not sell on Day One move into Day Two, where we glaze them. Honey-dipped, we call it, though we use no honey. The same donut as Day One, now transformed. Many people wait for Day Two, the shiny donut.

Santa Three: (*grabs bullhorn, to* DAUGHTERS) Is there a point to this?

SANTA FOUR *rises. Appreciative applause heard over the sound system, perhaps an electric applause sign overhead.* SANTA FOUR *steps out of character for just an instant, acknowledges the applause, tiptoes behind the counter and swipes a donut, then continues stumbling over to the jail cell, which he lets himself into using the oversized skeleton key hanging beside the bars. At the door he turns to audience.*

Santa Four: (*holds up donut*) Do you realize that the latest theory of the universe is that it's shaped like a donut? Fucking amazing. (*He enters cell, curls up and snores loudly over the rest of the donut-process recitation.*)

Daughter Three: Day Three we dust the remaining honey-dipped with confectioner's sugar—it is now a sugar donut. The faux honey has begun to skin over, like a caramel apple—it has some bite now, the sugar floating upon the surface like pollen dusts a pond in spring.

SANTA FOUR *takes his pillow and covers his head, attempting to block out the sound. Muffled curses.* SANTA FIVE *stands before* DAUGHTERS, *motions for a cup of coffee.* DAUGHTERS *ignore him. When they look away* SANTA FIVE *gives them the double finger.*

Daughter One: Day Four—

Santa Three: (*bullhorn*) For the love of Christ can't you move this along?

The SANTAS *adjust the pillows that make up their bellies.*

The projection on the scrim flickers, becoming the wall of a morgue, small stainless freezer doors stacked five high, maybe eight across, lit in the same way as the donuts. The DAUGHTERS *exchange their flour-coated aprons for black industrial rubber aprons. Each rolls a gurney beside* SANTAS ONE, TWO *and* THREE, *who climb aboard and are covered with a white sheet. All barefoot, we now notice, with a tag hanging from their big toes, now revealed in their prone positions.* SANTA FOUR *stays in cell,* SANTA FIVE *huddles along left wall. The* DAUGHTERS *wheel the bodies into position, lined in a row, feet forward. One* DAUGHTER *stands behind each head. A blinding overhead light lowers over each body. One by one* DAUGHTERS *read the vital stats off each toe tag, and as they read each* SANTA *sits up briefly, winks, tells story, lays back dead.*

Daughter One: Fell on a broken bottle and bled to death—his last words were about robbing a bank.

Santa Two: The whole enterprise—the hoo-hoo, the ha-ha, the goo-goo, the ga-ga—my idea, my brainchild. Those other morons did what I told them. Dippy-do Doyle?

Couldn't find his way out of a paper bag. I made millions, kid, millions. Lived well, drank in Joe Kennedy's hangout in Palm Beach. I walk in, bartender throws me a Johnnie Walker Black, asks, What're you writing these days? Mostly checks, I tell him, ha ha.

SANTA FOUR *exits cell, again to applause, picks up the bullhorn, coughs into it, rubs sleep from his eyes. He sits on the floor, begins to play close 'n play Christmas carols quietly, experimenting, scratching a song. It begins to snow lightly.*

Daughter Two: Froze to death, couldn't pry the bell from his hand.

Santa One: I was a goner from the first moment, the first check. Doyle set me up. He knew about you kids, knew where you lived, threatened to kill both you and Taddy-tu-tu if I didn't keep going along with it. Said he'd kidnap you, for chrissakes, what was I supposed to do? I only got a few thousand out of the whole gig, nothing, really.

Santa Three: (*sits up suddenly, speaks to* SANTA ONE) Now, wait a minute, dryballs. There I was, in front of the Great God Giggles Garrity, the greatest judge in the U.S. judicial system. . . . (*to* DAUGHTERS) Write it down, dryballs, it's classic.

DAUGHTERS *look at each other, confused, mouthing the word "dryballs?"*

SANTA FOUR *stands up and attempts to hold bullhorn before* SANTA THREE.

Santa Three: He never smiled until the day he sentenced me. (*bullhorn to* DAUGHTERS) Turn the page, dryballs, you need a new page.

DAUGHTERS *slowly begin transcribing on clipboards.*

Santa Three: Six U.S. marshals brought me in, in shackles, penis included. (DAUGHTERS, *confused, mouth the word "penis"*) A two-million-dollar case. I was arrested going into the Breakers with a beautiful broad.
(*through bullhorn to* DAUGHTERS) Hey, numbnuts, you don't write fast enough, you're all losing your brains. I was in love with the broad, said I'd be right back, after I spoke with the police. Dumb bunny's probably still waiting for me, ha ha.

Santa Four: Any donuts left?

Lights flicker.

Daughter Two: We drove at night, the city locked, subdued, steam breathing from the sewers, steam from the sides of buildings. The steam drew him to it, a cipher until he spoke, a shape, the shape of a man asleep. I am here to check his breathing, to watch the blanket rise and fall.

Santa Four: (*through bullhorn*) When the mind's free the body's delicate.

Daughter Three: The wind means something here, the snow means something. Footprints in the snow mean something. No footprints lead to this man. The snow began falling at midnight. He lay down before then. This means something.

Santa Three: Buried most of it below a tree—I'm not telling you where, you bastard—but know it's waiting, waiting for the dust to settle.

Daughter One: The engine running, hot air blowing on my legs. Art cold? Thou art the thing itself, methinks. Inhale, exhale, the body's steam, the engine inside, the soul manifest, the dream's white cloud. I am cold myself.

Daughter Two: For a few months after I got back from Mexico I seriously considered buying him a one-way ticket to Mexico City. Get him drunk one night and pour him into a bus while he's passed out.

Santa One: (*morose*) If there was any way I could snap my fingers and bring your mother back into this room. . . .

Daughter One: (*touching* SANTA TWO) We got a live one here, I tell Jeff, as if it's the first. I reach out and touch the shoulder, only after having whispered near, Hey, you need anything—

Santa Two: (*sits up*) How about a fuckin apartment? You got one?

Santa One: (*to* SANTA TWO) Don't say a word, you cocksucker, don't say word one.

Daughter One: It's Malachi, and Malachi's barred for life, no parole. Attacked a cop in the building with a knife.

Santa Four: (*bullhorn*) Man's life is cheap as beasts'.

Daughter One: Ah, Malachi, you pissed everyone off.

Santa Two: You think I'll weep? No, I'll not weep.

Daughter Two: Many do not know they have climbed a steep hill and now stand overlooking the rocks and sea below.

Santa Five: (*grabs bullhorn from* SANTA FOUR) What is the cause of thunder?

They all stop and stare at SANTA FIVE. *Lights flicker.*

Daughter Three: On Day Five those still unsold are coated with chocolate. Very popular, especially among children and junkies, they line up on the Day Five, singing and scratching.

The scrim flickers between donuts and morgue, stutters like it's short-circuiting.

Santa Four: (*wrests bullhorn back from* SANTA FIVE, *then whispers to* DAUGHTERS) Watch this. (*whispers through bullhorn*) Martin. Martin. Martin.

SANTA FIVE *starts, looks around frightened, covers his ears, runs behind mountain of shoes. Lights flicker.*

Santa One: Jesus Christ I miss her. I'm talking straight talk, numbhead.

Daughter Two: It'd never work. I'd never get him to Mexico. Not enough vodka in the world to keep him unconscious that long. I'd have to kill him.

Daughter One: Something must be sacrificed.

Santa One: With the ass, with the ankles, with the feet. God, I miss her.

Daughter One: Even moonshots jettison the spent engines to get home.

Daughter Two: Buy him a jug, make sure he kills it. When he falls, make sure he falls face-first into a snowbank, take off his shoes, lose the jacket. But . . . but . . . but someone will find him, a samaritan, a Florence-goddamn-Nightingale. How to disguise the body as the heat dribbles out of the flesh?

Daughter Three: By Day Five each donut was maybe twice its original size, it had become a real meal, and it cost no more than Day One. Good value.

Santa One: Shut up! Don't speak!

SANTA FIVE *pokes his head out from behind the shoes, tries to get* DAUGHTER's *attention, rubs his belly, motions for a donut, points to his mouth, raises his eyebrows hopefully.*

Santa One: Look at that picture, she's holding you in her arms. I talk to her, you cocksucker.

Daughter Two: Bleeding must be quicker than freezing. But

the snow, it will brighten beneath him like an alarm, like a goddamn slushie. Red snow, even the police would stop for that.

Santa One: If she were alive I know we'd be together.

Daughter Three: Day Six—colored sprinkles! They sink into the chocolate like jewels in a crown. The original donut is a mere vehicle at this point for the sprinkles, the scaffolding can now be removed. Most of us really just want the sprinkles.

Santa Four: How many goddamned days are there? (*sees* SANTA FIVE, *whispers through bullhorn*) Martin. Martin. Martin. (*chuckles*) Gracious, my lord, hard by here is a hovel.

SANTA FIVE *looks around, confused.*

Santa Three: Wait a minute, dryballs, let me speak. Who you know is of vital importance in America. Who you know, how well do you know them. VITAL!!!

Santa Two: Methinks the ground is even.

Santa Four: Horrible steep.

Blackout.

Lights up on SANTA ONE, *his suit disheveled, the hat in his back pocket, the beard hanging around his neck, midway down his chest, the pillow no longer beneath his coat so he looks skinny. The pillow is on the gurney he pushes before him, along with a box of donuts, a toothbrush in a cup, a binder of papers—his novel. He is in the hallway of a storage unit now, the vaults of the morgue are now individual units, one of them his, where he keeps all the belongings he doesn't carry on his person. He opens the door to his unit, begins unloading. Projected on the scrim is the logo for* U-STOR-IT.

Santa One: (*stacking newspapers*) Grist for the mill. It'll all be in my book—*The Pine Street Palace*—and my son will be just another character in that book. Useless fuck. Leaving his blood outside to rot. Like one of those pollacks who lived beside the train tracks that carried the Jews to the camps, leaning on his shovel and waving as the train smokes past. My imbecile son, standing there waving. (*punches fist into palm*) Worthless fuck. If you don't believe in yourself all is lost.

SANTA FOUR *appears* (APPLAUSE), *no longer dressed as Santa, pushing his own gurney, transporting only a toothbrush in a cup, stops before a unit, opens it, takes out a bottle of water, brushes his teeth, spits on the floor, takes a shirt out of the unit, takes off his shirt, wipes his armpits with it, tosses it into the unit, puts on the other shirt. Turns to* SANTA ONE.

Santa Four: Where do I know you from, are you on tv or something

Audience laughter on sound system, perhaps a neon sign lights up, LAUGH.

Santa One: I've never seen you before.

Santa Four: Why're you dressed up like Santa?

Santa One: I said I don't know you.

Santa Four: Of course you know me, everybody knows me. Besides, we're neighbors now.

SANTA FIVE *appears, pushes past them, looking furtive, his gurney piled high with donuts. Lights short-circuit. Blackout.*

six

dharma

(1989) I lock myself away for a week at a time, trying to cultivate compassion. I listen to the Zen master speak, try to understand his words. *The mind created everything, the mind can repair anything.* I understand this as he speaks, take notes so I'll remember, and then he tells us not to try to understand, to let the "dharma" wash over us like rain. Cross-legged under an enormous tent, a three-ring circus tent, a few hundred of us listening, and all I can hear is that we must heal our relationships with our fathers. This is not what I came for, not what I want to hear. Is he saying that my mind created my father? Is he saying my mind will repair him?

I end up in the dharma tent after a year in therapy. At my first appointment, after a few background questions, Lou shook his head. Why had I taken so long to get help? he wondered. Did I think he was a miracle worker? I joked that I was afraid he'd lock me up, that I questioned my grip on sanity sometimes. For some reason tears were streaming down my face. Lou didn't laugh. In fact he said that he could and would commit me to a psych hospital if he felt I was a threat to myself. He said he would do that for me, that he wouldn't let me hurt myself. Thirty days with a phone call, he said. I shook my head, called his bluff, *No, no, no, wait, wait. I work with the homeless, it's nearly impossible to get a placement.* He lifted the phone—*I can*, he said. But I hadn't said anything about hurting myself, had I? The thought hadn't crossed my mind. During that first fifty-minute session he also told me I was an alcoholic, to which I agreed. I'd known it forever, though it seemed the least of my troubles. He explained that he wouldn't waste his time treating me unless I quit drinking and started going to twelve-step meetings. *Fine*, I said, anything to get this over with as quickly as possible. *It also means you can't get high anymore*, he informed me, *not ever again.*

No problem, I said, fully intending to give it all up.

Both Emily and Richard told me that I didn't have a drug or alcohol problem, that Lou sounded like a crackpot, that I should never see him again. For the next few sessions I'd get high in the pickup on the way home, which seemed to pleasantly erase any hard feelings that had risen to the surface. I took to drinking a six-pack of nonalcoholic beer a night. I went to meetings once or twice a week, feeling absolutely nothing on the walk over, only to leave feeling wretched. And I couldn't stop crying. I cried every day for a year, and then the flow lessened. I was fortunate that my job on the Outreach Van brought me in frequent contact with Jeff, who'd been sober for a couple years now, which seemed an impossibly long time. I'd tell Jeff how much I hated the meetings and he'd just nod. I'd tell him how awful they made me feel and he'd just smile.

One night Russell, still sporting his captain's hat and white shoes, takes another stick of gum, like a fish swallows a hook. Slowly, over the next year, we reel him in, we *track* him, seek him out, let him ride the Van with us. Eventually we find out he's seventy-six years old, that he's been on the streets for almost twenty years. In the '60s Russell had a girlfriend, Rosie, and Rosie had a sister Louise. The three of them were crossing Charles Street one day and a car hit Rosie. As Russell tells it—*She went up in the air and then she came down. Oh boy oh boy*. After that Russell wandered, eventually moving from doorway to doorway on Newbury Street, checking in on all the homeless women. *My girlfriends*, he calls them. The sister, Louise, is now in a nursing home, has been for years, and I begin driving Russell to see her. He tells me he's planning to propose to her, out of love and because he believes she has some money stashed away. He wants to know if I can help him to buy a car so he can drive her away from the home. Louise has grown batty, repeating herself endlessly, a tape loop jammed inside her. She calls Russell *My little Russell, my dear little Russell*, those days she remembers who he is, and tells him she thinks she's already married. I suggest to Russell that perhaps if he gets his own apartment his chances with Louise might improve. He's reluctant to leave his homeless friends, but the chance of marrying Louise is enough to convince him. We start the process. It takes months—endless paperwork, missed appointments, inscrutable evaluations, foot-dragging all around—but the day he unlocks the door to his subsidized apartment, his hand still on the knob, it hits him—*Ah, the key to heaven*, he whispers.

The Zen master tells me that my body is the continuation of my father's body. This is a hard fact, he says. By now I've already spent countless hours in twelve-step meetings, perched on a folding chair, listening to sorry-assed people tell sorry-assed tales in one church basement after another. I've heard a pilot talk about waking up in Paris, not remembering he had flown himself and three hundred passengers in the night before. I've befriended a guy who poured gasoline on his hand and lit it, just to get the morphine. It takes a year to realize I am no different from anyone else. The Zen master says that if I can understand the nature of my body I will understand the cosmos—this is one promise of Buddhism. Unfortunately, I learn, the path to understanding is through my father's body, which, it seems, is my body, inescapably. *To be caught in a notion of self is bad. To be caught in a notion of nonself is worse.* I saw him sleeping in the sun on a bench on the Esplanade. He rose and staggered to the edge of the river to piss. Jesus said, *Forgive!* Buddha said, *Awaken!* The first warm day of spring, families out for a Sunday stroll. I watched them watch him, saw how they steered clear. That fucking little girl.

In the mid-1970s, the years my father was in prison, I'd cruise the dark streets of my hometown with Phil in oversized cars we called "boats." One night we'd test-drive crystal meth cut with marijuana, the next was valium spiked with schnapps. Cheap Trick sang "I Want You to Want Me" from the eight-track, a love song, we understood the sentiment. *The present is made entirely of the past.* The Zen master looks at me as he speaks—*Dwell in the present but learn from the past.*

You must understand that Boston's essentially a small town, its streets unplanned, sinuous, cow paths paved over and widened. I could have risen from bed any night and walked directly to where my father slept. In fifteen minutes or less I could have found him, taken his hand, led him home. Instead I locked my door, got high, slept until the sun entered me again. The Zen master says that we are adrift in a river of forgetfulness, which still, some days, doesn't sound like the worst place to be.

many ways to brooklyn

(1990) Emily and I end it after I've been sober for a year. I can't give her a reason not to go to graduate school in California without me. It's been ten years since we found out who we were. She's ready to start a family. I'm ready to curl up in a ball for a few more years. That summer I live on the boat and by August Lou says that I have to stop working at Pine Street. Even though I've sworn that I'd outlast my father, that I'd be damned if I let him drive me from my job, I quit. Or, more accurately, I just never return when summer ends. For the next ten years I will not set foot in Pine Street. Instead, I go back to school, finish my undergraduate degree, get my diploma. Lou tells me this is a good idea. If Lou had told me to spend a year building sandcastles I would have moved into a sandbox.

• • •

One day, that first winter away from Pine Street, I see my father poking through a trashbarrel—something I'd never seen him do before. This will go on forever, I think, he will die outside like this. But within a year he qualifies for an apartment. The same program as Russell. One of the forms he'd filled out made it through the channels. Unbeknownst to me some strings had been pulled by those I once worked with. Lauretta. Tommy. Hilary. After five years on the streets my father's delusions have become more acute, his toes have been nearly frostbitten off and the damage from alcohol has moved into its next demented phase. But he has made it off the streets alive. I move to New York a year later, to Brooklyn, to begin graduate school. To study poetry.

Before I leave Boston I stop by and visit Russell every month or so. Russell has some problems adjusting to life inside—he can't figure out how to use the newfangled faucet in the shower, so he washes himself in the sink. He complains softly that the shower's broken, and I show him again how to work it. I give up trying to explain how to change channels on his television—it seems enough for him to plug it in to turn it on, unplug it to turn it off. His walls were stark when he'd moved in, so I gave him a crewelwork sunflower wallhanging that my grandmother had made years before. In the early winter dark I remember her spreading it out on her lap, a ball of bright yellow yarn unspooling at her feet, batted around by the latest kitten, *Dark Shadows* on tv. And then she would fold it up, go into the kitchen and return with her glass of ice and whiskey.

Jasper, of the expensive shoes, of the vintage suits, of the playing-at-being-homeless, appears in Brooklyn a few months after me. Offered a full scholarship to study art at Cooper Union, he moves to New York and falls immediately into heroin. Within a few years I will see him panhandling outside the Bedford Avenue L station. Thirty-three, still beautiful, *Jasper*, I'll say, *what the fuck are you doing?* He'll talk of this job that has fallen through or that gig that dried up, someone who owes him something, a debt soon to be repaid. Sleeping on the roof of his ex-girlfriend's building, things should turn around next week. The last time I saw him he told me he was moving to L.A., where the winters "aren't so brutal." Jasper had moved into the building in the Combat Zone just as Ivan was forced out. The Mafioso heard Ivan was selling heroin out of his building, and that could not be tolerated. I never wanted to know about Ivan's relationship to junk, perhaps afraid I'd fall into it myself. Ivan found a storefront in the South End, but within a year I heard he was in the hospital. I went to see him and he called it hepatitis but I knew it was AIDS. Norma, a co-worker, told me Ivan started showing up at Pine Street after I left Boston, but had refused to speak to her. And then he vanished, no word of him came from anywhere, for a year, then three, and then we knew he was dead. Richard died a couple years after I moved to Brooklyn. I drove back and sat with him in the hospital for a few days, but his breathing was already erratic, his eyes seemingly uncomprehending.

I stay in New York after getting my degree, teach poetry in the public schools. After the years in the shelter it's what I want, to work with children. I work in Harlem, in Crown Heights, in the South Bronx. Some of these neighborhoods look like Dresden after the firebombing. I thought I was getting away from the homeless, but you don't move to New York City to escape the homeless. In some schools half the kids I work with live in shelters. Some of these kids write the best poetry I've ever read, weird and alive, but some still can't read in the sixth grade. I get desperate with the nonreaders, want to grab them and say, *You don't have much time.* My father's letters follow me, forwarded from Boston to Brooklyn, psychic bombs. He's been housed for five years now, and I decide one day to visit him. I want to see his room, look in his face, ask him a few questions about my mother.

my cardboard box

The way he came to me first was as a letter, handwritten. It came addressed from federal prison, it came during America's Bicentennial. *The stamps were free*, he'd later tell me. A number written below his name, a few words strung together, an incomplete sentence. *Soon—very soon—*, he promised, *I shall be known*. Known? What did that mean? I was sixteen, I'd never asked for any such promise. I'd never asked him for anything, as far as I could tell. *Tell me of yourself—I regret our mutual loss*. Over the next twenty-five years he would send me hundreds more. Some fragments:

We are born to help others. (1980)

Read as much as you can. Write only when you feel the inner need to do so. And don't ever rush into print. (1981)

The American Dream is to never forget anyone. (1983)

I am a born writer. So are you. (1986)

I know I shall be able to do for America now what Mr. Solzhenitsyn has done for Russia. My works are waiting, it shall be soon. (1989)

I shall—soon—win the Nobel Prize for both Storytelling and Poetry—no fear. (1993)

Get this in your great head at once!—I am a classic storyteller. A great writer. (1996)

These letters make their way to me, first via my mother, then via Emily, then I begin sending him change of address forms whenever I move. I begin noticing the weeks between his letters, even if I never answer them, wondering if he has finally died. I keep every one of those letters in a cardboard box. In most he speaks of his book (*One of the three great books that America has produced*). In most he tells me the writing is going very, very (underlined twice) well (exclamation point!). But never a mention of alcohol, though his hand shakes as he writes.

When I say I receive a thank you letter from Senator Ted Kennedy—it is true! A letter he typed himself! This is of vital importance in life in America! Who you know! How well do you know them! Vital! (1999)

flawless
(how to rob a bank)

(1995) My father points to a name on a tombstone. *Isaac Goose? What a name.* We're in Boston's Old Burial Grounds, he stands before me, talking into my video camera. I'm here to ask him about my mother, anything he can tell me, but he doesn't seem to be getting to the point. *If I was still in the checking business I'd use that name. Who are you? Isaac Goose.*

I'm making a video documentary of my mother's ex-boyfriends, thirteen years after she died—the rotating cast of father figures who'd been her husbands, lovers, friends. I couldn't tell you what I'm hoping to find—as one of her ex-boyfriends says into my camera, *I don't know what it is you're looking for, and neither do you.* By using the phone-book and directory assistance, by asking my brother what he remembers and the last time he saw each one, I'm able to locate nearly all of them. Ten men. Two I already know where to find. We'd kept in touch with Liam, her next-to-last, who'd been in federal prison when she died. The other was my father. It's been nearly ten years since he'd walked into the shelter. I haven't spoken to him since he got off the streets five years ago. *Let me show you something,* he says, taking out his wallet. He flashes a Bank of Boston ATM card. *See that card? I robbed that bank of sixty thousand dollars. I'm proud of that card.*

He wasn't hard to find—the return address on his envelopes, an apartment building in Boston, his name on the bell. I videotaped the bell, taped my finger pressing it. He buzzed me in without a word, without asking who I was. I planned to ask him the same two questions I will ask each man—

1. How did you meet my mother?
2. How did you find out she had died?

With most these questions will be enough to get them to unreel the story of their relationship. Most seem grateful I'd asked, as if this were a story they longed to tell but never found the right ear. In the sixties Sam worked for the Concrete Pipe Corporation, the only industry in town. He tells me how she would come into this breakfast joint for coffee every morning, and that one day he ran out after her as she was pulling away and jumped into the front seat beside her. *I just have to know your name*, he blurted out. They stayed together for a year. Tim says they were more friends than in any sort of relationship, *Just two lonely people who spent some time together for a while.* I remember stopping by Tim's apartment on my way home from elementary school, letting myself in. A pool table. 4711 cologne. The unknown world of men. I don't know if he knew I was there, I might not have had permission. Don helped her buy her first motorcycle, hints that he doesn't fully buy the story that it had been suicide—*She was a lot stronger than that.* Travis tells the story of the blueberry pie, remorseful that she'd used his gun, which may or may not be true, as she had her own gun.

Father figurines. Then there's my real father. Lunchtime when I first stop by, I catch him on his way out. Each Monday, I discover, he eats the free lunch in the basement of a church on Arlington Street. He's nicknamed it "the Dwarf's Diner." Some who eat at the diner are homeless; some, like my father, simply don't have enough money to make it through the month. The first tape I have is of him walking to the diner down Commonwealth Avenue. Next on the tape he's eating, sitting at a folding table with six other men. I ask him some questions, he looks uncomfortable. I keep the camera trained on his face, don't let it wander to the others. My father introduces me as his son to a guy named Howard. Howard warms up—*Why didn't you say so? I thought you was just some student, making another documentary on "The Homeless."* It's more like a home movie, I say. The Dwarf (she is diminutive, but not a dwarf) comes by. *I can't believe a handsome kid like him belongs to you. You sure it wasn't the milkman?*

After lunch we walk to the Old Burial Grounds. Late April, tourists pose before winged skulls on tombstones. I try again to ask about my mother, but first he wants to tell me his three-step process for robbing banks. *Flawless*, he promises. Animated for the camera, clearly this is a story he has told many times before.

Step One—

You need checks. Dippy-do Doyle knew someone who worked at John Hancock Insurance. They spirit out a check which has the official three-color sig on it. Dippy-do brings the check to Suitcase Fiddler, who forges the sig on a copy of the check—Suitcase is an artist, a master. The next day Dippy-do spirits the original back to John Hancock.

In the days to follow, when I meet with the other men, at moments I will feel the tables turn—now I am the older man, the father figure, and these men, telling about their younger selves, are lost, needing direction. Some take half an hour to tell their story, some three. My father takes days, weeks, years. He's still telling it, whenever I stop off to see him. It seems like two simple questions, but I soon find there are no simple questions, not with my father. He never seems to want to know much about me, how my life has gone, what kind of man I've become. In front of a camera there is a lot he wants to say.

Step Two—

Open an account. Open an account. Where? Fall River and New Bedford. Classic American towns. A lot of money in those towns—in certain hands. It was this nation's bicentennial—I'd go to a teller with a camera around my neck—classically dressed, even in Levi's I was always classically dressed. Why did I have this insurance check? My father died, my mother got hit by a car, some bullshit story.

At the soup kitchen my father had said no to dessert. Howard teased him that it was the first time he'd seen him give up food. *The kid's got me nervous,* my father muttered, *he knows how successful his father is*—Memoirs of a Moron, *that's my masterpiece.* By the time we get to the cemetery he has transformed himself from moron to swashbuckler. Perhaps it's the camera, his last shot at fame. He leans into the lens, his hand cupping his mouth, whispers:

One thing—always go to a female teller. Always go to a young female teller. A man would never work. Most of them are homosexuals and I despise homosexuals and they despise me because they can tell that I despise them. An African-American? Me? I'd have never gotten off base with an African-American. They had to be young, good-looking women. Some of them even slipped me their phone numbers, because they wanted to have a little . . . relationship, you know—I even wrote a couple from prison. Never got any reply—

By this point in the taping I'm experimenting with all the functions on the camera—the slo-mo, the fade, the stutter. I have been with him for almost four hours, and he has yet to mention my mother.

Step Three—

(holds three fingers in the air, thinking) *Step One was getting the checks. Step Two was opening the account* (pause). *Oh, the cash. Step Three was withdrawing the cash. A week later I return. I had to have a story. Why cash? I was buying antiques, and they wouldn't take a check. I'd say it indignantly. They say they need cash. By then the insurance check would have cleared, I had money in the bank, they gave me the dough. Always under five thousand dollars. Remember that. Anything over five thousand trips off an instant federal investigation.*

Like an automated cowboy in a glass box at an arcade—put a dime in and he shoots his gun in the air, cackles. I let the camera stray, passing over tombstone and tourist, blurring. *So that's the whole plan. Absolutely, positively flawless.*

Except he forgot the surveillance cameras. And he never answered my questions. The amount the scheme generated hovers between sixty grand and four million. During these years he never sent a letter, at least not to me. At least not one that was passed on. And no money ever came our way, not a dime of the thousands or millions ever landed in my mother's hands. The bank job (his, not hers) transpired a few years after another brush with the law. That time my mother drove him to the Hingham Courthouse to answer *some bullshit charge—what was it—something—Oh, I remember—it was nonsupport* (laughs). *That's what it was* (looks into camera). *That's where I escaped—*. This was the years we were on food stamps, when my mother was taking home one hundred and twenty-seven dollars a week. As a bank teller. A young, good-looking woman.

I lower the camera. Tourists pass. *They keep looking at me like I'm some kind of movie star*, my father glows.

photogenic

For the next two years I will visit my father every few months, always with a video camera as a buffer. I will bring the tapes home and watch him, again and again. He writes me a letter after my first visit, says I can ask him anything about my mother, anytime, that his memory is *100% photogenic.* "Photogenic"—his word, not mine. I imagine he tells me this to establish himself as a reliable narrator, someone I can ask about any aspect of his life, any minutiae, and he will conjure it, build that thing before me with words. This is what my father means, it seems, by *photogenic.*

He does eventually talk about my mother. He tells me the story of asking her out on a date for the first time when she was working in the coffee shop, how he finessed a car. *She was beautiful, for chrissakes.* He tells how Ray called him when she died. *I guess your brother found her—Jesus Christ, that's awful. Jesus Christ.* The next time I see him he says that he's figured something out. *The reason someone commits suicide,* he tells me, *is because they don't like themselves—self-hatred—I think it's a very reasonable explanation.*

Scotty, his buddy from Portsmouth, had a similar insight, though it was about my father—*I always felt your father didn't like himself a lot, that he had a self-destructive side wider than most. That he carried around a sense of failure. You kids were an important part of his life, he would read to me the letters he wrote you, yet it always seemed like he was punishing himself for his failures as a father. Eventually he made a business of being a failure—if he was close to success he would sabotage it. The one role he held on to was that of being a great undiscovered writer—it allowed him to lash out in anger, it became his job to straighten the world out, to point to exactly how he'd been mistreated. The art world allowed him to get away with extravagant and excessive behavior, it encouraged it. His life became a raging performance piece, scripted by Jonathan Flynn. This allowed him to stay in control of something in his life. It became all presentation.*

One winter morning my father found me outside my gate in the Combat Zone as I was coming off the night shift on the Van—*I'm not going to die out here*, he hissed. *I'm not your poor sensitive mother. I'm a survivor.*

another way to think of fire

In making the documentary I find one of my mother's ex-boyfriends in a retirement community in Florida—acre upon acre of identical attached houses, seemingly held together by golf. Vernon had been the carpenter she'd been with when our house burned down, married with a couple kids. He left his family for my mother, and all he will say about it when I meet him is that it had been wrong. A Roman Catholic led astray by a disbeliever. Vernon is the only one who won't allow me to videotape him, or even record his voice. I got his address from his second wife. He'd become a recluse, she said, refusing to see even his own children. I remember he and my mother being together for five years, though he claims it was only two. I remember hanging off his neck, I remember watching him shave. He turned on the window washer in his car once and told me ours was the only car it rained on, and I believed him. Surprised to see me after thirty years, but he invites me in and we talk for three hours without a break. He digs out a photograph he took of me sitting beside my mother in 1965, the first photograph I've ever seen of the two of us together from when I was that young. She looks calm. I look like there's a coiled spring inside me and I'm about to shoot off into outerspace. I tell him I remember how he rebuilt our house after the raccoons burned it down, and he laughs. *Raccoons*, Vernon guffaws, *raccoons?* Outside the white Florida sky bears down on hapless golfers. *Raccoons didn't burn down your house*, he clucks, *your mother did.* He describes the house, before the fire, as even worse a ruin than I remember. *All it needed was a match*, he says. My mother had developed a flirtatious relationship with an insurance agent, Vernon claims, got the house covered for more than it was worth. The night of the fire my mother was wide awake in bed beside him at two in the morning. She smelled smoke before there was any smoke, he insists. Half an hour later smoke filled the downstairs. They ran into the room my brother and I slept in and carried us outside, the house now thick with it.

vodka, stamps, flowers

(1998) The corner of my father's bed is the only surface in his room not stacked high with newspapers or books, pilfered reams of paper or tchotchkes. I take off my coat, sit where his body must have lain a few hours before, ask how he's been. It's still early in the month, so he hasn't gone through his disability check yet. This means he's drinking, *good, Russian vodka, not that rotgut crap*. . . . His background is, as he will often point out, Russian and Irish, so he'd be a little weird not to drink, if you get his point. So for the first ten, fifteen days of each month he drinks. Occasionally he takes himself out for a meal, somewhere other than a church basement, maybe he buys himself some shampoo. The remaining four hundred dollars goes to vodka, stamps and cut flowers. Cheap bouquets from the 7-Eleven. Stamps to send out letters to those few people with whom he keeps contact. The rest of the money goes to half gallons of Smirnoff's, which he drinks with orange juice all day, days on end, until the money begins to run out, then for the last few days he drinks it straight. During this time he may have a friend crash on his floor, someone he knows from the streets—Mississippi Mike, Joe Kahn (I remember Joe from the shelter). My father points out the narrow passage on the floor, between his bed and a mound of clothes, where his visitors sleep, and it seems unlikely, though perhaps a relief from shelters or doorways.

After insisting I shake his hand properly, deep and firm, he launches into a familiar flurry of hate speech, paranoid fist-to-palm gesticulating, racial invectives, this time something about ten-year-old white girls getting raped night after night outside his window by *the blacks*. This tirade causes me to have trouble focusing, and I consider leaving quickly, but will myself to stay. I look at the one cleared chair, turned vaguely toward the snowy television, take in the disorder—every wall, every chair, every countertop, deep with worthless junk. My inheritance. The television, donated by Tommy the Terror, his pal from the Portsmouth days, is always on, even if the volume is down. A one-panel comic strip pinned over my desk passes through my mind—a king holds an ice pick up to a boy and declares, *Someday son this awl will be yours.*

My father negotiates the passageway between where he sleeps and the kitchen, keeping up a constant patter, pouring more orange juice into his vodka cup. I imagine Joe sitting in the one cleared chair, drinking the beer he's brought, nodding, maybe wedging a story of his own in between my father's endless stream. I tell my father I spoke with Tommy a few weeks ago. He answers that Tommy was sitting where I am, on the edge of his bed, not three days ago. But I know it was seven years ago, Tommy told me this, told me he's given up on my father. Even Ray no longer writes, no longer visits, and Jonathan is not welcome to visit him. I excuse myself, pick my way to my father's bathroom. The bathtub's jammed with more magazines and clothes, so much so that to bathe must require a considerable investment of time and energy. I ask him if he uses it.

Of course, he snorts.

It's just that it's loaded with stuff, I point out.

I move it, he growls.

His stovetop too is thick with unopened cans of food, arranged in aesthetic patterns and pyramids, but never touched, as evidenced by the ever-thickening layer of dust over it all. The canned food is a relief, for it seems he'll never starve. His refrigerator, unopened for years now, is barricaded by the ever-growing towers of saved magazines and newspapers. Even his bed's mostly covered during the day, stacks of magazines which must be moved onto the one empty chair before he can lie down.

It's a form of generosity that my father invites a street person, a friend, up for the night. He's even offered it to me, or my brother, anytime we need a place, something I never offered him when he was living on the streets.

But in his room there is no place, unless I sat upright in a straight-backed chair all night, or stretched out on the bit of floor beside his single bed, in the path to the bathroom. Or, the horror, crawled in bed with him. I would first sleep on a bench, or under a bush. I would risk rats and mayhem before I would spend a night in his room.

twelve doors
(the devil's arithmetic)

When I ask my father the story of how he met my mother he tells me the story of how to rob a bank. I ask him about his years sleeping outside and he tells me about scamming a room at the Ritz. Can I see your book? I ask, every time I see him. He feigns shock, indignant at my doubts, points to a corner of his room, to a box buried beneath his piles of unread newspapers. *It must be there, it's the only place untouched.* I offer to dig into it with him. He'll ask how much time I have and if I say a couple hours he'll say it'll take ten, if I say a couple days he'll say a week. Of course there's a book, the book he's been working on his entire life, *The Button Man*, though sometimes it's called *The Adventures of Christopher Cobb*. Letters from Little, Brown and Viking are framed on his walls. He walks to these framed letters and points to them as proof. One describes the book as "a virtuoso display of personality," but, unfortunately, "its dosage would kill hardier readers that we have here." At the bottom of one my father has written, "Ann Hancock and I are still close friends. She loves my work. The Adventures of Christopher Cobb!—It shall be an American classic! I never quit! I never give up!" Yes, I say, I can see the letters, you've sent them to me a hundred times, but can I see the book?

When she was still with us I asked my mother about *The Button Man*. He'd mentioned the title in one of his letters from prison. *He's still talking about that?* was all she'd say. At his sentencing for nonpayment of child support, the time he escaped through a bathroom window (*It's my duty to remain free, as a poet, as a human being*), he stood before the judge and cried, *Soon*, his book would be finished and he would be known. *Tears*, my mother hissed. The judge gave him two months.

Some days there are twelve chapters, other days there are twelve books. This is why he needs twelve desks, one for each chapter, one for each book. He learned this from Solzhenitsyn, who shared a cell with my father, in a metaphysical sense, both put away unjustly, both redeemed through words. When Solzhenitsyn got out of Siberia he moved to Vermont to write about life in the gulag. He set himself up in a barn, surrounded himself with eight doors supported on sawhorses, a door for each of his chapters, spread them out before him, to keep track of what belonged where. This is what my father plans to do with his advance—he'll buy twelve doors, and his own barn, a place where he can lay his life out and the next day it will still be there. On each door will be a typewriter—twelve doors, twelve typewriters. Once inside and settled, he will move between these doors, fashioning his stories into his masterpiece. Each year of his life is a chapter, the life itself is the book. This is his plan, but it takes time, he insists, it's all about time and space, as Einstein (apparently never a close friend) said. Have you written each chapter? I ask. *Of course, it's all written, every word.* I ask, Is there a notebook, a sheaf of paper, ink, words, does this novel have a body, can I see it? *Of course*, he snorts, indignant, waving a hand magisterially around his clutter, his organized chaos. Yet ask him the next day and he again needs more space, to spread out, to finish. He's holding out for an advance of two million from Little, Brown, because Kissinger got two million for his book, and Kissinger isn't even a writer. My father, who has slept in a cardboard box, is holding out for two million, holding out for a barn so he can begin, or finish, the project that defines his entire life, the book he's been writing since before I was born. His apartment is not big enough to contain his book, a book in part about living in a cardboard box. *Things cost money, kid*, he tells me. Seven figures. The devil's arithmetic. I am beginning to see I am asking the wrong question.

my brother waits for the tiny machines

Across town from my father's subsidized apartment, in the same city, in a parallel universe, my brother, who has no use for our father and has refused to see him, to even speak to him, for a quarter century, not since our mother drove them both to Peggotty Beach that time, waits for the future. "Nanotechnology" is its name, the creation of smaller and smaller things. In twenty years, my brother tells me, we will be immersed in a computer fog, millions of microscopic computers filling the air around us, answering our beck and call. There will be no chairs in this future, no elevators. In your room you will begin to sit and the fog will automatically form a chair below you. Raise your leg and the fog will be your ottoman. The door will open when you want it to open, you'll step into a seemingly empty shaft and the fog will be your elevator, carry you wherever you want to go. Maybe this fog can be shaped into apartments for the homeless, I venture, but my brother ignores this.

When I go to Boston I usually sleep on my brother's couch, and before we drift off we speak to each other through the half wall he's built to divide his studio. Often I have just come from an afternoon with our father. Though he seldom asks, my brother seems mildly curious, as much about my inclination to maintain contact as with the specifics of our father's life. *Photogenic,* our father promises, *smells, everything.* I tell my brother this through his bookcase, and we laugh. Since he's two years older he can remember a little about how it was when our father was with us, and those few years were apparently enough for a lifetime. I now find myself writing a book about an absent father who writes letters to a son about the novel he is writing. A novel the son doesn't believe exists. The Great Unseen American Novel. My brother never asks why I still visit our father—I couldn't tell him if he did. What *do* I hope to find? My father's photogenic memory, to recreate a world I can't quite remember? An envelope with a photograph of my mother inside, before . . . before what? Before she met my father? Before she was born? You might as well hold fog in your hands.

the book of jon

"Cobb" is the character my father has created to represent himself. His book is the story of his life. He is Christopher Cobb. *That's the way it always works. Look at Salinger, look at Twain, anyone who says otherwise is a liar.* When asked for a synopsis he'll tell you that it is a novel of an innocent dream of glory, of a man who believes that the world can be made whole again by a story, that he can change the world by what he makes. Like Noah. That if you stick with your word long enough it will become flesh. Amen. His father created a life raft where bodies were sinking into the sea. Noah built an ark miles from the nearest water. The offspring of Noah went on to build their way up to heaven, constructing their Tower of Babel. Noah needed to gather nails. My father writes his letters. These letters are all I know of his writing, my own little box of babble. Maybe this box of letters *is* the novel, a book that transmutes as you try to find it, the one you can never hold in your hands. Maybe I've had it the whole time.

30 December 1999

I am a Section 8—physically <u>not</u> mentally! I was completely investigated over 10 years ago by 4 of the best hospitals in America—MGH, and 3 others—all here in Boston. I live with full pain from head to toe—however—I still can write! I was declared—over ten years ago—in Federal Court in Boston as being <u>one</u> thing—a poet!—And that I am—always was and always will be!

Love to all, Nick—your father—Jonathan

My father's room is filled with boxes, inside the boxes are his masterpieces, his novels-in-progress, alongside notes for future masterpieces, the blueprints for his stories. But open the boxes and you will find only more emptiness. The elements are all there—torn photographs, notes scrawled on cocktail napkins, check stubs, ink on paper—all meaning shattered. No one could reconstruct a life from these scraps, no one would find the thread that would lead to the particular stories he tells. Only his voice does that, the air moving through him, vibrating out as words. *What is word made of but breath, breath the stuff of life?*

• • •

Maybe the whole time the book has been standing in front of me and I've failed to grasp it. If I could hold my father in my hands, bring him under the light—his stories are all there, each story is inside him. The transparency of the word, the transparency of the story, he is constructed entirely of the stories he tells, like the scaffolding around a building still unbuilt. The story of how to rob a bank. The story of sleeping on a bench. The story of his father inventing the life raft. The story of my mother, the love of his life. How many stories could you take from him and leave the building standing? Is there one essential story, is it the story of his masterpiece, as yet, forever, undone? Is there a deadline ticking inside him for when he must finish, a day marked, like Noah, when the rains begin? As I reread his letters, as I try to write out his life, I worry that his obsession has passed into me, via the blood, via the letters, via the vision of him rising naked from a tin tub. For the only book being written about my father (*the greatest writer America has yet produced*), the only book ever written about or by him, as far as I can tell, is the book in your hands. The book that somehow fell to me, the son, to write. My father's uncredited, noncompliant ghostwriter. Not enough to be stuck with his body, to be stuck with his name, but to become his secretary, his handmaid, caught up in a folly, a doomed project, to write about a book that doesn't, that didn't ever, that may not even, exist.

button man (the musical)

(2000) I'm living in Provincetown for another summer, no longer on the boat. I sold the boat for a dollar to a guy who swore to keep her afloat, who turned out to be either a liar or inept. A letter comes in which my father claims to have located *The Button Man.* I show up a few days later at his apartment, and he hands me four binders, four hundred pages, typed out. Not only does it exist, it turns out to be a musical. It starts with a song:

Clink/Clank/Clunk
I think that I am drunk
Clunk/Clank/Clink
I really need a drink.

This first musical number is dated 2/15/64, the day after he blacked out and stole the sheriff's car. The singing starts the moment he awakes in his cell, hungover. I bring *The Button Man* home and read it in an afternoon. A page-turner. Each day he is in jail gets its own chapter. His first day continues:

> I'm writing this on paper given to me by the bicycle thief. I'm in jail. I don't know why. And until a short time ago I didn't know where. And I don't know how long I'll be here. I'm in, however, and still a bit drunk. In the Slammer, the Pokey, the Cooler, the Clink. . . . The only thing that I remember about last night is the Valentine's Day party at Palm Beach.
>
> Roses are red
> Violets are blue
> I'm in the jailhouse
> What did I do?
>
> Get a little drunk and you land in jail, get a little drunk and . . .
>
> Clink Clinkus
> Clank Clankus
> Clunk Clunkorum
>
> Get a little drunk and you land in jail, get a little drunk and . . .
>
> Clink/Stink

For thirty pages or so *The Button Man* shows promise—a hybrid of songs, letters, found documents and scrawlings smuggled out of a county jail, woven in with a tone and ideas sampled from *Catcher in the Rye*—a *meta-text*—but, like his life, it soon falls apart, dissipates into incoherence. What would I do if it was a masterpiece, an overlooked classic? What then? Would our blood be redeemed? Would time be made whole? Would I still have such ambivalence about calling myself a poet? Would I have more? Would I have some idea of what it means to be a father, would I still be terrified of becoming one? He cannot die, he tells me, until his work is complete. Perhaps I am digging his grave, perhaps the book you have in your hands is the coin for his eyes. Perhaps the story of his masterpiece is his life raft, what he's invented to keep himself afloat.

heroic uses of concrete (the city that always sleeps)

To invent anything you need an idea. See the wooden lifeboats lined up on the deck, slipping silently into the cold sea as the ship goes under—some capsize, some upend, some shake out their cargo to their new life below. Imagine you live on the streets, that you have no key, no door with a metal number tacked to it. Imagine wandering down by the river or the piers, to seek out a likely place to crawl into for what's left of the night. Listen to the water heave and sigh, lap and break. You might dream of a life raft, a vessel to come and lift you out of this. What does my father imagine when he utters the words "life raft"? A thin skin between his ass and the shark's teeth? That the cavalry's on the way? Should he hold out just a bit longer? Does he see his father, coming back for him? Does he see his son, piloting the life raft now, here to ease him into old age? There are many ways to drown, only the most obvious wave their arms as they're going under.

The man who imagined Pine Street didn't see it as a life raft, more as a rock you could rest briefly upon, to catch your breath, get your bearings. A man named Paul Sullivan founded Pine Street, and he knew that his guys, many of them, were never going to find their way back to shore. The shelter was meant to be a waystation, a halfway house, but halfway to where wasn't specified. The cot and the roof and the plate of food were only meant to tide one over. It was never meant to be a life raft. Even a life raft is only supposed to get you from the sinking ship back to land, you were never intended to live in the life raft, to drift years on end, in sight of land but never close enough.

After months of calling the U.S. Patent Office in Washington, of asking where I might locate the original patent for the invention of the life raft, I am directed to the Science, Industry, and Business Library on Madison Avenue, just across the river. There I waste a few more days online before someone finally takes pity on me and directs me to the back room, which houses the actual books of all the patents issued for every year, starting before the Civil War. As I don't know the date of the supposed invention, I must look in each volume, under the last name Flynn, from 1900 on up. I find that in 1930 an Edmund J. holds the patent for the manufacture of zinc sulfide. I find that in

1925 Edmund P. of Eastman Kodak holds many patents for film processing. I get excited when I find that in 1929 Thaddeus J., who I assume is my great-grandfather, the one whose name is etched inside the grasshopper weathervane on the roof of Faneuil Hall, secures the patent for a new and improved roof drain. After a few more fruitless hours I assume this roof drain is the extent of the inventions in my bloodline. Fifteen minutes before closing time on my third day I find it:

> *To all whom it may concern:*
>
> Be it known that I, Edmund T. Flynn, of Cambridge, in the county of Middlesex and State of Massachusetts, have invented a new and useful Life-Raft.

This patent was granted in 1918. Then, in 1942, my grandfather is granted a second patent:

> This invention relates to improvements in life rafts . . .

The problem was to keep the body above the waves. The trick was to breathe only air. My grandfather's patent was used by seven countries during both World Wars. Thousands of heads floating above the waves. I'll be damned.

June 23, 1942. E. T. FLYNN 2,287,518

LIFE RAFT

Filed Oct. 6, 1941 3 Sheets-Sheet 1

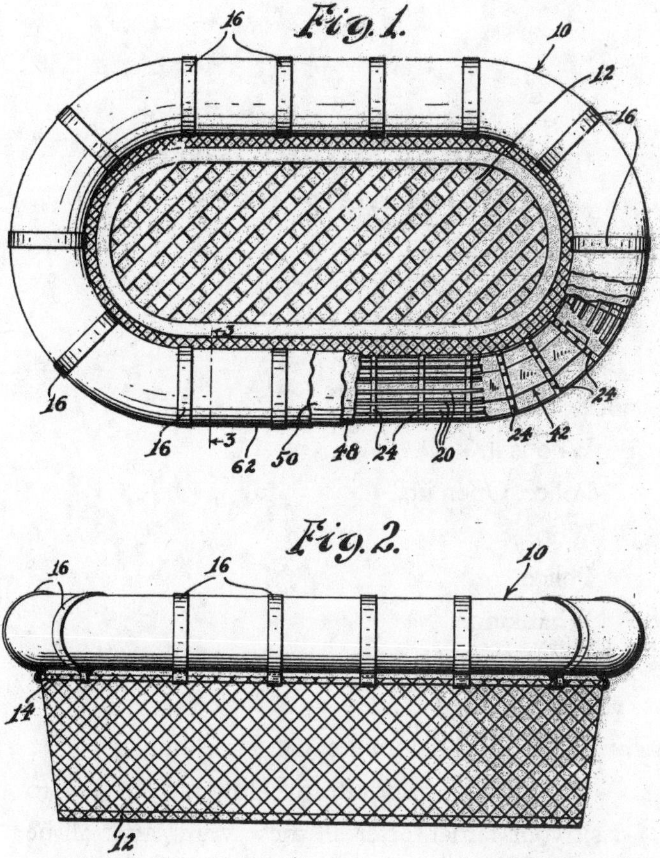

Edmund T. Flynn

INVENTOR

BY

Attorney

the boy stood on the burning deck

I knock on his door.

Who is it?

Police. Open up.

Who?

Police.

What kind?

Federal marshals. Open up, tough guy, we got you surrounded.

He opens the door a crack, peeks out.

Oh, it's little Taddy-tu-tu. How nice of you to visit your father, after all these years, after all he gave up for you.

A little game of misidentity we sometimes play. I'm unannounced, as always.

Come in, Nicholas, come in. Good to see you.

Trickier and trickier to enter without toppling something.

Look at the hair, he says, not bad in the hair department.

I shrug. His is white now, still longish, combed back from his face.

What about Thaddeus? Do you see him?

I just came from him, I say.

Is he ever going to learn to write his father a letter?

I shrug. You'd have to ask him that.

Ask him? Ask him? Are you joking? I don't even see him, how the Christ am I supposed to ask him?

I look blankly into his face.

Do you know how much your brother has broken my heart, for never coming to see me?

I come, I remind him.

And it's a delight, I'm honored. Is he healthy, physically, your brother?

Seems to be, I say.

Tell him Daddy-doo-doo loves him.

Last summer, when I found my father groggy and red-faced in a heatwave, I bought him an air conditioner. Now it's January and still it's cranked up full-blast, doing battle with the radiators. I haven't touched it, he swears. I take out my first book, a collection of poetry. Many of the poems deal with my mother's suicide, some deal with him.

It's the reason I'm here, to give him a copy. Now that I no longer videotape him I need to tell myself I have a reason to visit. He turns it over in his hands as if it's a holy relic.

Christ, I'm being beaten by my own son at poetry. Who would ever believe this bullshit?

He thumbs through the pages.

I've been in touch with Little, Brown, he says. They're doing my book. Four million.

Great, I say. Congratulations.

They said it's a masterpiece. Everything I write is a masterpiece.

So I've heard.

He reads a poem to himself.

That's heavy about the gun.

Neither my brother nor my grandfather have said a word about my book. Like dropping a pebble into a very deep pond. Just as neither of them has a photograph of my mother on display in their homes, yet there she is, beside my father's bed.

No, that's great. I'm being scooped by one of my sons. I'm delighted.

He reads another poem.

It is an inherited quality. If you didn't write I'd be surprised.

someday this awl will be yours

(2002) Music's blasting from an apartment below. My father's been stewing over it in his room for a couple days. After his check comes, after a day of solid vodka, he takes the club he keeps by his front door, the same club he used to carry in his cab, a spike in the business end, and lurches downstairs. He raps on the door the music's coming from and when a guy opens it my father swings the club at the guy's head. It misses, but shakes the guy up enough that he calls the cops, who come, inform the management company, and now the company wants my father out.

Twelve years now my father has been inside, housed, *sure glad that's behind us*, though I realize he's still lost, adrift in his own wrong ocean. But at least he isn't sleeping under a bush, at least I know that if I choose to I can drive into Boston and find him. I know if I wait until after the fifteenth of the month he most likely won't be completely hammered. But now I've been tracked down by Dawn from the management company, and she's told me what he's done, and that he has to go. I ask about the procedure, how long it takes. A month to serve the papers, she says, then another month in court, and then he's out. It must be a burden, I say, to be the one to put people on the street, and I really mean it, but she says it's no burden at all. I offer to go up there and tell him about his impending eviction, because I don't know what else to say. I also tell her that I'll take away his weapon, which I'm familiar with, as he has brandished it at my head once or twice in the past (*bammo*) in case I forgot he was a tough guy. I offer to go simply because I'd hate for him to do any actual damage. Dawn implies that if I can disarm him then perhaps she'll reconsider the eviction, though she makes no promises, and I don't ask for any. After I hang up I lay on the floor for a while as if rabbit-punched.

But I arrive too soon—the vodka still in abundance, he doesn't remember police or music or attacking anything. When a dim flicker does cross his face he goes into a familiar harangue, about how dangerous the neighborhood is, how just yesterday he got on the elevator and there was a loaded .38 magnum on the floor, which he, of course, didn't put a finger on, he's not stupid. When I tell him that I've come for his weapon, that if he gives it up there's an outside chance he won't be evicted, he begins to scream about being left defenseless in this murderous city, that he will never leave his apartment, showing his resolve by fishing the club out and brandishing it, once again, a foot from my head.

I ask him to put the club down.

What do you think I am, he screams, a homicidal maniac?

I ask him to put it down.

He lowers the club to his side, begins telling me about a twelve-year-old white kid who knocked on his door the other day, asked him where the rental office was. *What the fuck was that about?* he asks. *Out of all the apartments in this building, he comes to my door? Tell me it's not harassment, pure and simple.* His door is papered on the outside with letters sent to him, from Ted Kennedy, from Patty Hearst, to show the other tenants that he's someone, that he's known. A twelve-year-old might mistake it for an office, the letters for official notices. *I'll tell you something, though, that boy will never knock on my door again.* I tell him that if I leave today without the weapon I'll have to tell Dawn that he refused, and she will begin eviction proceedings, and I won't blame her or be able to do anything to help him. He screams some more, about the Supreme Court case he'll initiate, about them not knowing who they're up against. At one point he offers to hand it over, if I promise to give it back. As I turn to leave, he follows me into the hallway, calls me back, whispers, *Hey, I've got a hammer*, as if I could give this to Dawn and everything would be hunky-dory. As I start down the stairs he screams, *FATHER MURDERER, FATHER MURDERER*, at my retreating back.

• • •

Bitter cold walking down Boylston, the cold feels good in my head. I pass the piece of sidewalk where I first encountered Ida, a black southerner in her sixties, who ended up in Boston one winter, broke with no place to live. Ida had a shopping cart and, *No, thank you*, she didn't want to come on the Van with us to the shelter. All she wanted, once we'd established a rapport, was a grill so she could cook the rutabagas she'd acquired and now took up a good bit of her cart. She just wanted to start a little fire right there on the sidewalk and cook her rutabagas. Farther on I pass a man in the bus kiosk beside the library, hands deep in his pockets, his hood pulled tight over his face, three notes carefully safety-pinned to his yellow parka, pencil scrawl across each page. I don't know what the notes say because I don't stop to read them. In an hour I'm on a train to New York, and on the way back to Boston a few days later, I decide to give my father one more chance. I still haven't called Dawn. He buzzes me in, thanks me for trying to help him out, hands over the club, says he'd appreciate whatever I can do.

my tree

(2003) My father answers the door with a huge gash above his eye—swollen, bruised. Here we go. I mention the gash, unsure I want to know the details. *This?* he barks, pointing to his eye. *I got nailed. But you should see those two cocksuckers, tried to rob me, I'm stepping on their motherfuckin' heads. Off to Charles Street jail, they're in for twenty years.* I nod, look at the last of the day's sunlight coming through the ivy that fills his three windows with green. Cartoons on tv, coffee gone cold. How does he keep those plants so healthy? *You don't want any vodka?* he asks, hoisting the jug. *Fine, it's evil shit.* A room without corners, without a place to sit. After a few minutes of listening to this latest installment in his endless unraveling his room begins to feel especially suffocating, cramped. A seventy-three-year-old man in trouble with the law for the umpteenth time. I suggest a stroll, offer to buy him a sandwich. He mentions my book, the poems in it that deal with him, says he's impressed. I wonder if he's thinking of the one where I say I want to "*bend / each finger back, until the bottle / falls, until the bone snaps, save him / by destroying his hands.*"

On the sidewalk I notice how gnomelike he's become—cross-eyed, stiff gait, smaller and smaller, as is the way with all parents, perhaps, though my father is smaller yet cocky still, cocky and paranoid at once. Not a formidable presence, except in that madman way that drunks wield, that *does-it-look-like-I-give-a-fuck-about-anything?* look. First we walk to the 7-Eleven to replenish his stash of orange juice, where he introduces me to the guy behind the counter as his son. The cashier smiles, a bit reservedly, says only, Your son? Along with the o.j. he buys two bunches of cut flowers, one for his room, one for Jasmine, the seven-year-old girl who lives next door to him. A note from Jasmine is taped to his door—"Dear man that lives in 21, I love you." Once he knocked on their door while I was there, insisted I meet Jasmine and her mother. The mother gave me a look much like the one this cashier is giving me, of weary exasperation. Jasmine hid behind her mother's leg, waved *hola*. As we leave the cashier tells me my father is a good customer. *Damn right I am*, my father says, as he ambles back out. Next door is a junk store, a CLOSED sign hanging in the window. My father bangs on the sign with his fist. A man opens the door and is introduced as Sharkey. Nice to meet you, I say, and take his offered hand. *This is my son*, my father says. Sharkey squints into my face, confused. *He teaches at Columbia University*, my father says, *do you believe that?* Sharkey leans in to me, squints. That's a fuckin' miracle, he says. This block of Boston is mostly students, and they all seem to have somewhere to go. *The kid's got a book out*, my father tells Sharkey, then turns to me—*I don't understand how you did that. What promoted you?* When my mother was seventeen my father sent her a flurry of letters, just days before he would get her pregnant—*My future depends on my talent to write—I have periods of doubt and fear. I do not want to fail.* Sharkey tells me to keep an eye on him, that he gets in trouble sometimes, as my father staggers away from us down the sidewalk. I catch up, stop briefly to glance at an outdoor table covered with used CDs, but he orders me to keep walking. *Suck city*, he explains, *full of fuckers*, the two bouquets of flowers tucked under his arm. We pass the bank, where he cashes his government check, one of the banks he claims to have robbed many years before. He takes out his bank card, *See that?* I know, I tell him, you showed me. We're in front of a pizza joint now. I'm hungry, I say, you hungry?

He orders the steak bomb, I get a slice. He seems to know the woman at the register, or at least he acts like he does, giving her a demented stare. I drift away. She asks him if he needs anything else, if he's all right, and my father replies, loudly, *My name is Flynn, of course I'm doing all right, here in Boston. I'm Irish*, he sneers, *not African, or Spanish, or Chinese, who I love.* The woman smiles wanly,

That's good you love them, passing the bag of food into his hands.

We sit on his stoop in the fading sun, his sandwich difficult for him to negotiate, bits of fatty steak dropping to the concrete. I ask him about his father again, about the life raft. He tells the same story, nearly word for word—how he watched his father test it, dropping it over and over from a crane into Scituate Harbor until he got it right. I am now the age my father was when he entered his first bank, which is the same age my mother was when she killed herself. The sun is setting on us now. My father tells me that he has the original blueprints for the life raft. I know, I say, I gave them to you. *You did? I was wondering where I got them. You're Thaddeus, right, named after my grandfather?* No, I say, I'm Nicholas, named after the Czar.

After half an hour I tell him I have to shove off, I'm parked illegally, no sense pushing my luck.

Don't worry, he insists, just give the ticket to me, I'll tell them you were visiting.

Great, I say, I'll remember that next time.

As I stand to go he stands with me, points to a tree growing from a hole in the sidewalk—

See that tree? I'm responsible for that. I made a call, got the city to plant it. My tree.

Beautiful tree, I say.

And these steps, he says, pointing to where we were sitting, I had them replaced. My steps.

Nice steps, I say.

He walks me to my car, points to the tree beside it—*That tree too*—he's leaning into my window now, if I were to pull away I would drag him with me—*even though it's not in front of my door. I was feeling generous.*

aftermath (one year later)

questions often asked, and some possible answers

Q: Was writing the book cathartic for you?

A: In my experience, whatever happens clings to us like barnacles on the hull of a ship, slowing us slightly, both uglifying and giving us texture. You can scrape all you want, you can, if you have money, hire someone else to scrape, but the barnacles will come back, or at least leave a blemish on the steel.

Q: Why didn't you label your father mentally ill?

A: Another reader, whose father apparently was manic-depressive, criticized me for this, though my father was never diagnosed thus. It would be easier, I sometimes think, if I *could* label him mentally ill, and point to that and say, That's why he was homeless, and we could all sleep easier, knowing he was not like us.

Q: How do you deal with making people sad with what you write?

A: I'm beginning to believe that nearly all questions are projections of some inner need on the questioner's part, as if he had a movie projector inside his head, showing the same movie over and over. I thought I was the only one who did this, and it's comforting to know I'm not alone.

Q: Do you feel you shot yourself in the foot with the title?

A:

Q: What did you feel the first time you saw your father homeless?

A: Not to be coy, but there was no moment I could nail down for you—it was more a series of steps, a progression, one moment flowing into the next, which I believe is the experience, for most, of finding oneself in a difficult situation—you cannot believe it is really happening, that all roads have led to this, and that you may be stuck there for an undefined number of days or even years. And so, for me, there was also no single emotion, even if I could find a moment to attach it to—one emotion transformed into another, often in a more associative rather than a logical way—confusion into giddiness, outrage into an inappropriate joy, numbness into hyperawareness—which is the way life has been for me, so far at least, though I expect not even that will remain fixed.

Q: Your father identifies himself as a storyteller. What is the purpose of telling stories?

A: If one were a Buddhist, one might say we spend much of our lives in "monkey-mind," swinging from story to story, our thoughts never quiet. Perhaps it is our fear, that in the silence between stories, in the moment of falling, the fear that we will never find the one story which will save us, and so we lunge for another, and we feel safe again, if only for as long as we are telling it.

Q: You've said elsewhere that you based the structure of the book on Moby-Dick, *comparing Ahab's obsessive search with your own circling of your father. Can you say more about this?*

A: In *Moby-Dick*, the eponymous whale doesn't appear until the last fifty pages. The story of the whale appears earlier, but the actual whale only breaks the surface for a moment at the end, just long enough to wreak havoc and pull Ahab under. The whole book is about a whale and the whale isn't there. In the end the central mystery remains unfathomable—what was it exactly that Ahab gave his life to? We know he lost his leg, and that that loss became a story, and the story became the obsession that in the end defined, and ended, his life. We have to be careful of the stories we tell about ourselves.

Q: Do you give money to panhandlers?

A: Sometimes, even though I know I'm not supposed to. Sometimes I don't give, even though I can feel the quarters in my pocket, and the person looks really hungry or in bad shape. Then I don't feel good for awhile, or else I forget about it immediately. Sometimes I give only to someone who looks ill, sometimes only to someone who looks healthy. I am completely confused and overwhelmed by the whole transaction.

Q: Has your father read the book? How does he feel about it?

A: I've answered that question in many ways, and each answer I gave seemed true when I said it, but now I marvel at my certainty. I said that since the book came out it seemed that he was, to my surprise, more lucid, more compassionate, and that he seemed, when I saw him, not to be as drunk as other times I'd seen him (placing me, by comparison, once again firmly in the "normal" end of the spectrum). I might have even said, with a straight face and more than once, that perhaps the book had given some meaning to his life (ah, the transformative powers of art!), a reason not to drift so far out, to hold it together (aka "my Jesus complex").

After having seen him again ten months after the book came out, raging and incoherent, I realize it was all a self-aggrandizing delusion, though perhaps it was simply the wrong time of the month.

Q: Do you think your father had talent?

A: Several people have gotten in touch with me since the book came out, people who knew my father years before I did, and some have testified to how much they admired his drive and talent as a writer. My father's not dead yet, so there's always still the chance the Nobel committee will call.

Q: Do you still blame yourself for your mother's suicide?

A: Do you really think I'm going to answer that here?

bullshit afterword aka twenty years later

When I was just starting out, I heard it took Joyce seven years to write *Ulysses*. I thought, *How could anyone spend that much time inside one book?* Then I began trying to write this one, and it took seven years, from the first words scrawled into a notebook in Ireland to the day I held it in my hands. As those years began to pass, I saw what a miracle it was that Joyce was able to create that masterpiece (*Ulysses!*) in only seven years.

In Ireland, I read those first few pages to my then-girlfriend. She said, simply, *keep going*. Sometimes this is all it takes. I was in Ireland, in part, to find my ancestral homeland. My father had claimed his (our) family was from Enniskillen, which he called an island, but a glance at a map plainly showed it was landlocked. I told that to the taxi driver who picked me up at the airport, and he pointed out that my father was right, that Enniskillen is an island in the middle of two rivers. That was the first lie my father told me that turned out to be true.

Those first few words in Ireland came almost ten years to the day after my father walked into the shelter, demanding a bed, though versions of it had been rising up inside me my entire life, trying to find purchase. It's likely that any project needs to spend some time inside us, before it becomes manifest, but how to pinpoint the moment it begins? Did it begin two years before Ireland, when I found my father and videotaped him answering those two questions (*How did you meet my mother? How did you find out she had died?*). Did it begin when he walked into the shelter, or did it begin when I was a teenager, reading the letters he'd write me from prison? Or did it begin when my mother first kissed him, on that strip of beach between the Cliffs? *In dreams begin responsibilities*, as Delmore Schwartz reminds us.

When I began, I didn't know what this book would become . . . it could turn out to be a poem, or a screenplay, or a performance. Memoir, at that time (maybe still?) felt like a bastard genre, a Wild West of charlatans and fakers and bad writing, where the rules were not fixed. There were, of course, a few models of what it could be (*I Remember*, *My Life*), but there were even more examples of how wrong it could go (*A Million Little Pieces*). For the first few years I wandered in that wilderness, allowing it to lead me where it may, allowing one thing to lead to another. It was, at first, all questions. *How did my father end up on the streets? Was anything he said true? How did I end up working in a shelter?* I'd written two books of poetry (neither had been published when this book began), so I approached it as a poem, allowing associative energy and intuition and dreams to lead me into it. I had my memory of what had happened, as imperfect as it was, and that's where I began.

In some ways, once this book appeared, it felt like it had existed forever, that it just needed to be found. The inevitability of it—though this, of course, is another illusion. It could just as easily not been so, just as I could have just as easily not been so. I want to say all this to you, Dear Reader, in case you are also at the beginning of a project. To say, simply, *keep going*. To say that it is all right, no *better*, if you do not know exactly where it is you are headed. To remind you to trust those moments that feel inevitable.

• • •

At the end of this book, my father is off the streets and settled (somewhat) into his Section 8 apartment. He'd live in this apartment for nearly sixteen years, until some excessively erratic behavior (after years of erratic behavior) led to a hospital visit he never came back from. It seemed there was something going on with him that precluded him living on his own any longer. From the hospital he was discharged into a long-term care facility, where he held on for another five years or so.

Over the years I'd had to intervene fairly regularly to keep my father in that apartment. I got to know the manager of his building, asked her to call me if he got out of hand, and he got out of hand all the time (I assume if I drank as much as he did I'd get out of hand pretty regularly as well). He ended up spending time at the beginning of each month with a woman he dubbed *Fancy Nancy*. I never met this Nancy, but from what I know she was one of those who prey on guys when their checks come in, offering some service in exchange for that check. She would spend his check on crack, which she would smoke in his apartment, and when the money was gone she would be gone as well. It's a sad story, but somehow just the fact that he had an apartment to act out this sordid arrangement was an improvement.

He died ten years ago, on the same day Lou Reed died—that means he was in the world with this book for ten years.

• • •

Mary Gaitskill made this comment to an interviewer who was confused how to feel about a character in her (great) novel *Veronica*:

> You don't know how to feel? You're an adult, you feel what you feel. It's not my job as an artist to tell you what to feel.

It's not my job as an artist to tell you what to feel became a mantra for me. It's pinned over my desk as I write. In early drafts I was asked how I felt the moment my father walked into the shelter. I was confused by the question—was I allowed only one emotion, like on some daytime talk show? What if I felt a Rolodex of emotions, what if one emotion transformed into another as each second passed, what if what I felt made no sense? What if it would take an entire book to answer that question?

I've come to believe that for a memoir to succeed it needs to be the least ego-driven of all the genres, because it's already so dangerously close to being pure ego. I've gotten a few letters from folks after they've read this book. Some are a version of *Dear Nick, I too have had a miserable life, let me enumerate the ways.* Most have seen something in the book that mirrors something in their lives. I find it an honor to be able to take these letters in, to reply when I can, to offer something, even if it all remains somewhat incomprehensible to me . . . what do you do with a drunken sailor? I don't know why some people get it (by "it" I mean "sober"), and some don't. Some say it is simply a matter of *grace.* It is, for me, an eternal question.

Whitman calls the act of reading:

> Not a half-sleep, but, in the highest sense, an exercise, a gymnast's struggle . . . the reader is to do something for himself, must be on the alert, must himself or herself construct indeed the poem, argument, history, metaphysical essay—the text furnishing the hints, the clue, the start or frame-work. Not the book needs so much to be the complete thing, but the reader of the book does.

This is what I attempted—to create (find?) something that the reader (you) would have to actively engage with, something that would not provide answers (I didn't have any anyway), but would, hopefully, become a scrim that you could project yourself upon. My wife had told me that when we first met, that my job was to create the scrim that others could project themselves upon, and that I had to find a way to carry that projection with grace. It was hard at first, when I was first going out in public to read from this book, to feel so exposed, until I realized that the readers of this book, of any book, are not looking for the writer in it. We are looking for ourselves. By giving readers space, by not telling them what to feel, the hope is that they can find themselves in these words.

Here is the obit I wrote for him, which never made it into any newspaper:

> JONATHAN ROBINSON FLYNN, the self-proclaimed "greatest writer America has yet produced," died on a Sunday morning at the end of October in Boston. At the time of his death he was living at Roscommon, the nursing home where he'd spent his last five years of his life.
>
> He was the subject of his son Nick Flynn's 2004 memoir, *Another Bullshit Night in Suck City*, which chronicled his father's life as an absent father, a bank robber, and as a federal prisoner, as well as the five years he lived as what we now call "the working poor," sleeping in shelters and on the streets of Boston, working day labor. He made it off the streets with the help of several social workers and organizations, including Eileen O'Brien of

Elders Living at Home, Jim O'Connell of Health Care for the Homeless, the Pine Street Inn, and many others. His success in getting off the streets is a model for the current Housing First movement, which has the potential to end homelessness in America.

Jonathan Robinson Flynn was born in 1929 in Scituate, Massachusetts, and always had a complicated and contentious relationship with his own father, Edmund Flynn, although Jonathan was proud that his father had, in response to the sinking of the *Titanic*, invented the life raft—the *Titanic* only had lifeboats.

A ghostly, inscrutable, charming, frustrating, narcissistic, alcoholic, damaged, and damaging presence, Nick Flynn tried to understand his father in nearly all of his writing, especially in the subsequent memoirs *The Ticking Is the Bomb* and *The Reenactments*. Jonathan spent most of his life on the East Coast, between New Hampshire and Florida, often working on docks or on fishing boats in order to support his writing and his drinking. While serving time in federal prison, it is likely he was subjected to CIA-funded torture experiments, which likely contributed to his later paranoia. Nick Flynn's *The Ticking Is the Bomb* chronicles this time in his father's life. After prison, he remained in Boston for the last twenty-five years of his life.

Being Flynn, the feature film based on *Another Bullshit Night in Suck City*, starring Robert De Niro as Jonathan Flynn, was released in 2012. Jonathan was impressed with De Niro's performance and enjoyed imitating

De Niro ("You are me, I made you") as he taunted Paul Dano, his on-screen son.

At the time of his death Jonathan Flynn remained convinced he would win the Nobel Prize for "both storytelling and poetry." His one completed novel, *The Button Man*, remains unpublished. Along with his son Nick, he is survived by another son, Thaddeus, as well as a daughter, Anastacia.

For no good reason he outlived both of his ex-wives.

[born 7 dec 1929, died 27 oct 2013, age 83, R.I.P.]

Antonio Machado offers this: *In order to write poetry, you must first invent a poet who will write it.* Some of the years of working on this book were spent trying to invent the person who could write it. As Thich Nhat Hanh once said, *You must heal your relationship with your father.* I can say that in order to write this book I needed to develop a relationship with my father, something I never had. On my deathbed, I'm pretty sure that will be what matters most, more than this book—the fact that, in the end, I had a relationship with my father.

—Nick Flynn, June 2024

[extracts]

Perhaps to lose a sense of where you are implies the danger of losing a sense of *who* you are.

—Ralph Ellison, *Invisible Man*

. . . certain diseases—such as alcoholism— . . . tend to devour memories in reverse order to their acquisition.

—Forrest Gander

Haimon: If you were not my father, I'd say you can't think.

—Sophocles, *Antigone*

I find there is nothing ridiculous in dying in the streets, as long as one doesn't do it on purpose.

—Stendhal

Tell me what you fear and I will tell you what has happened to you.

—D. W. Winnicott

Fatherhood is a mystical state, an apostolic succession, from only begetter to only begotton.

—James Joyce, *Ulysses*

BULLSHIT
BULLSHIT
BULLSHIT

[some notes]

p. 59 "Look! here comes a walking fire!"—*King Lear.* "A map the size of the world"—Jorge Luis Borges. **p. 79** "Trigger-hippie"—Morcheeba. **p. 125** Lines in italics—*King Lear* (approximately—original is "that wants the means to lead it"). **p. 126** "pruno"—usually made by fermenting ketchup in a plastic bag (the kick is formidable, but the taste, they say, is wretched). **p. 143** "Who is it that can tell me . . ."—*King Lear.* **p. 155** "It wasn't any woman . . ."—William Faulkner, *Light in August.* **p. 198** "I have plenty of places to go . . ."—Mike Leigh, *Naked* (approximately). **p. 205** ". . . a box imagined into a house"—an idea lifted from Gaston Bachelard, *The Poetics of Space.* **p. 220** "We arouse pity . . ."—Jean Genet, *The Thief's Journal.* **p. 221–24** "same again"—a collage of many voices, including friends, Homer Simpson & the band Acrophobe. The phrase "Sadder Budweiser" was stolen without permission from the artist David

Brody. The form is adapted from a Kato Indian Genesis myth (found in *Technicians of the Sacred*, Jerome Rothenberg, editor). **pp. 274–86** Many lines lifted from *King Lear.* **pp. 274–75** "Accursed fornicator! . . . ," & "Grain upon grain . . ."—Samuel Beckett, *Endgame.* **p. 300** *Flawless (how to rob a bank)*—title of a documentary video written & directed by NF, produced by the Kitchen, edited by David Anzarch (1997). **p. 321** "What is word made of but breath . . ."—*Hamlet* (approximately). **p. 323** Excerpts from Jonathan Flynn, *The Button Man* (unpublished). **p. 330** "the boy stood on the burning deck"—Elizabeth Bishop, *Casabianca.* **p. 338**—"bend / each finger back . . ."—NF, *Father Outside.* **p. 359** The illustration is from the hand and mind of Josh Neufeld.

[debts]

impossible without tom draper, bill clegg, jill bialosky, frances richard, lee brackstone, oscar van gelderen, jessica craig, mark adams, dorothy antczak, sarah messer, thich nhat hahn, jacqueline woodson, johnny cash, maggie nelson, mark conway, dana goodyear, doug montgomery, hubert sauper, eli gottlieb, danella carter, dave cole, martin moran, debra gitterman, arlo crawford, suzanne bach, robbie cunningham, sarah moriarty, rodney phillips, deirdre o'dwyer, padgett-marbens, marisa pagano, anna oler, josh neufeld, the macdowell colony, michael carroll, the schoolhouse center, sylvia sichel, the corporation of yaddo, peggy gould, pat oleszko, daniele bollea, nicola bollea, jen liese, alex blumberg, shane dubow, billy loos, everyone I worked beside & with at the pine street palace, all my friends who have become fathers, tad flynn, talaya delaney ***impossible without***

[bragging rights]

Nick Flynn is the author of thirteen books, most recently *Low* (2023). Other recent books include *This Is the Night Our House Will Catch Fire* (2020) and *Stay: threads, collaborations, conversations* (2020), which documents twenty-five years of his collaborations with artists, filmmakers, and composers. His bestselling memoir *Another Bullshit Night in Suck City* (2004) was made into a film (*Being Flynn*, 2012) starring Robert De Niro and has been translated into fifteen languages. He has received fellowships from (among other organizations) the Guggenheim Foundation, the Fine Arts Work Center, and the Library of Congress. His work has won two PEN/America prizes and been a finalist for France's Prix Femina. Some of the venues his poems, essays, and nonfiction have appeared in include *The New Yorker*, *The Paris Review*, and National Public Radio's *This American Life*. His film credits include artistic collaborator and "field poet" on the film *Darwin's Nightmare* (2004), which won a César in France and was nominated for an Academy Award for best feature documentary. In 2023–2024 he was the artist in residence at the BMO Lab for Creative Research in the Arts, Performance, Emerging Technologies & Artificial Intelligence at the University of Toronto. Since 2004, he has spent each spring in residence at the University of Houston, where he is a professor on the creative writing faculty, focused on poetry and collaboration among the arts. The rest of the year he is based in or around Brooklyn, NY. (www.nickflynn.org)

Andre Dubus III's nine books include the *New York Times* bestsellers *House of Sand and Fog, The Garden of Last Days,* and his memoir, *Townie.* His most recent novel, *Such Kindness,* was published in June 2023, and a collection of personal essays, *Ghost Dogs: On Killers and Kin,* was published in March 2024. He is also the editor of *Reaching Inside: 50 Acclaimed Authors on 100 Unforgettable Short Stories.*

Mr. Dubus has been a finalist for the National Book Award and has been awarded a Guggenheim Fellowship, the National Magazine Award for Fiction, three Pushcart Prizes, and is a recipient of an American Academy of Arts and Letters Award in Literature. His books are published in over twenty-five languages, and he teaches at the University of Massachusetts Lowell.